ornwall

with your family

From breathtaking coastlines to tranquil villages

by Sue Viccars

Copyright © 2008 John Wiley & Sons Ltd, The Atrium, Southern Gate, Chichester, West Sussex PO19 8SQ, England
Telephone (+44) 1243 779777
Email (for orders and customer service enquiries): cs-books@wiley.co.uk. Visit our Home Page on www.wiley.com

UK Publisher: Sally Smith
Executive Project Editor: Daniel Mersey (Frommer's UK)
Commissioning Editor: Mark Henshall (Frommer's UK)
Development Editor: Mark Henshall (Frommer's UK)
Content Editor: Hannah Clement (Frommer's UK)
Cartographer: Tim Lohnes
Photo Research: Jill Emeny (Frommer's UK)
Wiley also publishes its books in a variety of electronic formats. Some content that appears in print may not be available in electronic books.

Library of Congress Cataloging-in-Publication Data
Viccars, Sue.
    Frommer's Devon & Cornwall with your family / Sue Viccars.
            p. cm.
    Includes bibliographical references and index.
    ISBN 978-0-470-51894-6 (pbk. : acid-free paper)
    1. Devon (England)—Guidebooks. 2. Cornwall (England : Country)—Guidebooks.
3. Family recreation—England—Devon. 4. Family recreation—England—Cornwall
(County) I. Title.   II. Title: Devon & Cornwall with your family.   III. Title:
Frommer's Devon and Cornwall with your family.
    DA670.D5V44 2008
    914.23'50486—dc22   2007050391

British Library Cataloguing in Publication Data
A catalogue record for this book is available from the British Library

ISBN: 978-0-470-51894-6

Typeset by Wiley Indianapolis Composition Services

Printed and bound in China by SNP Leefung Printers Ltd.

5 4 3 2 1

Contents

About the Author

After family holidays in Devon and Cornwall as a child Sue Viccars returned to the southwest to study geography and archaeology at Exeter University, and apart from a brief spell with a London publishing company (mainly working on a tourist guide to Devon) has lived on Dartmoor's eastern fringes ever since. She has always had a passionate interest in the outdoors, sparked off by camping holidays and exploring the Surrey hills on horseback as a child. A 20-year career at David & Charles publishers commissioning walking and outdoor books has been followed by a successful freelance career as an editor and author specialising in the southwest. Her first book, *50 Walks in Devon* (AA Publishing), led to family walking books on Dartmoor, Exmoor and Cornwall (Jarrold Publishing) and she has worked on guides to the southwest for Time Out and the AA. Sue has written about family cycle routes in Devon and Cornwall, many articles for both national and local press, and was former editor of *Dartmoor: the country magazine* (Halsgrove) – a real chance to immerse herself in this beautiful area. She has explored Devon, Cornwall and Dorset extensively through her regular work revising Pathfinder walking guides (Jarrold) – she originally discovered many of the places covered in this guide on foot! She also wrote Aurum's National Trail Guide to the Pennine Bridleway, the first National Trail designed to accommodate walkers, cyclists and horse riders. Further afield she has trekked in Morocco, walked across Corsica, been to Everest base camp, scrambled on Skye and in Snowdonia – and in the autumn of 2007 trekked to Kangchenjunga base camp in the Himalayas. Sue lives in a cottage on the eastern edge of Dartmoor with her two sons.

Acknowledgements

It would be impossible to list everyone I've talked to in connection with this book, so perhaps it's best just to say a big general 'thank you' to all those accommodation providers (in particular) who plied me with coffee, showed me round and answered endless questions – and to those who loaned me photographs on those days when the weather was too grim to let me take anything decent. Thanks too to the owners of dozens of attractions who admitted me free of charge and enabled me to happily revert to childhood status... Special thanks are due to Suzi Browne of Hammond PR and Sophie Hughes of the Isles of Scilly TIC for enabling my Isles of Scilly trip – the hospitality I received on Scilly was second-to-none. Thanks too to Jane for putting me up (and providing the wine...!) when I was researching mid Cornwall, and to Brenda for helping me on our Exmoor trips. My biggest thank you goes to my other half Stu, who has steadfastly supported me both emotionally and practically throughout the preparation of this book. Every Sunday, come rain or shine, he has ridden on steam trains, watched sheep racing, taken giant steps through model villages, sampled ice cream and cream teas – and (most importantly) uncomplainingly donned a fleece gnome hat at Devon's Gnome Reserve!

Dedication

For Nick and Joffy

An Additional Note

Please be advised that travel information is subject to change at any time and this is especially true of prices. We therefore suggest that you write or call ahead for confirmation when making your travel plans. The authors, editors and publisher cannot be held responsible for experiences of readers while travelling. Your safety is important to us however, so we encourage you to stay alert and be aware of your surroundings.

Star Ratings, Icons & Abbreviations

Hotels, restaurants and attraction listings in this guide have been ranked for quality, value, service, amenities and special features using a star-rating system. Hotels, restaurants, attractions, shopping and nightlife are rated on a scale of zero stars (recommended) to three (exceptional). In addition to the star rating system, we also use five feature icons that point you to the great deals, in-the-know advice and unique experiences. Throughout the book, look for:

FIND	Special finds – those places only insiders know about
MOMENT	Special moments – those experiences that memories are made of
VALUE	Great values – where to get the best deals
OVERRATED	Places or experiences not worth your time or money
GREEN	Attractions employing responsible tourism policies

The following **abbreviations** are used for credit cards:

AE   American Express
MC   MasterCard
V   Visa

A Note on Prices

In the Family-friendly Accommodation section of this book we have used a price category system.

An Invitation to the Reader

In researching this book, we discovered many wonderful places – hotels, restaurants, shops and more. We're sure you'll find others. Please tell us about them, so we can share the information with your fellow travellers in upcoming editions. If you were disappointed with a recommendation, we'd love to know that too. Please write to;

Frommer's Devon & Cornwall with Your Family, 1st Edition
John Wiley & Sons, Ltd
The Atrium
Southern Gate
Chichester
West Sussex, PO19 8SQ

Photo Credits

1 Family Highlights of Devon & Cornwall

It's hard to pinpoint quite when my love affair with Devon and Cornwall started. I think it all began long ago with family holidays on a farm in the countryside near Mevagissey, days on the beach at Caerhayes and Gorran Haven, and memories of stopping for a picnic on Dartmoor on the way home. When I was a little older we spent family holidays in a caravan near Woolacombe in north Devon, then in a cottage at Constantine Bay near Padstow in north Cornwall. Trips with friends to explore Penwith and Exmoor followed; then there were weeks of conservation work on Lundy Island and sailing holidays in Salcombe. I was lucky enough to move to Devon in my early 20s and have lived on the eastern edge of Dartmoor for more than 20 years, along with my two sons. Together we have cycled the Camel Trail, walked on Dartmoor and camped on Bryher on the Isles of Scilly. Over the last 10 years my work has concentrated on researching (mainly on foot) and writing about the southwest peninsula for a number of books and articles, and it's clear to me why Devon, Cornwall and the Isles of Scilly – and Exmoor – together provide ideal locations for all kinds of family holiday, from simple bucket-and-spade fun on the beach to more active pursuits such as walking, cycling or sailing on the Salcombe estuary. A stunning coastline, some of the best beaches in the country, tranquil wooded estuaries, wild moorland, picturesque villages, historic fishing ports, ancient castles, colourful local customs, and an equable maritime climate give this region an edge. Add to that good family attractions, a huge choice of places to stay, from beachside camping to top-class family hotels, sunshine, ice cream, pasties and clotted cream – what more could any family want?

DEVON & CORNWALL FAMILY HIGHLIGHTS

Best Family Events Sidmouth FolkWeek brings together singers, dancers and musicians to this elegant east Devon seaside town. You don't have to go to an official concert: musicians, dancers and street theatre perform for free all over town, especially along the seafront. Special children's events are held all day every day in Blackmore Gardens. See p. 23.

Best Cities Cities are pretty thin on the ground, but visit Exeter for its shops, museum, underground passages and historic quay, and Plymouth for the Barbican and amazing National Marine Aquarium. See p. 24 and p. 109.

Best Natural Attractions Where to start? The Valley of Rocks on Exmoor; Dartmoor's tors; Lundy Island (p. 48); the Penwith Moors; the Helford River; the Isles of Scilly (p. 219); and just about the whole of the 1000-km Southwest Coast Path.

Plymouth Barbican

Best Animal Parks Paradise Park in Hayle: a myriad of exotic birds, small animals for toddlers, plus indoor play for wet days – and a strong educational element. Living Coasts in Torquay: all manner of seabirds in a virtually natural environment. The Big Sheep near Bideford for animal fun and frolics for all ages. See p. 205, p. 115, and p. 50.

Best Aquarium The National Marine Aquarium in Plymouth: the biggest and best aquarium in the country. See p. 110.

Best Beaches There are dozens, from quiet sandy coves to wide surfing beaches: Blackpool Sands near Dartmouth; Rickham Sands near Salcombe; Lantic Bay near Polruan; Sennen Cove, Gwithian Towans, Watergate Bay at Newquay; Widemouth Bay near Bude and so on. See area chapters.

Best Islands Lundy Island off the north Devon coast for those looking for adventure; St Agnes on the Isles of Scilly, the most southwesterly island in the UK. See p. 48 and p. 224.

Best Boat Trips Three hours along the World Heritage Jurassic Coast from Exmouth on a Stuart Line cruise, spotting peregrine falcons and dolphins. See p. 30.

Best Forest Haldon Forest near Exeter: cycle tracks and walks, sculptures, special events for children – and good refreshments. See p. 96.

Paradise Park, Hayle

Land Ahoy!

Best Outdoor Activities
Cycling along the Camel Trail from Wadebridge to Padstow; **sailing** on the Salcombe estuary with the Island Cruising Club; **horse riding** on Exmoor. See p. 115, p. 118, and p. 51.

Best Museums
The **Wayside Museum**, Zennor – memorabilia of life in rural west Cornwall; **Dingles Fairground Heritage Centre** near Launceston; Falmouth's **Maritime Museum** has a huge range of hands-on activities for children. See p. 203, p. 90, and p. 174.

Best Castles
Berry Pomeroy near Totnes for places to hide – and ghosts; **Castle Drogo** on Dartmoor – the youngest in the country – for location. See p. 112 and p. 88.

Best Gardens
Trebah Gardens on the Helford river: gunnera tunnel, bamboo maze, Tarzan's Camp, beach, children's trails and activities; **Tresco Abbey Gardens** in the Isles of Scilly features sub-tropical splendour. See p. 179 and p. 225.

Best Farmers' Market/Shop
Tavistock – farmers' market and huge daily pannier market. **Trevathan Farm Shop** at St Endellion, plus café and children's play area. See p. 102 and p. 165.

Best Miniature Train Rides
Take a ride on the **Lappa Valley Steam Railway** near Newquay to all sorts of family fun; the **Beer Light Railway** trundles through beautiful gardens at Pecorama above the sea in east Devon. See p. 177 and p. 27.

BEST ACCOMMODATION

Best Family-Friendly Option
For the best hands-on experience with small animals Torridge House in north Devon is pretty well unbeatable. See p. 76.

Best Grand Hotels
Fowey Hall Hotel in southeast Cornwall is totally committed to the needs of families, with very flexible accommodation options. See p. 141.

Best Seaside Hotels
For the best indoor and outdoor facilities for children – and parents are well catered for too – try the **Bedruthan Steps Hotel** near Newquay. See p. 187.

Best B&Bs
Trevone Beach House near Padstow: bright, cheerful, environmentally aware; **Mincarlo** on the Town Beach, St Mary's on the Isles of Scilly. See p. 161 and p. 227.

Torridge House, North Devon

Best Self-Catering

Accommodation Masses! **North Bradbury** at Chittlehampton for that personal touch, **Bosinver** near St Austell for large groups of children and mass animal feeding; **Gitcombe** near Totnes; **Burnville Farm** in West Devon and **Cot Manor** near St Just for peace, tranquillity and a spot of luxury. See p. 76, p. 186, p. 121, p. 100, and p. 212.

Best Campsites

Gwithian Farm and **Kenneggy Cove Holiday Park** in southwest Cornwall for straightforward camping and good facilities near the beach; **Wooda Farm Park** near Bude if you're after a little more onsite entertainment; **Westermill Farm** on Exmoor for wildlife and landscape. See p. 209, p. 209, p. 158, and p. 56.

BEST EATING OPTIONS

Best Child-Friendly Restaurants

Cap'n Flint's in Salcombe is deservedly popular; **The Springer Spaniel** near Launceston genuinely welcomes children; the **Wheelhouse Restaurant** in Mevagissey has life-size pirate models! See p. 123, p. 143, and p. 190.

Best Child-Friendly Cafés

Mother Meldrum's on Exmoor serves Witches' Fingers; **The Old Dairy Café** at Downes Traditional Breed Centre has a good family room – and animals; **Channel View Café** in Exmouth has an indoor play area. See p. 60, p. 79, and p. 35.

Best Vegetarian Food

Willow Vegetarian Garden Restaurant in Totnes (with dedicated family room); and **Herbies** in Exeter – both long

Traditional Cream Tea

established and brilliant. See
p. 122 and p. 38.

Best Teashops Particularly
good are the **Quay Café** at
Fremington (turn up by bike);
The Corn Dolly in South Molton;
and **Anne of Cleves** in Totnes.
See p. 61, p. 78, and p. 111.

Best Ice Cream Roskilly's on
the Lizard; **Salcombe Dairy** in
south Devon; and **Callestick
Farm** in mid Cornwall. See
p. 213, p. 109, and p. 177.

Best Outdoor Eating
The Three Mackerel, above
Swanpool beach near Falmouth;
Juliet's Garden Restaurant on
St Mary's; **Stein's Fish & Chips,**
Padstow; BBQ at the **Smugglers'
Rest,** Talland Bay. See p. 192,
p. 233, p. 166, and p. 142.

Best Views The **Porthgwidden
Café Bar** in St Ives; the **Seabreeze
Café** at Torcross; the **Turk's Head**
on St Agnes; the **Beach Café** at
Sennen Cove, looking out across
the Atlantic Ocean. See p. 218,
p. 122, p. 234, and p. 214.

Enjoying a bite to eat

2 Planning a Family Trip to Devon & Cornwall

DEVON & CORNWALL

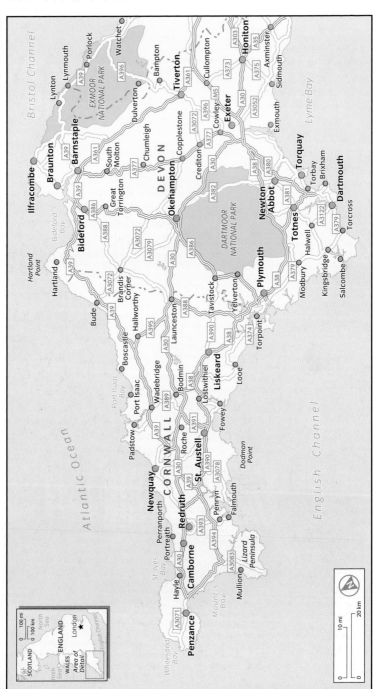

VISITOR INFORMATION

The Internet has made researching any holiday destination very easy, but that doesn't mean that every website listed via your search engine gives accurate information. The area chapters in this guidebook contain details of websites specific to that area, but if you want to find out more about the southwest as a whole visit *www.westcountry now.com* or *www.visitsouthwest. co.uk*, which cover southwest England, from Gloucestershire all the way west to the Isles of Scilly (also linked to *www.sw tourism.co.uk*). There's a useful link to *www.familyholidaysouth west.co.uk* for information on family beaches and attractions. Moving further west Devon's official tourist information site, Discover Devon (*www.discover devon.com*), is the place to go for comprehensive and up-to-date information. The family page details accommodation, activities, attractions, events, food and drink in Devon, plus an online booking facility for accommodation, travel and activities, and information on green tourism. Devon Connect (*www.devon-connect.co.uk*) has a good section on tourist attractions all over the

How This Book Works

The counties of Devon and Cornwall, together with Exmoor and the Isles of Scilly, make up a huge area – Devon alone is the second-largest county in the country, and Cornwall measures 128 km from the Devon border to Land's End – and it would be impossible in any book to present a comprehensive survey of family attractions, accommodation and eating places. However, it is possible to give an idea as to what's on offer.

I have divided the book into 10 area chapters – East Devon, North Devon Coast & Exmoor, Devon's Heartland, Dartmoor & West Devon, South Devon, Southeast Cornwall, North Cornwall, Mid Cornwall, Southwest Cornwall and the Isles of Scilly. Each chapter starts with an overview of that area, highlighting its special qualities, with information on its location and on how to get there, and particular family highlights. There follows a selection of attractions and accommodation possibilities available in that area, ranging, for example, from a simple campsite or Scandinavian-style lodge to fairly elaborate self-catering on a working farm or a top-quality family hotel. The same applies to suggestions about places to eat. In general most cafés, pubs and restaurants in the southwest will accommodate children, and there will be hundreds of suitable places not covered in this guide, but I have given a snapshot of the possible options. Accommodation and eating places have been grouped according to average price: inexpensive, moderate and expensive; attractions show the suggested suitable age range.

Fun for Free

One of the best things about family holidays in Devon and Cornwall is that although there is a wealth of attractions to visit if you wish – some ideal for wet days – it's not necessary to spend a fortune. The area is blessed with so many natural attractions that if the sun shines it's easy to occupy children by spending the day on the beach, having a picnic or flying a kite. An excellent little book published in Cornwall in 2006, **Happy Holidays** by Alix Wood (Truran Books, **www.truranbooks.co.uk**) is packed with ideas on how to occupy your children without resorting to artificial attractions: the cost soon mounts up. On a walk, on a car journey, on the beach, in the garden, on a rainy day... it's full of brilliant ideas. Another vital source of information on both paying and free family activities in the areas covered by this guidebook is **Let's Go with the Children South West**, aimed at 3–16 year olds (**www.letsgowiththechildren.co.uk**). Attractions are price coded, and split into themed sections; there are money-off vouchers to some, plus masses of useful information and contacts. Another inexpensive publication, **Kids Cornwall** (**www.kids.cornwall.co.uk**) lists '50 brilliant ways to entertain your children', a wealth of ideas put together by a group of mums with young children, with extra information on places to eat, easy walks, and handy tips. Essential reading.

county, and top attractions are covered by **www.lotstodo.co.uk**.

Cornwall Tourist Board's official website **www.cornwalltouristboard.co.uk** or **www.visitcornwall.co.uk** doesn't have a specific family page, but there's a children's welcome facility on the 'things to do' and 'accommodation' listings. **www.cornwall-online.co.uk** has good general information; **www.chycor.co.uk** details travel and accommodation, plus links to a good range of accommodation providers.

www.bbc.co.uk/devon or **/cornwall** will give you details about what's going on in the county, plus weather information. For everything you need to know about the Isles of Scilly visit **www.simplyscilly.co.uk**.

ESSENTIALS

Getting There

For all general details on travel by train, coach and bus to and within Devon and Cornwall contact Traveline (℡ 0871 200 2233; www.traveline.org.uk).

By Road The vast majority of holidaymakers come to Devon and Cornwall by car (for details on getting to the Isles of Scilly see p. 221). During peak holiday times travelling to or from the southwest via the M5 and A303 can be a nightmare (see also Family Travel p. 238), and hold-ups and long travelling times on Fridays and Saturdays unavoidable.

After decades of discussion and planning the new Goss

Moor bypass in mid Cornwall finally opened in mid July 2007, avoiding the notorious 'low bridge' bottleneck between Bodmin and Indian Queens. This stretch of the A30 carries 30,000 vehicles per day in the high summer, and was constructed at a cost of £93 million. It's now possible to travel from Edinburgh to Hayle on dual carriageways, apart from a couple of brief stretches in Cornwall.

Once you get off the A roads and onto B roads and minor roads the pace of life slows down. Many B roads (and some As) have single-lane stretches; many lanes are only wide enough for one car, with odd passing places. Brush up on your reversing skills in advance – and don't rely on in-car sat nav – you may find yourself negotiating a narrow, overgrown green lane (from which cars are banned). Some rural areas are relatively free of signposts; get hold of a good Ordinance Survey (OS) map, and learn how to use it. Thousands of people live and work in the West Country, and not every driver you come across will be on holiday; over 30,000 people, for example, live within Dartmoor National Park. Locals may not appreciate trickling along at 15 mph while the inmates of the car in front drink in the view. Be aware of other road users and considerate to their needs.

Driving in rural areas (especially Dartmoor, Exmoor and Bodmin Moor) brings with it specific hazards. Roads across moorland areas are generally

A Protected Landscape

In terms of landscape quality the southwest has it all – apart from mountains! The officially Protected Landscapes of Devon and Cornwall comprise a large percentage of the land area, reflecting the high regard in which this unique part of the country is held at national level (**www.south westlandscapes.co.uk**).

National Parks Dartmoor National Park in Devon (Chapter 6) and Exmoor National Park (Chapter 4) which straddles the north Devon–Somerset border.

Areas of Outstanding Natural Beauty The region – including the Isles of Scilly – is home to eight AONBs.

Heritage Coast Sixty percent of the Heritage Coast is found in the southwest.

World Heritage Sites – the Jurassic Coast (p. 26) and the Cornish Mining World Heritage Site (p. 133).

UNESCO Biosphere Reserve – the first to be designated in the UK – in North Devon (p. 47).

The South West Coast Path Britain's longest national trail, runs for more than 1,000 km from Minehead in Somerset to South Haven Point near Poole in Dorset.

unfenced; animals wander at random. Watch out for the temptation to slow down suddenly to look at an especially appealing foal – there may be a car right behind you. Sheep have a tendency to settle on the road to lick salts from the surface, and will seek out the shade from bridges on hot days and warmth from the road surface when it's cold. Keep your eyes peeled and your speed down.

By Rail

London and the Southeast:

First Great Western Trains provide services from South Wales and the south of England from stations including Bristol (Temple Meads and Parkway), Swindon, Reading and London Paddington (✆ *08457 000125; www.firstgreatwestern.co.uk*). **South West Trains** provide services from the south of England including Brighton, Southampton, Guildford and Bournemouth. They also provide direct services from London Waterloo (✆ *08456 000 650; www.southwesttrains.co.uk*).

The Midlands, the North & Scotland:

Virgin Cross-Country Trains provide all services to the southwest from north of Gloucester. Stations include Birmingham, Derby, York, Newcastle, Edinburgh and Glasgow (✆ *08457 222 333; www.virgintrains.co.uk*).

Useful Contacts:

National Rail Enquiries provide service and ticketing information with booking facilities for train services across the country (✆ *08457 484950; www.nationalrail.co.uk*); **The Trainline** provides the same service (*www.thetrainline.com*).

Once you've reached your destination take a trip on one of Devon and Cornwall's scenic branch lines – the Maritime Line Truro–Falmouth, St Ives Bay Line Penzance–St Ives, Looe Valley Line Liskeard–Looe, Atlantic Coast Line Par–Newquay, Tamar Valley Line Plymouth–Gunnislake, and Tarka Line Exeter–Barnstaple (*www.carfreedaysout.com*). Check out their Rail Ale Trails (✆ *01752 233094; www.railaletrail.com*).

By Bus If travelling to Devon and Cornwall by coach, contact **National Express:** a huge network of services exists between major towns across the whole country (✆ *08705 808080; www.nationalexpress.com*).

For bus journeys within Devon, **Stagecoach** (*www.stagecoachbus.com/devon*) services mainly originate in Exeter, and cover east Devon as far as Axminster, most of Devon's Heartland (Tiverton, South Molton), south Devon (including Dartmouth, Torbay and Plymouth), Dartmoor, and Barnstaple in north Devon (via South Molton). **First** (*www.firstgroup.com*) provide a number of services, such as along the River Taw to the north Devon coast; Westward Ho! to Barnstaple via Bideford; Exeter to Bude; Barnstaple to Woolacombe,

Ilfracombe and Combe Martin; Plymouth to Looe; Plymouth to Tavistock, Barnstaple, Okehampton.

First provide extensive services across Cornwall: Truro to Penzance, St Ives, St Austell, Camborne, Redruth, Newquay; St Ives to St Just, Land's End; Falmouth to Redruth, Camborne; Falmouth to Newquay, Penryn, Truro; Newquay to Truro.

First links up with **First Great Western** to offer various special train and bus deals in Cornwall (*www.firstgreatwestern. co.uk*). For details of local bus services contact Tourist Information Centres (TICs).

By Air
To Exeter:
Flybe ☏ 0871 522 6100; *www. flybe.com*

Aberdeen, Belfast City, Dublin, Edinburgh, Glasgow, Guernsey, Jersey, Leeds, Bradford, Manchester, Newcastle, Norwich

To Plymouth:
Air SouthWest ☏ 0870 241 8202; *www.airsouthwest.com*

Bristol, Jersey, Leeds Bradford, London Gatwick, Manchester

To Newquay:
Air SouthWest ☏ 0870 241 8202; *www.airsouthwest.com*

Bristol, Leeds Bradford, London Gatwick, Manchester
BmiBaby ☏ 0871 224 0224; *www.bmibaby.com*

To Manchester:
British Airways ☏ 0870 850 9850; *www.ba.com*

London Gatwick

Flybe ☏ 0871 522 6100; *www.flybe.com*

Edinburgh
Ryanair ☏ 0871 246 0000; *www.ryanair.com*

London Stansted

To the Isles of Scilly:
British International
☏ 01736 363 871; *www.isles ofscillyhelicopter.com*

Penzance Heliport (the world's longest-running scheduled helicopter service)
Skybus ☏ 0845 710 5555; *www.ios-travel.co.uk*

Bristol, Exeter, Land's End, Newquay, Southampton

ACCOMMODATION & DINING

Accommodation

So how do you decide where to stay? If you've already been to Devon and Cornwall and know which part of which county would provide the best holiday experience for your family, finding accommodation is pretty simple: just type 'Mullion cottages', for example, into your search engine, and you'll be rewarded with *www.mullion cottages.co.uk*, and more than 100 properties to choose from. The same goes for different types of accommodation in towns and villages all over Devon and Cornwall (or contact the local tourist office).

The problems start if you're a newcomer to the area and have no idea which part of which county would best suit your needs. The area chapters in this guidebook start with a rundown of that area's special qualities – whether it's good for surfing, quiet family beaches, sailing and so on – followed by details on information centres and websites that will provide accommodation options. Another point to consider is ease of access and how far you want to travel: if driving from upcountry, for example, east Devon will obviously be reached more easily than, say, west Cornwall.

Then there's the question of what sort of accommodation to go for, depending on taste and budget, and what type of facilities you're after, from simple inexpensive camping to a relatively costly family hotel with all kinds of onsite activities included. During recent years there has been a vast increase in the number of self-catering options on working or former farms, offering additional animal care and feeding (very popular with young children – see below), and the general standard of

accommodation available has vastly improved. If you want to stay on a working farm *www.farmstayuk.co.uk* details B&B, self-catering, camping and hostel accommodation on farms all over the country, with a good spread across Devon and Cornwall; **Cornish Farm Holidays** (*www.cornish-farms.co.uk*) and **Devon Farms** (*www.devonfarms.co.uk*) offer B&B and self-catering options. Another excellent site (working and non-working farm holidays) is *www.cartwheel.org.uk*, with a special toddler-friendly section. If you have young children you have a definite advantage in that you can holiday outside the main Easter and summer school holiday periods: *www.easypreschoolsouthwest.co.uk* is a very good source of information on baby- and toddler-friendly accommodation.

Self-Catering

It all depends on what you want: a remote cottage tucked away in the depths of the countryside, or

Halsbeer Farm

to stay in a complex of cottages on a farm where the children can join in with daily animal feeding and egg collecting, with swimming pool, games room and soft play area.

It's quite hard to find a non-working farmyard in Devon and Cornwall that hasn't been converted into holiday accommodation! There's a huge range of self-catering possibilities, from simple and relatively inexpensive chalets to a grand converted coach house on a country estate. Prices vary enormously, and rocket over the summer holiday period.

Two particularly good websites are **Child-Friendly Cottages** (*www.childfriendly cottages.co.uk*) and **Baby-Friendly Boltholes** (*baby friendlyboltholes.co.uk*): all the properties listed are specifically equipped for families – some more obviously geared towards the pre-school market – with a good range of additional facilities. Visit **Helpful Holidays** (*www.helpfulholidays.com*), a specialist West Country provider, for explicit details on a huge number of very lovely self-catering properties; **Farm and Cottage Holidays** (*www.holidaycottages.co.uk*), **Classic Cottages** (*www.classic. co.uk*) and **Toad Hall Cottages** (*www.toadhallcottages.co.uk*) have cottages in Devon, Cornwall and Somerset; **Marsdens Cottage Holidays** (*www.marsdens.co.uk*) covers north Devon and north Cornwall specifically; *www.south westholidaycottages.com* offers a range of properties in Cornwall. If you already know where you want

to go contact the local TIC for accommodation information, or visit the relevant websites.

Camping

Campsites too vary enormously in price, location and facilities; two or three I visited no longer accept tents and are building lodges instead in order to attract holidaymakers all year round, so it's worth checking in advance. Some campsites only accept tents; others have a separate camping field for them; some have static caravans for hire (an inexpensive self-catering option); some have bars, restaurants, swimming pools and fishing lakes. Once again, it all depends on the make-up of your party and what you want, but camping is always going to be the cheapest family holiday option.

Most of the general Devon and Cornwall websites (see above) give details of camping and caravanning parks; try *www.chycor.co.uk* and *www. cornwall-online.co.uk* for Cornwall, *www.caravancamping sites.co.uk/devon/devon.htm* for Devon, plus local area websites. Book well in advance if you're holidaying during the peak season, and check whether the campsite accepts couples or families only. Be clear about the size of your tent: pitches on most sites are now large enough to accommodate extensive family tents, but it would be unfortunate to turn up and find out that your tent was too large for its appointed spot!

Beach Safety

SLIP on a T-shirt
SLAP on a hat
SLOP on the suncream!

Days on the beach play a large part in any family holiday in Devon and Cornwall. If the weather is good all you need to do is pack up a picnic, grab towels and sun cream, buckets and spades, and head for the nearest expanse of golden sand. But apart from the obvious need to protect the family from the effects of too much sun – keep out of it altogether between 11am and 3pm – it's worth taking a quick look at some other important aspects of beach behaviour.

Keep safe in the sea Never swim alone; it's safest to swim where there is lifeguard cover, especially if you have young children (see below). Different coloured flags are displayed to indicate when and where swimming is safe: red and yellow flags denote the bathing area covered. Never swim when red flags are flying.

The sea is immensely powerful; be aware that every now and then there may be a wave that will knock you off your feet. Err on the cautious at all times. Never dive off piers or rocks: it's impossible to see what's beneath the surface.

The Royal National Lifeboat Institution (RNLI) has lifeguard cover at a large number of beaches in Devon and Cornwall; find out which ones are covered, and get more tips of beach safety by visiting ***www. rnli.org.uk***.

Beach streams Be aware that beach streams can carry unpleasant bacteria. Don't let children drink from them, or splash water in their mouths; wash hands in clean water before eating.

Inflatables These are much better used in a pool. If you do bring them to the beach only use them within the safe bathing area, and make sure they are attached to a line, held firm by an adult on the beach.

Recycling Many beaches now have recycling facilities during the summer season. Take all your litter to a bin or take it home with you.

Sand safety All children love digging holes in the sand, but when they've finished fill them in to avoid some unsuspecting person tipping in headfirst. Never let a small child crawl into a deep hole – the sides could collapse at any time.

Weaver fish Although it doesn't happen that often, people do get stung by weaver fish. This nasty little creature has a line of venomous spines along its dorsal fin, and hides under the sand at low tide. Standing on one is an extremely painful experience, and the affected foot should be immersed in very hot water for 15 minutes (it may be worth taking a thermos flask of hot water to the beach). Lifeguards will be able to assist.

B&Bs

B&Bs can get pretty pricey for families unless you only have a baby or toddler who can share your room in a travel cot, or the room is large enough to take an extra bed for an older child. Some B&B providers have interconnecting rooms; many pubs offer B&B accommodation, but few have specific facilities for children. B&B on a West Country farm is probably the best bet: check out *www.cornishfarms.co.uk*, *www.devonfarms.co.uk* and *www.cartwheel.org.uk*.

Hotels

Hotel accommodation is usually – but not always – the most expensive holiday option. Many hotels now offer a range of accommodation – half-board, full-board, B&B – or even self-catering apartments, with full use of the hotel's facilities. There are some fantastic family-friendly hotels in Devon and Cornwall with every possible need catered for – crèche, children's club, swimming pool, sporting activities for older children and so on – ideal if parents want a real break too. At the luxury end of the scale visit *www.all4kidsuk.com*, or check out local area websites and TICs.

Dining

There's been a growing interest in local food from Devon and Cornwall during recent years, as evidenced by the growth of farmers' markets and farm shops, many of which now have cafés too (see area chapters; see also Responsible Tourism, p. 238). Overall standards of food on

Fun in the Forest

The Forestry Commission (*www.forestry.gov.uk*) runs a varied programme of activities for adults and children in woods and forests all over the country, including three in Cornwall and five in Devon:

Cardinham Woods near Bodmin (North Cornwall)
Deerpark Woods near Liskeard (Southwest Cornwall)
Idless Woods near Truro (Mid Cornwall)
Abbeyford Woods near Okehampton (Mid Devon)
Cookworthy Forest near Holsworthy (Mid Devon)
Eggesford Forest between Exeter and Barnstaple (Mid Devon)
Haldon Forest Park near Exeter (South Devon)
Lydford Forest between Okehampton and Tavistock (West Devon)
Family bike rides, wildlife walks, moonlit stargazing, pond dipping, mini beat safaris, and stalking games are loads of fun for all members of the family. Go online to find out more, or contact the Peninsula District Office in Exeter (☎ *01392 834200*).

Tiddy Oggies & Thunder and Lightning

When holidaying in Cornwall it's obligatory to eat at least one tiddy oggy (or Cornish pasty) during your stay. Although there has recently been an outrageous claim (some would say) that the pasty originated in Devon, most still believe that the Cornish pasty is just that – Cornish. In the mining communities of the 19th century the pasty provided a complete meal for men working long hours underground – meat, potato, swede and onion in a pastry case – the thick crust providing a good handhold. Miners' hands were often tainted by arsenic, so the crust was rarely eaten as a result and often saved to appease the 'knockers' (ghosts) who lived down the mines. Pasties became the staple diet of miners, farmers, blacksmiths and fishermen – although fishermen believed it was bad luck to take a pasty aboard their boats.

And so to Devon...although cream teas are widely available throughout Devon and Cornwall (and Dorset and Somerset too, for that matter) it is believed by some that the tradition was inadvertently invented by the monks at Tavistock's Benedictine Abbey, when they rewarded local people with bread spread with clotted cream and strawberry preserves, in gratitude for their help in restoring the abbey when it was plundered by the Vikings in AD997. Another ancient myth is that Jennie, the fourth wife of the giant Blunderbus, who resided on Dartmoor, fed her husband clotted cream to win his affection. Whatever the truth of the matter, there is no doubt that scones (or if you're a traditionalist, Devonshire splits), clotted cream and strawberry jam is an unbeatable combination – and, certainly if you live in Devon, not merely a holiday treat! Clotted cream is made by gently heating full fat cream until it starts to wrinkle, resulting in a thick, smooth substance softer than butter but denser that whipped cream, often with a yellowish hue and delectable crusty topping. 'Thunder and lightning' is the term used when strawberry jam is replaced with treacle, or more usually today, golden syrup.

offer have improved enormously. Many pubs, cafés and restaurants make a point of using local producers wherever possible. There has also been an explosion of beach cafés and bars, and all along the coast cafés serve excellent food in pretty idyllic locations, many starting the evening menu from around 6pm to cater for the needs of families with younger children. Don't expect all pubs to serve food all day, however; although some may be open all day, many have specific food times. In terms of family-friendliness the vast majority happily accept children; not all have children's menus, but most will serve half-portions of adult dishes where possible.

3 East Devon

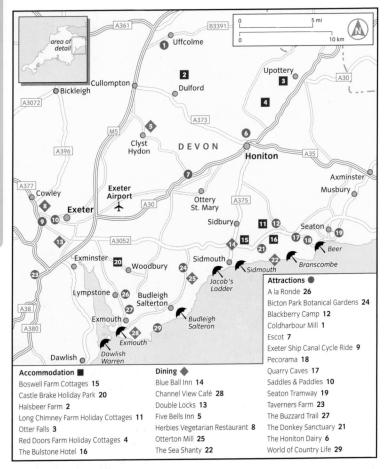

Attractions ●

A la Ronde **26**
Bicton Park Botanical Gardens **24**
Blackberry Camp **12**
Coldharbour Mill **1**
Escot **7**
Exeter Ship Canal Cycle Ride **9**
Pecorama **18**
Quarry Caves **17**
Saddles & Paddles **10**
Seaton Tramway **19**
Taverners Farm **23**
The Buzzard Trail **27**
The Donkey Sanctuary **21**
The Honiton Dairy **6**
World of Country Life **29**

Accommodation ■

Boswell Farm Cottages **15**
Castle Brake Holiday Park **20**
Halsbeer Farm **2**
Long Chimney Farm Holiday Cottages **11**
Otter Falls **3**
Red Doors Farm Holiday Cottages **4**
The Bulstone Hotel **16**

Dining ◆

Blue Ball Inn **14**
Channel View Café **28**
Double Locks **13**
Five Bells Inn **5**
Herbies Vegetarian Restaurant **8**
Otterton Mill **25**
The Sea Shanty **22**

The rolling hills and valleys of East Devon feel civilised, familiar and safe. It's an exceptionally beautiful part of the county: inland plateaux, ridges and hills, often topped with woodland and heathland, give way to a spectacular coastline – red sandstone cliffs in the west, white chalk in the east – and the tranquil fertile river valleys of the Exe, Otter, Sid and Axe, renowned for their birdlife. One-third of the East Devon district is a designated AONB, stretching from Lyme Regis in west Dorset, west to Exmouth and north to Honiton. Woodbury and adjoining commons form the largest single block of lowland heath west of the New Forest, affording ample opportunities for walking and exploring.

The Blackdown Hills AONB straddles the East Devon and south-east Somerset border north of the A30, a remote area characterised by narrow, twisting lanes, few signposts, and a mosaic of fields edged by ancient hedgerows. The north-facing scarp rises to beechwoods and pastureland, and the remains of the ancient royal Neroche Forest; population is sparse, with remote hamlets and small farms rather than compact villages.

Space to roam freely, family-friendly accommodation, all-weather attractions, safe beaches and a number of small, attractive towns – Ottery St Mary and Honiton inland, and coastal settlements such as Sidmouth and Exmouth – make this part of Devon an appealing holiday destination for young families. You'll find country pubs and traditional teashops here, not beach bars and bistros, while the county town of Exeter provides the necessary 'buzz' for those seeking more lively entertainment.

VISITOR INFORMATION

The free publication **Essential Devon** (*www.essentialdevon. co.uk*) covers East Devon and part of mid Devon and is packed with useful information, as is the **East Devon Holiday Guide** (*www.devon24.co.uk*). The Blackdown Hills AONB Partnership publishes a free booklet of guided walks and activities (℡ *01823 680681; www.blackdown-hills.net*); it's worth checking out the East Devon AONB (℡ *01404 46663; www.eastdevonaonb.org.uk*). **What's On Exeter** (*www. whatson-exeter.co.uk*) is a handy guide to events in Exeter and its environs. The best maps are OS Explorers 115 Exmouth & Sidmouth, plus the eastern section of 114 Exeter & the Exe Valley, and the western section of 116 Lyme Regis & Bridport.

Information Centres

Axminster, The Old Courthouse, Church Street ℡ *01297 34386*

Budleigh Salterton, Fore Street ℡ *01395 445275; www. visitbudleigh.com*

Exeter, Civic Centre, Paris Street ℡ *01392 265700; www. exeter.gov.uk/visiting*

Exeter Quay House Visitor Centre, Exeter Quay ℡ *01392 271611*

Exmouth, Manor Gardens, Alexandra Terrace ℡ *01395 222299; www.exmouth-guide. co.uk*

Honiton, Lace Walk Car Park ℡ *01404 43716*

Ottery St Mary, 10b Broad Street ℡ *01404 813964; www. otterytourism.org.uk*

Seaton, The Underfleet ℡ *01297 21660; www.seaton.gov.uk*

Sidmouth, Ham Lane ℡ *01395 516441 www.visitsidmouth.co.uk*

Orientation

East Devon is the most accessible part of the county when travelling from 'up country': when on the M5 heading for Exeter look out for the Wellington monument to the left – you can't miss it – the Somerset–East Devon border runs close by. Further south the A303 and then the A30 crosses East Devon from east to west, running through Honiton to Exeter (passing Exeter airport en route); the A35 runs from the coast at Lyme Regis in Dorset northwest to reach Honiton. The B3052 follows the coast from Lyme Regis via Seaton and Sidford to link with the M5 east of Exeter.

Getting Around

Road links are better in East Devon than in the rest of the county, and unless you delve into the remote countryside north of the A30 towards the Blackdown Hills you shouldn't have too many problems finding your way around. Mainline trains run through East Devon into Exeter St David's from Waterloo via Axminster and Honiton, with a branch line along the Exe estuary to Exmouth. Buses link East Devon's main towns, and the **Jurassic Coast bus service** runs through the south of the area, linking Exeter, Sidford, Beer and Seaton (**www.jurassiccoast.com**). For information on bus and train timetables ask in the local TIC or ☎ Traveline *0871 200 2233; www.traveline.org.uk*.

Child-Friendly Events & Entertainment

Devon County Show

Mid May, Westpoint, Clyst St Mary, near Exeter. www.devoncounty show.co.uk

This huge three-day show – the biggest agricultural county show in the country – gives a real taste of how rural Devon works, and is a virtual tour of country life. The show features livestock competitions, marquees full of cattle, pigs, sheep, goats, poultry – and flowers – local foods, every sort of

Sidmouth Folk Week

agricultural item under the sun, children's activities, family entertainment.

Exeter Festival

Mid June, mainly central Exeter.
☏ *01392 493493; www.exeter.gov. uk/summerfestival*

Music, concerts, comedy, workshops, children's events, wonderful craft market on the Cathedral Green, local foods, fireworks... Exeter comes alive during the two weeks of the festival.

Sidmouth Folk Week

Early Aug, all around the town.
☏ *01395 578627; www.sidmouth folkweek.co.uk*

Eight days of fun: concerts, ceilidhs, dances, workshops and impromptu music sessions take over this gentile East Devon town. There's a wonderful atmosphere and special events for children in Blackmore Gardens: puppet theatre, storytelling, craft and music activities, plus family concerts. You can join a lantern-making workshop and take part in the last night's torchlight procession – not to be missed.

WHAT TO SEE & DO

Children's Top 10 Attractions

❶ Riding through the gardens at Pecorama on the Beer Light Railway. See p. 27.

❷ Choosing one of 45 different ice creams at The Honiton Dairy. See p. 34.

❸ Cycling beside the Exeter Ship Canal on the way to the Turf Hotel. See p. 30.

❹ Stroking the nose of a donkey at the Donkey Sanctuary. See p. 28.

❺ Whizzing down the giant slides at Exmouth's World of Country Life. See p. 28.

❻ Fossil hunting on Charmouth beach, just over the Devon–Dorset border. See p. 26.

❼ Face painting during Sidmouth Folk Week. See above.

❽ Creeping through Exeter's medieval Underground Passages. See p. 24.

❾ Not getting lost in the beech maze at Escot Fantasy Gardens. See p. 26.

❿ Looking out for rabbits from the Seaton Tram as it trundles through the Axe Valley. See p. 27.

Towns & Villages

Beer

Beer is one of East Devon's most attractive seaside villages, with a long history of smuggling, a pretty beach and lots of places to eat and drink. Beer is also famous for Honiton lace, a craft brought here by Flemish refugees in the 16th century. The village's other claim to fame is the **Quarry Caves** (*www.beerquarrycaves. fsnet.co.uk*). Beer stone has been produced here for 2,000 years and was used to build Exeter and

Beer

St Paul's Cathedrals, and the Tower of London. There's an hour-long guided tour – take warm clothes and sensible footwear; children under 12 must be accompanied by an adult.

Exeter

One of the most attractive aspects of Exeter is the fact that from most parts of the city centre you have a distant view of green hills! It's a manageable town: the city centre and old West Quarter (leading to the River Exe and historic quayside with good cafés and cycle and canoe hire at **Saddles & Paddles** (see p. 30), plus the **Quay House Visitor Centre** (☎ *01392 271611*) with ducks to feed is compact and easy to explore. The town has all the usual amenities and high street shops, plus three cinemas, while the **Royal Albert Memorial Museum** in Queen Street (☎ *01392 665858*) has children's quiz sheets and activity boxes. There has been a settlement here

(the lowest crossing point of the Exe) since before the Romans arrived in AD50; about two-thirds of the Roman city walls are still visible. The magnificent cathedral church of St Peter dates from Norman times (great café in the cloisters – excellent carrot cake!), and Cathedral Close is flanked by fine Tudor and Georgian buildings. Take a trip through the unique 13th-century Underground Passages off the High Street (☎ *01392 665887*), built to bring fresh water into the city. The passages reopened late in 2007 after extensive city centre redevelopment. Join a **Red Coat guided tour,** and if you're feeling brave go on an evening 'Ghosts and Legends' or 'Murder and Mayhem' tour to find out about grizzly happenings in Exeter's past (☎ *01392 265203; www.exeter. gov.uk/guided tours*). Younger children will enjoy **Dinky's Pop In & Play Café** behind St George's Hall (☎ *01392 252253*), suitable for 1–5 year olds.

Exmouth

Exmouth, situated on the east side of the mouth of the River Exe, is a fairly typical seaside town that has expanded enormously in the last few years – the town's main claim to fame is the fabulous 3.2 km sandy beach. For boat trips contact **Stuart Lines** (p. 30). **Edge Watersports** (☎ *01395 222551; www.edgewatersports.com*) offer courses in windsurfing, kayaking, kitesurfing and the like, some suitable for children as young as six. Along the Esplanade you'll find a putting green and **Jungle Fun** (soft play) (☎ *01395 273312*) and **Exmouth Fun Park** adventure playground (☎ *01395 222545*), as well as **Exmouth Model Railway** (☎ *01395 278383*). A quirky place to visit is **A la Ronde**, just north of the town (☎ *01395 265514; www.nationaltrust.org.uk*). This interesting little 16-sided house, built in the late 1790s, was home to two spinsters who collected all kinds of objects on their Grand Tour of Europe. There are lots of fun bits and pieces for children to look at – plus quiz, trail and a tearoom – and the scale of the building makes it more manageable than many other National Trust properties.

Sidmouth

Sidmouth is a delightful, unspoilt Regency seaside town. It became a popular holiday venue in the late 18th century, but lost favour to Torquay in the mid-19th century, so missed out on further development. There's a very civilised feel here, with none of the 'tackiness' associated with some seaside settlements. The best beach for families is **Jacob's Ladder**; check out the Jungle and Rock Garden in lovely **Connaught Gardens** just above the beach, where you'll also find the **Clocktower Tearooms**. For excellent fish and chips (eat in or takeaway) go to

Exmouth Beach

The Jurassic Coast

The coast of East Devon and Dorset has a real claim to fame: in late 2001 this 152-km stretch of coastline – where the oldest rocks, at Orcombe Point near Exmouth, date back 250 million years – was designated the UK's first natural World Heritage Site. The friable red sandstone cliffs of East Devon (the Triassic Coast) run into the chalk cliffs of the Jurassic Coast, named as a result of the wealth of fossils found in the Jurassic chalk where it meets the coast, most famously around Lyme Regis and Charmouth in West Dorset. Go fossil collecting on the beaches there, particularly after stormy weather, and you may well come home with an exciting find – most likely a spiral-shaped Ammonite. In Devon you can find wonderful quartzite pebbles to the west of the sea front at Budleigh Salterton, brought here by ancient rivers in Triassic times. Much of East Devon was dry and arid 250–200 million years ago, giving rise to the rusty red colour of East Devon's soils (*www.jurassiccoast.com*).

Prospect Plaice which has quick service, sea views and welcomes children. There's a swimming pool in Ham Lane (☎ *01395 577057*) and the **Radway cinema** (☎ *01395 513085*), and lovely, gentle walks along the banks of the River Sid through **The Byes,** where expectant ducks wait to be fed.

Fun Days Out

Escot Fantasy Gardens, Maze & Woodland ★★ ALL AGES

Fairmile, Ottery St Mary, Devon EX11 1LU; ☎ 01404 822188; www.escot-devon.co.uk. Signed from the A30 between Exeter and Honiton.

Drive through the gates into the historic Escot estate – the present house was built in 1837/8, but the estate dates from the 1680s – and you enter a different world. The Victorian two-acre walled vegetable garden is home to beautiful rose-covered bowers, plus birds of prey (flying demos twice a day), pets' corner and chattering otters. Don't miss the fantastic beech maze – very easy to get lost, but four wooded bridges inside give you a bird's-eye view of where you are! Follow the fantasy trail through the woods to find wild boar, pot-bellied pigs, pheasants, 'upside-down trees', swinging ropes, woodland playground, giant trees... Escot still feels very much part of an English country estate, aided by the fact that a 'natural' approach to family entertainment has been taken by utilising fallen trees, wilderness paths and so on: a day spent here is a real adventure (don't miss the letter-box trail). The shop and restaurant are in the Victorian stables and courtyard, where there are children's games – and seahorses!

Open 10am–6pm daily summer, 5pm rest of year. **Admission** £5.95 adult, £4.95 child (3–15), under 3 free, £4.95 OAP, £18.50 family. **Credit** AmEx,

MC, V. **Amenities** disabled access possible, parking, picnic areas, restaurant, shop, aquatic centre.

Pecorama ★ ★ ★ FIND ALL AGES

Beer, Devon EX12 3NA; ☎ 01297 21542; www.peco-uk.com. Signed from the centre of Beer. Bus from Exeter and Seaton.

A fantastic place to visit at any age, in a superb position overlooking the historic little village of Beer and out to sea. Model railway buffs will spend hours in the exhibition and shop, where clever layouts are demonstrated – even one in a fish tank – and buttons to press to get trains moving. Children and adults will love riding on the Beer Heights Light Railway from Much Natter station, which trundles through beautifully landscaped and flower-filled gardens before running through a very dark tunnel out into the countryside. There are the magnificent and innovative Peco Gardens to explore, including the Sun, Moon and Rainbow Gardens, linked by bridges and enticing narrow paths – and the very special Secret Garden. And then near the Wildway Park – tucked away out of sight– there are children's activity areas for toddlers to teens, a crazy golf course and fitness trail for adults. Refreshments can be taken in a luxury Pullman car or in the Garden Room. A delightful, magical place.

***Open** 10am–5.30pm (4.30pm Oct) Mon–Fri, 10am–1pm Sat early Apr– end Oct; 10am–5.30pm Easter Sun, Sun end May to early Sept (gardens and railway; model railway exhibition 10am–5.30pm Mon–Fri, 10am–1pm Sat all year).* **Admission** *£6 adult, £4 child (4–14) under 4/over 80 free, £5.50 OAP; reduced prices for gardens only, extra train rides etc.* **Credit** *MC, V.* **Amenities** *café, disabled access, parking, picnic area, restaurant, shop, outdoor play area, special events: jugglers, clowns, magicians, Thomas the Tank Engine story days.*

Seaton Tramway ★ ★

Harbour Road, Seaton, Devon EX12 2NQ; ☎ 01297 20375; www.tram. co.uk. Follow signs off the A3052 into the centre of Seaton, or from the centre of Colyton.

Take a gentle 4.8 km tram trip along the unspoilt Axe Valley between the seaside town of Seaton and historic Colyton (infamous since the Monmouth Rebellion of 1685). You can catch the tram at either end; I would recommend starting from Colyton station (excellent shop and café, picnic tables on the platform, free parking and Motoring Memories Museum). The trams are scaled-down versions of metropolitan trams, with steep, narrow stairs leading to the open top (for the less

Escot Otters, Fairmile

Colyton tram station

agile – and rainy days – there is plenty of room inside). Wave at the traffic as the tram passes over the A3052 – or alight here for a drink at the White Hart Inn, and catch the next tram (they run every 20 minutes). Keep an eye out for wading birds – and hundreds of rabbits – as you trundle through Seaton Marshes. The seafront is only a five-minute walk from the Seaton terminus.

Open *10am–5pm (later in summer holidays) Feb half-term, end Mar–end Oct; weekends Mar/Nov.* **Return fare** *£7.95 adult, £5.55 child (4–14), under 4 free, £7.15 OAP, discounts for families.* **Credit** *MC, V.* **Amenities** *disabled access, parking, café, shop, parking, disabled access at Colyton station.*

Animal Attractions

The Donkey Sanctuary ☆

Sidmouth, Devon EX10 0NU; ☎ *01395 578222; www.thedonkeysanctuary. org.uk. Follow signs off the A3052*

just east of Sidford. Bus from Exeter and Axe Valley.

There's hundreds of donkeys here! They come to the sanctuary from all over the country, some rescued, some retired, and you get the feeling that those living here are the lucky ones. Some of the residents are around 40 years old, living in peaceful retirement. A handy leaflet gives a guide to donkey behaviour and explains their different coloured collars (displaying each donkey's name): red for boys, yellow for girls, pink for blind and so on. The best way to make sure you see everything is to follow the numbered walks around the site – and try not to let your child get too attached to any of the donkeys that are up for adoption...

Open *9am–dusk daily. Restaurant open 10.30am–5pm spring/summer, 11.30am–3.30pm autumn/winter* ☎ *01395 514996).* **Admission** *free.* **Credit** *MC, V.* **Amenities** *café, disabled access, parking, picnic area, shop, maze, nature centre, walks.*

World of Country Life ☆☆
ALL AGES

Sandy Bay, Littleham, Exmouth, Devon EX8 5BU; ☎ *01395 274533; www.worldofcountrylife.co.uk. Signed from B1378 Exmouth–Budleigh Salterton. Bus from Exmouth.*

First impressions can be a little misleading here. Situated by Sandy Bay holiday park, the World of Country Life has something for every age (and all weathers – much of the site is under cover). There's a fascinating mix of rural and agricultural memorabilia – a reconstructed Victorian village street and a huge collection of farming machinery, plus working steam engines, vintage and veteran vehicles. Outside children can enjoy exotic birds, Shetland ponies, wallabies, pets' corner – or take a pygmy goat for a walk. There are tractor and trailer rides to hand-feed red deer, llamas and Soay sheep, and a huge selection of indoor and outdoor activities: radio-controlled boats, crazy golf, trampolines, soft play, a wonderful pirate ship, bouncy castles, and some brilliant slides (for adults too!). The site is much bigger than you think at first, and I cannot imagine it ever feeling overcrowded. Those interested in nostalgia can happily while away the hours while the rest of the family indulge in more frivolous pastimes!

Open *10am–5pm early Apr–end Sept.* **Admission** *£9 adult, £7.50 child (3–17), under 3 free, £7.50 OAP, £30 family.* **Credit** *AmEx, MC, V.* **Amenities** *café, disabled access, parking, picnic area, restaurant, shop.*

Gardens

Bicton Park Botanical Gardens ★★

Budleigh Salterton, Devon EX9 7BJ; ☎ 01395 568465; www.bicton gardens.co.uk. From the A3052 at Newton Poppleford follow signs on the B3178 for 4.8 km. Bus from Exmouth, Budleigh Salterton, Sidmouth.

A botanical garden may not be somewhere you'd think

particularly entertaining for children – but Bicton is full of fun things to do for the whole family. The historic gardens are wonderful, and include a Stream Garden, Mediterranean Garden, Palm House and pinetum, a huge lake and superb collection of (often enormous) trees. There's a wonderful 19th-century summerhouse for under 12s, and picnic tables by the lake. There are huge indoor (with an area for under 5s) and outdoor play areas, with snack shacks; there's mini-golf, a maze, football pitch and five brightly coloured playhouses for the under 8s. And to top it all there's the Woodland Railway, a lovely 25-minute ride behind the *Sir Walter Raleigh* engine. On wet days take a look inside the Countryside Museum where boys of all ages will delight in tractors, steam rollers and a hand-operated fire engine, last used at Bicton around 1931. Note: children must be supervised at all times, and are not allowed to climb the trees.

Open *10am–6pm summer, 10am–5pm winter (closed Christmas Day and Boxing Day).* **Admission** *£6.95 adult, £5.95 child, £22.95 family.* **Credit** *AmEx, MC, V.* **Amenities** *Orangery Restaurant, snack bars, disabled access, parking, picnic areas, shop, garden centre, 60 acres of woodland and garden, woodland railway.*

Best Beaches

Beer Pebble beach, natural suntrap. Café, car park up hill.

Branscombe Shingle and pebble beach, steep shelf into water. Café, car park.

Budleigh Salterton Pebble beach, red cliffs. Café, car park.

Exmouth Long sandy beach, good for watersports. All amenities.

Jacob's Ladder, Sidmouth Popular family beach, sheltered, pebbles with sand at low water. Café, car park.

Sidmouth Town beach 1.6 km long, pebble beach. All amenities. Sand at low water.

INSIDER TIP

Stuart Line Cruises (℡ 01395 222144; www.stuartlinecruises.co.uk) run lovely boat trips from Exmouth Marina and Sidmouth – a great way to explore the Exe estuary and to see the **Jurassic Coast** (p. 26). You can cruise along the Jurassic Coast and return via the Jurassic Coast bus on a combined ticket, or take a day trip to Torquay or Brixham in South Devon.

For Active Families

Exeter Ship Canal Cycle Ride AGES 5 AND UP

This is one of the best short family cycle rides in the area in terms of interest, landscape quality (and pubs en route). The easy ride follows well-surfaced paths from Exeter's historic quayside, then strikes south along the old ship canal through Royal Society for the Protection of Birds (RSPB) nature reserves (good information boards) and marshes to pass the Double Locks (p. 36) and finally reach the Turf Hotel, situated on the Exe estuary (a great place for lunch). You follow the canal for most of the way; it was extended to Topsham (a port since Roman times) in 1676, and in the early 19th century reached the Turf Hotel. The fortunes of the canal deteriorated when the railway reached Exeter in 1844. Considering this ride starts in the centre of Exeter it is remarkably rural, with only one controlled road crossing (A379) by the swing bridge. In summer the canal is bordered by swathes of yellow flag and purple loosestrife plants. The return is by the same route, but this is such a lovely ride it's a real treat to do it twice!

Exeter Quay to the Turf Hotel 10 km. Cycle hire Saddles & Paddles, Exeter; ℡ 01392 424241; www.saddlepaddle.co.uk

The Buzzard Trail AGES 5 AND UP

This easy route follows part of The Buzzard, a 130 km circular cycle route through East Devon. Much of this section follows the line of the old Exmouth–Budleigh Salterton railway line (1903–67). Cycle as far as you like before turning round, depending on the make-up of your family group. The first part through Exmouth isn't particularly attractive – the best bit is out in the countryside beyond Littleham – but be aware that to reach that section there is some pavement work and a fairly busy road crossing (at traffic lights). Families with older children can cycle onto Budleigh Salterton from Bear Lane (but the B3178 is very busy) or – probably better – take a detour from the route towards the coast at Littleham,

Exeter Ship Canal

and return to Exmouth along Maer Lane (narrow), which is followed by a lovely run along Exmouth's beach. Another alternative is to take in the World of Country Life at Sandy Bay (p. 28).

Phear Park, Exmouth to Bear Lane. Knowle 8 km. Cycle hire Knobblies, Exmouth; ☏ 01395 270182; Bikeworks, Exmouth; ☏ 01395 223242.

FAMILY-FRIENDLY ACCOMMODATION

INEXPENSIVE

Castle Brake Holiday Park ☆

Woodbury, nr Exeter, Devon EX5 1HA; ☏ 01395 232431; www.castle brake.co.uk. Between Woodbury and Exmouth; signed from A3052/A3180 Halfway Inn.

A campsite with a little bit extra for those families who want to stay in a quiet, rural location and learn about local wildlife. This medium-sized family site is on the edge of Woodbury Common in East Devon AONB, with ample opportunities for walking and wildlife spotting. Each year the park supports a different wildlife charity, and produces a leaflet on local wildlife, as well as a nature trail for children, which teaches them about their local environment. There's a woodland walk, wildflower meadows, a cycling trail and a wealth of wildlife – roe deer are often spotted in the lower field. On less clement evenings visitors can take advantage of Mr Badger's Bar and Restaurant (takeaway service 6pm–9.30pm in peak season). Children under 14 are not allowed in the bar, but there's a big family room, with games and toys, TV and Internet access. Food is home-made and locally sourced wherever possible.

*25 camping pitches, £8–12.50 per night (2 people), £2 child over 5. 12 static caravans, 2–3 bedrooms, £224–440 per week. **Credit** MC, V. **Amenities** parking, shop, laundry, dogs welcome, bar/restaurant, adventure playground, cycle trail, croquet lawn, sauna/steam room.*

MODERATE

The Bulstone Hotel ★ ★

*Higher Bulstone, Branscombe, Devon EX12 3BL; ☎ 01297 680446; **www.childfriendlyhotels.com**. Follow signs off the A3052 Exeter–Lyme Regis at Branscombe Cross.*

This homely, practical, 'no frills' hotel caters essentially for families with children under eight, and is a real old-fashioned family-friendly establishment. Up to nine families can be accommodated at one time; rooms are well-appointed, with children in an adjoining room. The needs and demands of small children are paramount: guests have their own kitchen where babies' bottles and snacks can be prepared; there is a children's TV lounge (good selection of videos), large playroom, and children's tea served at 5pm. Parents dine from 8pm (all rooms have baby monitors), and can relax in the adults-only lounge. The large child-friendly garden has tractors, swings and climbing frames, beaches and a number of good attractions – Bicton (p. 29),

Pecorama (p. 27) and Exmouth's World of Country Life (p. 28) – are within easy reach.

*7 family suites and 2 family units (2 adults/2 children). **Rates** £769 (low)–£859 (high). **Amenities** babysitting, bar, cots in all rooms, extra bed possible, laundry service, parking, restaurant, guests' kitchen, Internet access (in office). **In room** shower/bath. TV (TV/DVD in children's TV room).*

Boswell Farm Cottages ★ ★

*Sidford, nr Sidmouth, Devon EX10 0PP; ☎ 01395 514162; **www. boswell-farm.co.uk**. From Sidford head east on the A3052; just past the Blue Ball Inn turn left, signed Harcombe; after 200 m, turn right for Boswell Farm.*

Drive into the yard at Boswell Farm and you just can't stop yourself from saying 'Wow!'. This beautiful Grade II listed 17th-century farmhouse and its holiday cottages – converted from period farm buildings – nestle in the secluded Sweetcombe Valley by the Snod brook ('snod' = Old English for 'pretty'). The magnificent Bank Barn (c.1710) is reputed to be the only threshing barn in the country still standing on its original sandstone piers. This is a glorious place: the care put into the conversions (each has a private garden) extends to the rambling roses and flowering creepers that tumble over each one. Each cottage is different, retaining original features while conforming to modern expectations in terms of comfort and equipment. There's an under 10s play area and the chance to collect eggs and feed chickens, geese

Try These Too!

- **Long Chimney Farm Holiday Cottages:** Two recently converted semi-detached stone cottages in the grounds of a beautiful country house.
  Beech Tree Lane, Salcombe Regis, Sidmouth, Devon EX10 0PE;
  📞 *01297 680636*; *www.longchimneyfarmcottages.co.uk*

- **Halsbeer Farm:** Four thatched cottages near Blackborough supplying everything one might require for a tranquil family holiday.
  Cullompton, Devon EX15 2HD; 📞 *01647 433593*; *www.helpful holidays.com*

- **Five Bells Inn:** A lovely traditional 16th-century thatched, low-beamed pub, tucked away in rural East Devon.
  Clyst Hydon, Cullompton, Devon EX15 2NT; 📞 *01274 277288*;
  www.fivebellsclysthydon.co.uk.

and goats. The extensive meadow is ideal for ball games and kite flying; a fishing lake, all-weather tennis court and pilates classes complete the picture, with the beach at Sidmouth just a few kilometres away.

7 s/c cottages: 2–6 people (+ cot). **Rates** *£275 (low)–1,142 (high) (2 properties can be combined to sleep 12).* **Credit** *MC, V.* **Amenities** *babysitting, cot (free), DIY laundry, parking, tennis court, children's play area, trout pond, 45 acres of farmland.* **In cottage** *fridge, cooker and microwave, dishwasher, shower/bath, TV/video, private enclosed gardens/ garden furniture.*

INSIDER TIP »

If you're staying in East Devon in May visit **Blackberry Camp,** an Iron Age settlement at Southleigh. It will take your breath away: beautiful beech trees in early leaf rise above a magnificent carpet of bluebells, the deepest of purple-blues. Well worth making the effort.

Otter Falls ☆

New Road, Upottery, Honiton, Devon EX14 9QB; 📞 *01404 861706; www. otterfalls.co.uk. Upottery is signed off the A30 east of Honiton.*

In a part of the country where converted farm buildings are the norm for holiday accommodation, Otter Falls is something a bit different. If you're after a more intimate experience it might not be ideal, but it's a good destination for families with older children who are looking for on-site entertainment (and others of a similar age): there's tennis, pool, table tennis, pitch and putt, coarse fishing on three lakes, and a bar and bistro during peak seasons. The coast at Beer is 22 km away, so this is a place for those families who are happy to spend some days on site. Otter Falls does have self-catering cottages, but also nine wooden single-storey open-plan Finnish-style

FUN FACT ›› Homemade Ice Cream ‹‹

You can't visit East Devon without trying one – or more! – of The Honiton Dairy's (☎ *01404 42075*) superb homemade ice creams. The family has been producing ice cream since 1935, and makes over 45 different flavours with new ones every year. You can't miss the shop – it's on the High Street and has huge ice cream cones outside. Try choc chip, honeycomb, black cherry, banoffee pie, white choc and malteser, apricot...or go for the soft whipped ice cream, freshly made every day.

lodges overlooking the fishing lakes, each with its own veranda. Accommodation is flexible: in the two-bedroom lodges extra children can sleep on a sofa bed. Electricity and gas is extra, calculated at the end of your stay.

9 s/c lodges, 4–6 people, + 12 self-catering cottages, 2–10 people. **Rates** *£265 (low)–925 (high) lodges; £180 (low)–925 (high) cottages.* **Credit** *MC, V.* **Amenities** *cot (charge), disabled access, parking, indoor pool/sauna, launderette, fishing, bar/bistro, games rooms, pitch and putt course, tennis court.* **In lodges** *cooker/microwave, dishwasher, washing machine/tumble dryer (in 3-bed lodges), garden furniture.*

EXPENSIVE

Red Doors Farm Holiday Cottages ★★

Beacon, Luppitt, Honiton, Devon EX14 4TX; ☎ *01404 890067; www.reddoors.co.uk. Luppitt is signed off the A30 at Monkton, just east of Honiton: Beacon is passed en route.*

The countryside north of the A30 to the east of Honiton, towards the Blackdown Hills, has a remote, 'step-back-in-time' feel: deep valleys, narrow twisting lanes, tiny hamlets tucked away into the folds of the hills. Yet beautiful 500-year-old Red Doors Farm lies just a 10-minute drive

Red Doors Farm Holiday Cottages near Honiton

(mainly uphill!) from the A30 – easily accessible yet peaceful, with lovely views over the Otter valley. The farmhouse and tastefully converted flint and thatched buildings sit around the big cobbled yard; you can almost imagine working horses clumping through the gate. A huge amount of care has gone into the conversions and furnishings. One cottage has a first-floor sitting room to take advantage of the view; some have views to the National Trust's Dumpden Hill (good for flying kites). Each has a pretty garden, with flowering shrubs and creepers; there are two play areas, one partially covered; trampoline; giant chess and croquet; and big indoor swimming pool, a real bonus in poor weather. There's a really intimate, personal atmosphere. Highly recommended.

7 s/c cottages: 2–8 people (+ cot). **Rates** *£325 (low)–1650 (high) per week.* **Credit** *MC, V.* **Amenities** *babysitting, cot (free), extra bed (child – free), parking, indoor pool, children's play areas, games room, home-cooked freezer meals, Internet access in games room.* **In cottage** *welcome hamper, fridge/freezer, cooker/microwave, dishwasher, washer/dryer, shower/bath, TV/DVD/satellite.*

FAMILY-FRIENDLY DINING

Channel View Café ★★

The Esplanade, Exmouth, Devon EX8 2AZ; ℡ 01395 279238. On the seafront near Exmouth Pavilions. Bus from Exeter. Sidmouth.

A really fun place for a family meal, situated over the road from Exmouth's lovely beach – and with its own indoor toddlers' play area to occupy small children. Pirate scenes adorn the walls, and the indoor play area is set up like a pirate school – great artwork, wooden floors, barrels and ropes, all nicely unfussy. The children's menu (£3.45) has a clever pick 'n' mix element: three of, for example, bacon, sausage, peas, beans, fish fingers, hash browns. There's also healthy options and the needs of 'picky' children are met wherever possible! Adults can enjoy the very reasonably priced all-day breakfast and daily specials: West country smoked mackerel salad (£8.45) and homemade cauliflower cheese (£6.95). Opposite are swingboats, a merry-go-round, and the beach.

Open *9.30am–5pm (to c.10.30pm school holidays, depending on weather) Easter to end Oct; Sun in winter.* **Main course** *£5.95–8.95.* **Credit** *No – cash machine in café.* **Amenities** *children's menu, indoor play area, highchair, disabled access, small car park.*

INSIDER TIP
Sidford's fine old 14th-century pub The Blue Ball Inn (℡ *01395 514062; www.blueballinn.net*) was razed to the ground by fire in March 2006. A wonderful thatched building, the pub had been in the same family since 1912 and had built up an excellent reputation for good food and friendly service – and for welcoming children.

Happily, the pub was rebuilt during 2007 on the same lines, and in 2008 normal service will be resumed from 8am to midnight every day (plus nine en suite bedrooms).

Double Locks ★★★

Canal Banks, Exeter, Devon EX2 6LT; (01392 256947; www.doublelocks. co.uk. Difficult to find from Marsh Barton trading estate (along Alphinbrook Road) – best on foot, by bike or boat.

The Double Locks pub – originally a lock-keeper's cottage (built 1701) and stabling for barge horses – sits by the earliest English lock canal, begun in 1563, linking Exeter to Matford Brook, and extended to Topsham in 1676. The one lock is big enough to accommodate two ships at once, hence 'Double Locks'. Today it provides a fabulous setting for a very popular pub (packed with students during term-time). Under 18s are not allowed in the bar but there's lots of inside space for families, and extensive seating along the banks of the canal and also a large grassy area and playground where children can play at a safe distance from the water. The menu is original and varied: chili bean pot (£6.50), goat's cheese and roasted vegetable ciabatta (£4.95) and mango, feta and chickpea salad (£7.25).

Open *11am–12 pm daily.* **Main course** *£6.50–10.50.* **Credit** *MC, V.* **Amenities** *half portions of many dishes, volleyball, beer festivals, barbecues, outdoor adventure play area, bike racks, disabled access possible, parking.*

INSIDER TIP

The best way to get to the Double Locks is by foot, bike or boat. You can hire bikes and canoes from Saddles & Paddles on Exeter Quay, or take a leisurely ride along the canal with Exeter Cruises (07984 368442; www. exetercruises.com). And if once you get to the Double Locks you're still feeling energetic, cycle on for another km or so to the lovely Turf Locks Hotel, situated at the junction of the canal with the River Exe – or onto Powderham Castle (p. 114). The White Heather launch operates daily from Exeter Quay to the Double Locks, and onto the Turf.

Otterton Mill ★★

Otterton, Budleigh Salterton, Devon EX9 7HG; (01395 567041; www. ottertonmill.com. On the edge of Otterton, signed off B3178 Newton Poppleford–Budleigh Salterton.

Otterton Mill – the last working mill on the River Otter – has been working for more than 1,000 years, using waterpower to produce stoneground flour. Today the mill and its buildings (occasional milling days) have been tastefully converted into a spacious craft gallery, workshops, a bakery and wonderful local food shop. Delicious (often organic) food is available: breakfast (until 11am); pâté, hummus, Devon cheese, wonderful soups, all served with wonderful home-baked bread; original and substantial 'chunky' salads (£5.95); red onion and goat's cheese tart (£7.30), beef casserole (£8.15). If you can't fit in

Orange Elephants «

South Devon cattle are known as 'orange elephants' because of their long faces and rusty red-coloured coats, and **Taverners Farm** (📞 *01392 833776; www.tavernersfarm.co.uk*) near Kennford (just off the A38 southwest of Exeter) produces delicious Orange Elephant ice cream. There's an excellent café and farm shop too.

pudding drop into the Devon food shop where you'll be tempted by cider apple cake, flapjacks (oat cakes) and lemon drizzle cake, and a huge range of Devon produce. Two large courtyards, one partially covered, increase the available seating: there's a wonderfully relaxed feel (but it's very busy at holiday times). There are also easy walks lead along the tranquil River Otter toward Budleigh Salterton.

*Open 10am–5pm summer; Nov onwards 10am–dusk daily. **Main course** £5.95–8.25. **Credit** MC, V. **Amenities** half portions, music evenings, highchair, disabled access, reservations accepted, parking, craft shops, bakery.*

INSIDER TIP »

Look out for traces of otters if you go for a walk along the River Otter. Strangely this was the last Devon river on which the return of the otter (after several years' absence) was recorded.

The Sea Shanty ★ ★

Restaurant and Shop, Branscombe Beach, East Devon EX12 3DP; 📞 01297 680577; www.thesea shanty.co.uk. Follow signs for the beach from Branscombe village (signed off the A3052 east of Sidford). Bus from Exeter and Lyme Regis to Branscombe; level walk to beach.

Round off your exploration of East Devon's Jurassic Coast with a visit to the thatched Sea Shanty, situated on Branscombe's shingle beach. The café is housed in an old coal yard (coal imported from South Wales), and has been serving refreshments for more than 70 years. Although the beach isn't ideal for small children – it's pebbly and steeply shelving – the Sea Shanty is worth a visit for good family food. Crab, lobster and fish come straight off the beach; 'small fry bites' appear on the children's menu (£3.95). There are daily specials from £7.95 – fresh salmon, homemade steak and kidney pie, lobster (when available) – and delicious puddings. With a walled suntrap courtyard, an open fire inside, tables by the beach and wonderful views, this café caters for all the vagaries of the British climate.

*Open 10am–5pm daily week before Easter–end Oct; shop open weekends all year. **Main course** £5.95–9.50. **Credit** MC, V. **Amenities** children's menu, highchair, disabled access, reservations accepted, parking, outside seating overlooking beach.*

INSIDER TIP »

Coldharbour Mill at Uffculme, near Cullompton, a 200-year-old woollen mill (📞 *01884 840960; www.coldharbourmill.co.uk*) has

Keeping It Local – Farmers' Markets & Farm Shops

Culm Valley Farm Shop, Cullompton; ☏ 01884 38513
Darts Farm Shoping Village, Clyst St Mary; ☏ 01392 878000
Exeter Farmers' Market, South Street/Fore Street, Thurs
Exe Valley Farm Shop, Thorverton; ☏ 01392 861239
Exmouth Farmers' Market, Strand Gardens, 2nd Wed
Honiton Farmers' Market, St Paul's Church, High Street, 3rd Thurs
Joshua's Harvest Store, Ottery St Mary; ☏ 01404 815473
Kenniford Farm Shop, Clyst St Mary; ☏ 01392 875938
Millers Farm Shop, Kilmington, Axminster; ☏ 01297 35290
Ottery St Mary Farmers' Market, High Street car park; 1st Fri
Powderham Country Store, Kenton; ☏ 01626 891883
Seaton Farmers' Market, Town Hall, 3rd Fri
Slow Food Market, Exeter Quay, 3rd Sat
Taverners Farm Shop, Kennford; ☏ 01392 833776
Wallaces' Farm Shop, Hemyock, Cullompton; ☏ 01823 680307

a lovely riverside picnic area. The mill – unique in the southwest – stopped working in 1980, and is a fascinating place. Guided tours are available ((phone for details), and refreshments served in the Gill House restaurant overlooking the millstream.

Herbies Vegetarian Restaurant ★ ★ ★ FIND

15 North Street, Exeter, Devon EX4 3QS; ☏ *01392 258473. North Street runs between the High Street and Paris Street at the western end of the town centre.*

Vegetarian food that – if it doesn't bring about total conversion – moves carnivores a step nearer to going veggie! This bistro-style restaurant has satisfied the needs of Exeter's vegetarians (and vegans) for years, but dispels any outdated notions of vegetarian food being dull. Food is locally sourced, freshly prepared, and organic wherever possible; dishes are bright, colourful, varied, beautifully presented and always delicious – and very reasonably priced. Beer, wine and cider is organic; coffee is organic and fair-trade. The children's menu is healthy and tasty (£1.75–3.75) – organic beans on toast, jacket potato with hummus, a platter of homemade crisps, hummus, pitta bread, sultanas, cheese and fruit. Main courses are creative and cater for every taste: Greek vegetable pie, Herbies chilli, Moroccan tagine, served with generous portions of interesting salads.

*Open 11am–2.30pm Mon–Fri, 10.30am–4pm Sat; 6–9.30pm Tue–Sat. **Main course** £7.75–8.25. **Credit** MC, V. **Amenities** children's menu, highchair, disabled access possible (not to toilets), reservations accepted, vegan diets catered for.*

4 North Devon Coast & Exmoor

NORTH DEVON COAST & EXMOOR

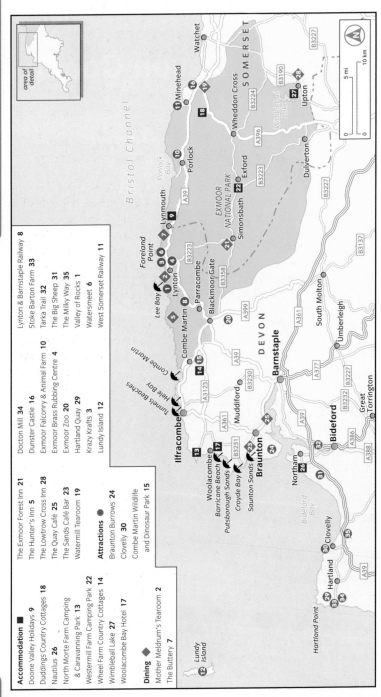

Accommodation ■

Doone Valley Holidays **9**
Duddings Country Cottages **18**
Nautilus **26**
North Morte Farm Camping
& Caravanning Park **13**
Westermill Farm Camping Park **22**
Wheel Farm Country Cottages **14**
Wimbleball Lake **27**
Woolacombe Bay Hotel **17**

Dining ◆

Mother Meldrum's Tearoom **2**
The Buttery **7**
The Exmoor Forest Inn **21**
The Hunter's Inn **5**
The Lowtrow Cross Inn **28**
The Quay Café **25**
The Sands Café Bar **23**
Watermill Tearoom **19**

Docton Mill **34**
Dunster Castle **16**
Exmoor Falconry & Animal Farm **10**
Exmoor Brass Rubbing Centre **4**
Exmoor Zoo **20**
Hartland Quay **29**
Krazy Krafts **3**
Lundy Island **12**

Lynton & Barnstaple Railway **8**
Stoke Barton Farm **33**
Tarka Trail **32**
The Big Sheep **31**
The Milky Way **35**
Valley of Rocks **1**
Watersmeet **6**
West Somerset Railway **11**

Attractions ●

Braunton Burrows **24**
Clovelly **30**
Combe Martin Wildlife
and Dinosaur Park **15**

The coast of North Devon has much to recommend it for families. Much of it is a designated Area of Outstanding Natural Beauty (AONB): dramatic sea cliffs, long sandy beaches, rocky coves, tranquil estuaries and the UK's first UNESCO Biosphere Reserve (p. 47). It's a wonderfully varied coastline too: jagged rocks, wild seas and stories of shipwrecks round Hartland Point (p. 46), sheltered harbours at Clovelly and Lynmouth, and wonderful long, sandy beaches at Saunton and Woolacombe. There are historic ports – Bideford, Barnstaple, Fremington Quay – opportunities for exploration by bike along the Tarka Trail, and great surfing at Croyde and Woolacombe. This is one of the most impressive (and in places the most taxing) sections of the Southwest Coast Path, which starts (or finishes!) at Minehead on Exmoor's eastern edge.

The North Devon coast continues east and enters Exmoor National Park at Combe Martin. One of Exmoor's greatest delights is its coastline, where soaring hog's-backed cliffs rise to over 300 km with superb views over the Bristol Channel. Exmoor National Park covers 692 square km, a glorious mix of steep wooded valleys, ancient oak woodland, rounded heather moorland, and patchwork of small hedged fields, ancient farms and sheltered villages. The underlying sedimentary sandstone creates moorlands that are less harsh than the granite uplands of Dartmoor (p. 83) and Bodmin Moor (p. 151). Exmoor is a peaceful place: the National Park population stands at around 10,500, and it is one of the least visited National Parks in the country on account of its distance from main transport links – all the more reason to visit! It's a great destination for families looking for an active holiday, with excellent opportunities for walking, horse riding and cycling – with over 965 km of foot- and bridlepaths – yet with good beaches at Minehead and Woolacombe within striking distance.

VISITOR INFORMATION

As usual the TIC should be your first port of call (see below). The North Devon AONB website is worth a look (01237 423655; www.northdevon-aonb.org.uk), as is www.northdevon.com, the official website for more than 2,200 square km of coast and countryside. The Exmoor National Park Authority has a number of visitor centres, some doubling up as TICs; for the best coverage visit the one in Dulverton. There is a mass of free information: Tarka Country Visitor, North Devon & Exmoor Towns & Villages guide (www.northdevon.com); Scene North Devon holiday guide (www.northdevongazette.co.uk); ENPA's Exmoor Visitor is essential for exploring the National Park. The free Bideford Bay Companion guide covers Bideford, Appledore, Northam, Westward Ho! and surrounding areas (01237 425466). For

North Devon you will need Explorers 126 Clovelly & Hartland and 139 Bideford, Ilfracombe & Barnstaple; for Exmoor check out OS Explorer OL9.

Information Centres

Barnstaple, North Devon Museum, The Square; ☎ *01271 375000; www.staynorthdevon. co.uk*

Bideford, Victoria Park, The Quay; ☎ *01237 477676*

Braunton, The Bakehouse Centre, Caen Street; ☎ *01271 816400; www.braunton.co.uk*

Ilfracombe, The Landmark, The Seafront; ☎ *01271 863001; www.visitilfracombe.co.uk*

Porlock, West End; ☎ *01643 863150; www.porlock.co.uk*

Woolacombe, The Esplanade; ☎ *01271 870553; www. woolacombetourism.co.uk*

ENPA, Exmoor House, Dulverton, Somerset TA22 9HL; ☎ *01398 323665; www. exmoor-nationalpark.gov.uk*

Exmoor National Park Authority (ENPA) Information Centres

Combe Martin, Cross Street; ☎ *01271 883319; www.visit combemartin.co.uk*

Dulverton, Fore Street; ☎ *01398 323841*

Dunster, Dunster Steep; ☎ *01643 821835*

Lynton, Town Hall, Lee Road; ☎ *01598 752225; www.lynton-lynmouth-tourism.co.uk*

Orientation

Devon's north coast stretches from the Cornish border at Marsland Mouth north round Hartland Point, then east past the mouths of the Torridge and Taw rivers (Bideford and Barnstaple), then by Ilfracombe and Combe Martin to enter Exmoor National Park. The National Park extends east along the coast to Minehead, and south as far as Dulverton in West Somerset. The A39 runs right through the area from Minehead in the east via Lynton/Lynmouth to Barnstaple, then along the North Devon coast before bearing south to Bude in Cornwall. The A361 North Devon link road is the quickest way to access the heart of North Devon's coast – to Barnstaple – from Tiverton and the M5.

Getting Around

In practical terms a car is the easiest way of getting around the area, though check out bus timetables in the local TIC (or ☎ Traveline *0871 200 2233; www.traveline.org.uk*). The **Tarka Line** runs from Exeter St David's train station to Barnstaple. The **Tarka Trail** enters the area south of Bideford and runs on to Barnstaple and Braunton (p. 54), an excellent off-road walking and cycling route. A useful guide

Exmoor by Public Transport is available in information centres and TICs; the **Moor Rover Bus** covers two-thirds of the National Park and gives access (specifically to walkers) to areas away from scheduled bus routes (weekends and school holidays). In the summer the **Exmoor Explorer,** an open-topped vintage double-decker bus, follows a circular route from Minehead via Dunster, Exford and Porlock.

Child-Friendly Events & Entertainment

Lynton & Lynmouth Music Festival

An open-air, free music festival for all ages and musical tastes set in Lynton and Lynmouth (p. 45). Part of the North Devon Festival (see below), this event is the largest free music festival in Devon.

Early June, Lynton and Lynmouth. www.llama.org.uk

North Devon Festival

A month-long festival in various venues all over North Devon: music and dance, touring theatre and fairs, visual arts and literature, sport and leisure, plus the National Sandcastle Competition on Woolacombe Bay beach.

June, all over North Devon and Exmoor. ✆ *01271 324242; www.northdevonfestival.org*

North Devon Walking and Cycling Festival

Just over a week of 60-plus walking and cycling events, from long-distance treks over Exmoor to family-friendly explorations of Braunton Burrows (p. 47) and otter spotting on the River Torridge.

Early May, all over North Devon and Exmoor. ✆ *01271 883131; www. walkcyclenorthdevon.co.uk*

Lynmouth

WHAT TO SEE & DO

Children's Top 10 Attractions

❶ Betting on the sheep race at The Big Sheep. See p. 50.

❷ Playing pitch and putt on the seafront at Lynmouth. See p. 45.

❸ Spotting tree porcupines at Exmoor Zoo. See p. 51.

❹ Searching for cowrie shells on Barricane Beach. See p. 53.

❺ Cycling along the Tarka Trail for ice cream at Fremington Quay. See p. 54.

❻ Riding a pony through the valley of the Badgworthy Water. See p. 56.

❼ Kayaking on Wimbleball Lake. See p. 56.

❽ Enjoying 'wibble wobble jelly' at Mother Meldrum's tearoom. See p. 60.

❾ Taking a ride on the Cliff Railway. See p. 46.

❿ Ducking the squirting dinosaurs at Combe Martin's Dinosaur Park! See p. 52.

Towns & Villages

Bideford

In his novel *Westward Ho!* (1855), Charles Kingsley said of Bideford 'pleasantly it has stood there for now, perhaps, 800 years' – and that just about sums up this little working port on the banks of the river Torridge. Bypassed by the A39, unassuming,

a little run-down, but Bideford is a pleasant place to explore. Victoria Park has a putting green, paddling pool, playground and the **Burton Art Gallery and Museum** (free entry, café, shop, children's art workshops in the holidays; ℡ 01237 471455; *www.burtonart gallery.co.uk*). Bideford's pannier market is held on Tuesdays and Saturdays (℡ 01237 478777); wander down Mill Street to find Roly's Fudge Pantry (℡ 01271 459215; *www.rolysfudge.co.uk*) where you can watch fudge being made, taste it, and then buy it. The Tarka Trail (p. 54) runs along the other side of the Torridge, past old Bideford station at East-the-Water, and the Lundy Island ferry booking office (p. 48) is on the quay. Just downstream the pretty village of Appledore is worth a visit, with narrow cobbled streets, brightly painted cottages, artists' workshops and cafes: a few kilometres west along the A39 is the historic little fishing village of Clovelly, basically one very steep cobbled street clinging precariously to the wooded cliffs. Visit early in the day – or in the evening – to get a real feel for the place (*www.clovelly.co.uk*).

Dunster

The little medieval town of Dunster on the edge of the National Park gets very, very crowded in holiday times, but it's easy to escape along the main street – passing the wonderful

Old Yarn Market, built in 1609, en route – into the quieter environs of the National Trust's **Dunster Castle** (children's quiz, trail; ☎ 01643 821314; www. nationaltrust.org.uk), which sits on a wooded knoll overlooking the town. At the bottom of the gardens is the 18th-century working watermill, and just beyond the excellent **Watermill Tearoom,** with huge homemade cakes and a lovely garden with bantam hens. A little further on is **Gallox Bridge,** a medieval packhorse bridge, by the children's playground. Cross the bridge to enter **Dunster deer park,** with kilometres of footpaths to enjoy. From the deer park you'll hear the whistle of the **West Somerset Railway** (☎ 01643 704996; www.west-somerset-railway.co.uk), which runs from Minehead to Bishops Lydeard. Dunster has a lot to offer.

Ilfracombe

Ilfracombe is a typical Victorian seaside town: a bit run down in places, a little brash in others, but with a certain unpretentious charm. The most visitor-friendly – and crowded – part is round the harbour and promenade, where you'll find the **Landmark Theatre** (☎ 01271 324242; www.northdevontheatres. org.uk), TIC, museum (☎ 01271 863541) and famous **Tunnels Beaches,** with a tidal pool dating from Victorian times (☎ 01271 879882; www.tunnelsbeaches. co.uk), café bar and kayak hire.

The **Devon Wildlife Trust** sometimes runs rock pool rambles here (www.devonwildlifetrust.org). You can visit **Ilfracombe Aquarium** on The Pier (☎ 01271 864533; www.ilfracombe aquarium.co.uk), go on a wildlife cruise aboard the *Ilfracombe Princess* (☎ 01271 879727; www. ilfracombeprincess.co.uk) or take a day trip to **Lundy Island** (p. 48 – take warm clothing and waterproofs, whatever the weather on the mainland). **Ifracombe swimming pool** (☎ 01271 864480) is in Hillsborough Pleasure Ground to the east of the town, and the fully licensed **Embassy Cinema** in the centre (☎ 01271 862323; www.merlincinemas.co.uk), along with **Walkers Chocolate Emporium** (☎ 01271 867193; www. chocolate-emporium.co.uk) – a must! Finally lovely **Bicclescombe Park,** at the top of the town off the A361, has a children's playground, café, ponds, mill leat, and sensory garden.

Lynton & Lynmouth

Lynmouth – originally a small fishing port – and Lynton developed as a popular tourist destination from the late 18th century. The dramatic cliffs, steep-sided wooded valleys and sparkling rivers attract hordes of visitors: it's unique! In the late 19th century many new hotels were built and the area became known as 'Little Switzerland'. Today Lynmouth is a tranquil

Heading to Hartland

The area of North Devon known as Hartland – Devon's largest parish – lies to the west of the A39 between Clovelly and Bude. It's fairly off the beaten track, and often missed by those shooting along the Atlantic Highway towards Bude and North Cornwall – which is precisely why it is so wonderful! Devon's northwest tip is characterised by an extraordinary change in the nature of the coast: the cliffs along the coast from Clovelly, although high, are relatively calm and flat-topped; yet turn the corner at Hartland lighthouse (erected 1874) and you enter a different world, where the craggy rocks on the seabed run in jagged lines towards the unforgiving cliffs – you can understand why this area is peppered with shipwrecks. Hartland means 'stag island' and – although not an island – the feeling of space and remoteness here is made even stronger by the fact that on a clear day there are inviting views of **Lundy,** rising majestically out of the deep blue sea (p. 48). Hartland is not a place to go exploring by car unless you are happy negotiating very narrow, steep lanes and sharp bends – and not without an OS map. Better to get out of the car and set off on foot along the Coast Path – just about the most exciting part of the 1,000 km. But there are other delights for the less active (or those restricted by the needs of small children). There are good places to eat: enjoy a slice of the Queen Mother's favourite fruit cake in the tranquil surroundings of the beautiful woodland and wildflower garden at **Docton Mill** (*℡ 01237 441369; www.docton mill.co.uk*); strawberries, raspberries and salads are all grown in the garden. A little to the south can be found the wonderful **Rectory Farm Tearooms** at Morwenstow (p. 163), just over the border into Cornwall. Expect chips if you go to **Hartland Quay Hotel** (*℡ 01237 441218; www.hartlandquayhotel.com*), where the Wreckers Bar and Shipwreck

place (*www.lyntonandlynmouth scene.co.uk*): there's no sandy beach here (Exmoor's only accessible sandy beach, Lee Bay, is a few kilometres west), but you can play pitch and putt golf in Manor Gardens, visit **The Glen Lyn Gorge** to learn more about water power (*www.theglenlyn gorge.co.uk*), take a walk through the rocky gorge of the East Lyn for tea at the National's Trust **Watersmeet** (children's quiz, trail; *℡ 01598 753348;*

www.nationaltrust.org.uk), and sail from the quay with **Exmoor Boat Trips** (*℡ 01598 753207*). One of the town's most popular attractions is the unique water-powered **Cliff Railway,** opened in 1888, which takes visitors speedily up to Lynton, 152 m above (*℡ 01598 753486; www. cliffrailwaylynton.co.uk*). An easy walk along the North Walk leads to the **Valley of Rocks**; the **Lyn and Exmoor Museum** in Market Street is worth a visit;

Museum are full of stories and memorabilia about life here from the 16th to 18th centuries, when Hartland Quay was an important working port. When it was abandoned it was quickly destroyed by storms. The little village of **Hartland** is a mecca for artists and craftspeople; park in the square and take a good look round. Then there's **Hartland Abbey** (☎ *01237 441264/4412324; www.hartlandabbey.com*), dating from 1157 and a family home since 1539, which has children's quizzes, peacocks and a café. The delightful gardens – designed by Gertrude Jekyll – flourish in this sheltered spot, and there's a lovely woodland walk along the valley to a beautiful cove. And if you're into camping look no further than **Stoke Barton Farm** (☎ *01237 441238; www.westcountry-camping.co.uk*), a wonderful site just a stone's throw across the fields from Hartland Quay, where you can also enjoy superb cream teas in the summer months. In 2002 Braunton Burrows (the largest sand dune system in the UK – some up to 30 m high) to the west of Braunton was designated (with the Taw–Torridge estuary, Northam Burrows and Braunton Marsh) as the UK's first **UNESCO Biosphere Reserve.** Access for visitors is managed carefully to protect fragile areas, and the area is well worth exploring. The whole dune system is moving inland at a rate of around 3 m per year under the prevailing southwesterly winds. More than 500 species of flowering plant have been identified, including 11 orchids. The area is easy to reach by bike from the **Tarka Trail** (p. 54). Just to the east is Braunton Great Field, a rare example of medieval strip farming, and Braunton Marsh, enclosed in the 19th century for grazing cattle. (Braunton Burrows Biosphere Reserve; ☎ *01271 817349*).

Lynton's Cliff Railway

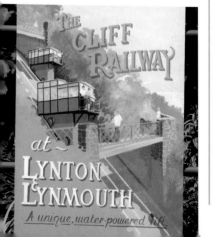

and if the storm clouds gather you can always visit **Lynton Cinema,** just up the road from the TIC (☎ *01598 753397; www.lyntoncinema.co.uk*).

Fun Days Out

The Milky Way ★

Nr Clovelly, Bideford, Devon EX39 5RY; ☎ *01237 431255; www.the milkyway.co.uk. On the A39 west of Bideford, near Clovelly.*

An excellent day out for those less-than-perfect days (most of the attractions are indoors) – and great for parents who have never quite grown up and enjoy going on rides too! This is a place for thrills and spills – last year saw the arrival of the biggest, tallest and fastest roller-coaster in Devon (quite terrifying). There are bumper cars (special sessions for parents and young children), the Clone Zone (ride in an alien spaceship) plus the Milky Way railway. For younger children there's toddler town and fantasy farm for the under fives, pets' corner and lamb feeding. You can get lost in the maze, have a go at archery or try driving a golf ball, watch a birds of prey show (the site is home to the North Devon Birds of Prey Centre), enjoy ferret racing, try sculpting and ceramic painting, or just have simple fun in the outdoor play area. All the rides (once you're inside) are included in the admission price.

Open 10.30am–6pm end Mar–end Oct, 11am–5pm winter weekends and school holidays. *Admission* £9

Lundy Island

Few people seem to have heard of the little island of Lundy – the name is Norse for puffin – but from various points along the north Devon coast this 122 m high stack of granite is visible, lying 18 km off Hartland Point at the meeting place of the waters of the Bristol Channel and the Atlantic. The island measures a mere 5.6 km from north to south by 0.8 km wide, but in terms of wildlife has riches beyond compare. Designated the UK's only statutory Marine Nature Reserve – most of the island is a designated SSSI – any visit is almost bound to be rewarded by the sight of Atlantic grey seals; the first puffins to breed for many years were recorded in 2005. Owned by the National Trust and leased to the Landmark Trust, Lundy operates as a working farm and has an excellent pub and shop, and a number of self-catering properties: you can camp, stay in the old lighthouse, in the 13th-century castle, or in the converted Admiralty lookout. The warden runs guided walks and rock pool rambles in the summer months; day trips run from Ilfracombe or Bideford (✆ *01271 863636; www.lundyisland.co.uk*); if you've booked accommodation you can pay a premium to ensure that you'll be flown out by helicopter should the weather prevent the MV *Oldenburg* from sailing (a frequent occurrence!). If you want to get right away from it all – no cars, no roads, no TV, no radio – with wildlife on tap, peace and quiet, endless space, a pond full of giant carp, a lighthouse to explore, wonderful rock pools in the Devil's Kitchen, Lundy ponies, feral goats and sika deer to spot...Lundy may be the right place for you. Any trip to Lundy, whatever the weather and whatever the outcome, is a real old-fashioned adventure.

The Milky Way, near Clovelly

adult, £8 child (under 1.2 m), under 3 free, 50p off per person family rate. **Credit** MC, V. **Amenities** cafés, disabled access, parking, shop.

INSIDER TIP »

Ideas for a wet day on Exmoor: try the **Krazy Krafts Workshop** (℡ 01598 753489) in Watersmeet Road, Lynmouth. All ages and abilities are welcome to join in over 30 crafty activities, especially card making and scrapbooks. Nearby the **Exmoor Brass Rubbing Centre** introduces all age groups to this fascinating art (℡ 01598 752529; *www.exmoor brassrubbing.co.uk*); phone in advance to ask for details.

Lynton & Barnstaple Railway
★★ **ALL AGES**

Woody Bay Station, Martinhoe Cross, Parracombe, Devon EX31 4RA; ℡ 01598 763487; *www.lynton-rail.co.uk*. On A39 between Lynton and Blackmoor Gate. Bus from Lynton, Ilfracombe, Combe Martin, Minehead.

The 30 km narrow-gauge Lynton and Barnstaple Railway opened in May 1898 and ran through the glorious west Exmoor countryside before slipping down wooded valleys to Barnstaple. The last train ran in September 1935, unable to compete with ever-improving road transport. In 2004 the Lynton and Barnstaple Railway re-opened, and today trains run along the restored mile-long stretch of line from Woody Bay – at 299 m the highest station in southern England, and the highest narrow-gauge station in the country – to Killington Lane near Parracombe. It's a fantastic ride, with wonderful views. The restoration programme is ongoing; every year sees more work on the line and original coaches being used. Special events are held throughout the year – 'Jack the Cat', a fun weekend for all the family, and 'Scary Steam Trains' round Halloween, when carriages are pulled by either a steam- or diesel-hauled train. Great fun for all ages – and a charity well worth supporting.

Open *11am–4pm peak season, early Apr–end Oct, plus weekends Feb/Mar/Nov/Dec.* **Return fare** *£4 adult, £2.50 child (5–14), under 5 free, £3.50 OAP, £9.50 family (single fares available).* **Credit** *MC, V.* **Amenities** *café, disabled access, parking, shop.*

INSIDER TIP ⟩⟩

The **Railways round Exmoor** ticket allows you to make one return journey on the Lynton and Barnstaple Railway, the Lynton and Lynmouth Clliff Railway (p. 46) and the West Somerset Railway (Minehead–Bishops Lydeard). **Prices** (2007) £18 adult, £9 (child), £16 OAP.

Animal Attractions

The Big Sheep ★ ★ ★ FIND
ALL AGES VALUE

Bideford, Devon EX39 5AP; ☏ *01237 472366; www.thebigsheep.co.uk. Signed off the A39 just west of Bideford. Bus from Barnstaple/Bude.*

I walked around this clever, innovative place just grinning from ear to ear. There's so much going on to amuse and occupy all members of the family; it's clearly been put together by someone with a great sense of humour – children even have their own currency: Eweros! You could definitely spend the whole day here. Apart from a mass of indoor and outdoor entertainment – an excellent indoor play area plus Internet café (Ewetopia), sheep to stroke and feed, live combat games, tractor track, train rides from Eweston station – every 30 minutes a new event takes place: duck trials, dog trials, sheep shearing, the Great Sheep Show, the 'Beer Experience' (beer is brewed on site), pony rides, culminating in the famous sheep racing (Red Ram, Aldernitti, and Woolly Jumper, among others), complete with bets and jockeys. The staff involve both children and adults in every event (and try to

The Big Sheep, Bideford

The Exmoor Pony

Unlike Dartmoor, where the majority of ponies spotted on the moor are cross-breeds, any ponies you come across on Exmoor will be pure-bred Exmoor ponies, identified by their stocky build, mealy-coloured muzzles, and absence of any white markings. One of the world's oldest breeds, these tough little ponies are believed to be the closest native breed to the indigenous British wild horse, and worldwide numbers at one time dropped as low as 50. Today's population stands at about 1,400. The Moorland Mousie Trust (01398 323093; *www.exmoor ponycentre.org.uk*) at Ashwick near Dulverton offers the whole family the chance to ride an Exmoor pony (despite their size they can carry up to 76 kg (12 stone)), or spend time grooming and handling one, and learning about tack and pony care – a bit like having your own pony for half a day! The Centre also runs schemes for adopting and sponsoring ponies.

embarrass parents wherever possible) – watching more than 60 children feeding 20 lambs has to be seen to be believed! There's a garden centre on site too, and free kennels for dogs. Unmissable!

Open *10am–6pm Apr–end Oct; phone for winter times.* **Admission** *£8.50 adult, £7.50 child (over 3), under 3 free, £30–40 family; £100–140 family season ticket.* **Credit** *MC, V.* **Amenities** *café, disabled access, parking, picnic area, restaurant, shop, free dog kennels.*

Exmoor Zoo ★ ★ ALL AGES FIND

South Stowford, Bratton Fleming, Barnstaple, Devon EX31 4SG; 01598 763352; www.exmoorzoo.com. Signed off A399 South Molton–Combe Martin, south of Blackmoor Gate.

Walk around the zoo and you get the definite feeling that someone – or something – is watching you! Winding paths lead between pens and cages, often screened from each other by high flowering hedges, giving a really jungly atmosphere. Monkeys run

through mesh tunnels high above the path: tree porcupines doze in the fork of a tree branch; and huge leopard tortoises amble over each other. Don't let small children rush too far ahead – there are lots of path junctions, and it would be easy to lose each other. Many pens have low-level glass panels so that toddlers and those in buggies get a good view. Every 30 minutes in summertime there's an animal activity – cheetah feed and talk, meet the alpacas, wallaby petting – where everyone can get close to animals and learn more about them. Children's trail quizzes are available for a small charge, with proceeds going to support various wildlife appeals. There's a really big picnic area with outdoor play equipment, and many of the animals can be viewed from covered areas.

Open *10am–6pm daily, end Mar–end Oct.* **Admission** *£7.95 adult, £5.50 child (3–16), under 3 free, £24.50 family.* **Credit** *MC, V (not in café).*

Exmoor Zoo

Amenities café, disabled access, parking, picnic area, shop.

Exmoor Falconry and Animal Farm ★ ALL AGES

Allerford, near Porlock, Somerset TA24 8HJ; ☎ 01643 862816; www. exmoorfalconry.co.uk. Signed off A39 Porlock–Minehead.

The animal and falconry centre is housed in a range of traditional barns on a 15th-century farmstead where a cream tea in the beautiful cottage garden is almost obligatory! This is a lovely place where you can wander gently through barns and paddocks enjoying all manner of animals at close quarters – rats, polecats, ferrets, rabbits and so on in a huge barn, goats, calves, ponies, lambs outside – or get more closely involved and join a falconry experience day (also available for children), learn about animal behaviour or how to keep parrots and reptiles. You can feed lambs, watch a flying display, take an

alpaca for a walk or adopt a blue-tongued skink – and pick up all kinds of fascinating facts about your favourite animal. Allerford and Bossington nearby are two of Exmoor's most picturesque villages.

Open 10.30am–5pm daily mid Feb–end Oct; 11am–4pm Nov–mid Feb. Admission £7 adult, £5.50 child (3–16), under 3 free, £6.50 OAP, £22.50 family. Credit MC, V. Amenities café, disabled access, parking, picnic area, shop, activity breaks.

Combe Martin Wildlife and Dinosaur Park ★★ ALL AGES

Combe Martin, Devon EX34 0NG; ☎ 01271 882486; www.dinosaur-park.com. On A399 just outside south of Combe Martin.

Time your arrival properly and your entrance – down a long flight of stone steps through almost sub-tropical vegetation – will be accompanied by ferocious roars! A group of brilliant model dinosaurs 'perform' at regular intervals (one or two have the odd trick to play – children love it!). The area round the dinosaur enclosure is a little daunting – museum and cinema, wolf education centre, Tomb of the Pharaohs – but beyond that you enter the amazing botanical gardens. Long (sometimes steep) paths wind downhill under huge trees, over bridges and waterfalls to find monkeys, racoons, pelicans, birds of prey, snow leopards, and wolves as well as a huge meerkat enclosure. This part of the park is really worth spending time in – there's a huge variety of special events (sea lion display, wolf talks etc.) every day. You feel miles away from the more commercial upper parts of the site – and you can catch a bus back to the car park if younger children are tired at the end of their jungle exploration.

Open *10am–3pm (last admission), mid Mar–early Nov.* **Admission** *£12 adult, £7 child (3–16), under 3 free, £8 OAP, £34 family.* **Credit** *MC, V.* **Amenities** *café, disabled access possible to some areas, parking, picnic area, shop.*

Best Beaches

Barricane Beach, Woolacombe Narrow, sheltered sand and shingle cove, rock pools, shells. Car park.

Combe Martin Safe sandy beach, shingle with sand at low water, rock pools. Café, car park.

Croyde Bay 800 m sandy beach and dunes, popular with families. Surfing. Café, car park.

Hele Bay, Ilfracombe Small beach, sand and shingle, rock pools. Café, car park.

Lee Bay, nr Lynton Only accessible sandy beach on Exmoor, sheltered, rock pools. Car park.

Putsborough Sands, Croyde Huge sandy beach, rock pools, great for families. Surfing. Café, car park.

Saunton Sands Long sandy beach, backed by dunes. Surfing. Café, car park.

Saunton Sands

Tunnels Beaches, Ilfracombe
Accessed by tunnels; popular with families, rock pool, tidal pool.

Westward Ho!, Bideford 3.2 km sandy beach, great for families. Café, car park.

Woolacombe 4.8 km of golden sands. Surfing. Café, car park.

For Active Families

Tarka Trail AGES 5 AND UP

The Tarka Trail is a wonderful 290 km figure-of-eight walking and cycling route through north and mid Devon. There's an easy 48 km off-road cycling route along disused railway lines from Braunton via Barnstaple and Bideford to Meeth in Devon's heartland (p. 74). Start from old Braunton station and follow the Taw estuary into Barnstaple (where you can visit Barnstaple Heritage Centre); or start from Bideford station and cycle down-river through Instow (Wayfarer Inn and beach café) and the RSPB's Isley Marsh reserve to Fremington Quay (p. 61) and onto Barnstaple. Information boards give details on local flora and fauna. Both routes are lovely, with stunning views, and the cycling equally easy, but I would pick the Bideford–Fremington stretch if you're limited by time (and short legs!) – there's more to interest younger riders, and more places to stop for a drink or ice cream.

Braunton to Barnstaple 9 km; Bideford to Barnstaple 12 km. Cycle hire Otter Cycle Hire, Braunton; 01271 813339; Tarka Trail Cycle Hire, Barnstaple station; 01271 324202; Biketrail, Fremington Quay; 01271 372586; www.biketrail.co.uk; Bideford Cycle Hire, East-the-Water; 01237 424123

Surfing

Devon's north coast has some fabulous surfing beaches. Contact the following for details of lessons; remember to check the lower age limit.
Barefoot Surf School, Putsborough; 01271 891231; www.barefoot surf.com
Nick Thorn Surf Coaching, Woolacombe; 01271 871337; www.nick thorn.com
North Devon Surf School, Barnstaple; 01598 710818; www.north devonsurfschool.co.uk
Point Breaks, Croyde Bay; 07776 148679; www.pointbreaks.com
Surfing Croyde Bay, Croyde Bay; 01271 891200; www.surfing croydebay.co.uk
Surf South West, Croyde Bay; 01271 890400; www.surfsouth west.com

Getting Active

Active Exmoor For information on a huge range of outdoor activities on Exmoor – cycling, canoeing, sailing, riding, mountain biking, even Nordic walking – visit *www.activeexmoor.com*, a great website which will tell you everything you need to know about what's going on and how to get involved. The company is based in Dulverton (**℡** *01398 324599*).

Horse Riding Horseback is one of the best ways to explore the moor. There are literally dozens of riding stables operating on Exmoor, most of which will take beginners and young children on lead reins. Get hold of ENPA's **Exmoor Visitor** for details.

Safaris For those who would rather see Exmoor the easy way join a **Discovery Safari** (**℡** *01643 863080; www.discoverysafaris.com*) on an overland tour of the moor and learn more about Exmoor's stunning scenery and wildlife, including red deer.

Walking Exmoor offers fantastic possibilities for all ages and abilities. Apart from the 55 km stretch of Coast Path, the 164 km **Two Moors Way** reaches the sea at Lynmouth from its start at Ivybridge on Dartmoor's southern edge; the **Coleridge Way** runs for 58 km from Nether Stowey in Somerset to reach the sea at Porlock on the eastern edge of Exmoor. There are lots of opportunities for short, easy walks, and books and leaflets available in TICs. **Dunster Forest,** for example, has waymarked trails from 2–15 km long, and a one-hour family cycle trail (*www.thecrownestate.co.uk*).

INSIDER TIP »
Want to try something different? **Skern Lodge** at Appledore (**℡** *01237 475992; www.skernlodge.co.uk*) provides outdoor activities, fun and adventure for all ages and abilities. Join one of their great adventure days, or have a go at canoeing, surfing and climbing. Children under nine must be accompanied by an adult. **Outdoor Education Training** at Bideford (**℡** *01237 471010; www.outdoortraining.co.uk*) specialises in family groups: have a go at sea kayaking, climbing, abseiling, coasteering and kayaking.

FAMILY-FRIENDLY ACCOMMODATION

INEXPENSIVE
Doone Valley Holidays ★★
Cloud Farm, Oare, Lynton, Devon EX35 6NU; **℡** *01598 741234; www.doonevalleyholidays.co.uk (accommodation) www.doonevalleytrekking.co.uk (riding). South of the A39 between Porlock and Lynton, between Malmsmead and Oare church.*

The Doone Valley has long been famous as the setting for R.D. Blackmore's novel *Lorna Doone*, based on the legend of a band of infamous outlaws who lived in

Hoccombe Combe, a little upriver from Cloud Farm. Jan Ridd married Lorna Doone in Oare church, a stone's throw away. It's a beautiful, sheltered spot, and Cloud Farm's campsite is perfectly positioned on the banks of the pretty Badgworthy Water. Three camping fields run along the riverside; plenty of shallow pools and waterfalls for splashing around in. Campfires are allowed – quite unusual – as are 'polite' dogs. Cloud Farm is perfectly situated for explorations of the 'Doone Valley' – a level track leads upriver on the opposite bank. Riding for all levels is available at the farm, from tiny children to experienced adults. A real bonus is the good campsite shop, plus off licence and tearoom, all of which have long opening hours. And if you can't quite trust Exmoor's weather the farmhouse has been divided into three comfortably furnished self-catering cottages.

Extensive flat riverside camping area. **Rates** *£5–7.50 adult per night, £3.50–4 child (5–12), under 5 free. 3 s/c cottages (2–8 people) £210–895 + static caravan (5 people) £185–525 per week.* **Credit** *MC, V.* **Amenities** *parking, DIY laundry, cot (for cottages), tea shop (breakfasts, BBQs) and shop, off-licence, riding.*

Westermill Farm Camping Park and Cottages ★

Exford, Minehead, Somerset TA24 7NJ; ☎ *01643 831238;* **www.exmoor farmholidays.co.uk.** *Just over 3 km west of Exford in the centre of Exmoor, signed off the road to Porlock. Bus from Tiverton, Minehead to Exford.*

A stunning campsite in the heart of Exmoor. The infant River Exe runs through four enormous camping fields – campfires allowed in the furthest flung – in a beautiful, peaceful valley just outside Exford (playground, two pubs, tearoom). Westermill is a working farm but there's been a campsite here for more than 20 years – people come back over and over again. You'll have a wonderfully natural holiday here: look out for buzzards, red deer and herons. Children love playing in the river (the first field is fenced off from the water); there are waymarked walks, and trout fishing. Even the drinking water comes from a natural spring. If camping's not quite your thing you can stay in Scandinavian-style wooden cottages, very comfortable and well equipped (with woodburners, TV, video, microwave, cooker, garden furniture) set in spacious yet secluded grounds separate from the camping fields. The farm has a small shop selling local produce, and breeds Aberdeen Angus cattle – good for BBQs!

60 camping pitches. **Rates** *£4.50 adult, £2.50 child. 6 s/c cottages and farmhouse wing, 2–8 people.* **Rates** *£170–540 per week.* **Credit** *MC, V.* **Amenities** *babysitting, cot, disabled access (some cottages), DIY laundry, parking, payphone, shop.*

Wimbleball Lake ★★

Angling and Watersports Centre, Brompton Regis, Dulverton, Somerset TA22 9NW; ☎ *01398 371460 (angling and watersports, 01398 371257 (tearoom and camping);* **www.swlakes trust.org.uk.** *Signed off the B3190*

Wimbleball Lake

northeast of Bampton and off the A396 near Dulverton.

The last thing you might expect to find at the end of a narrow country lane in the eastern fringes of Exmoor National Park is: (a) 372 acres of reservoir; (b) a bustling watersports centre and (c) a campsite! Wimbleball Lake was completed in the late 1970s to supply Tiverton and Exeter; today it provides excellent opportunities for fishing, bird-watching, sailing, windsurfing, rowing, kayaking, canoeing and power boating. There's a lovely camping area on the southern shores, next to the tearoom/gift shop, with modern shower, wash-up and disposal facilities. Packed lunches can be ordered from the tearoom. All levels of experience are catered for at the Watersports Centre: you can gain a Royal Yachting Association (RYA) adult or child qualification; children aged 6–10 can join the Nippers Club and learn to sail in specially designed fun boats, and there's a Wheelyboat available for hire. Those happier on dry land can enjoy one of the walking trails – it's 14.5 km round the whole lake! – or join an introductory family orienteering course.

30 lakeside camping pitches. **Rates** *£5 per night adult, £3 per night child 5–14, under 5 free, £13 per night family (4).* **Credit** *MC, V.* **Amenities** *tea room 11am–5pm Apr, Jun–early Sept; Mar Fri–Sun; May, Sept–early Nov Wed–Sun, adventure playground, walking trails, sailing, windsurfing, canoeing, kayaking, rowing, power boating, orienteering (phone in advance), angling (advance booking recommended).*

North Morte Farm Camping & Caravanning Park ★★

Mortehoe, Woolacombe, Devon EX34 7EG; ☎ 01271 870381; www. northmortefarm.co.uk. Signed from the centre of Mortehoe, off B3343 from Mullacott Cross.

North Morte Farm camping

A fabulous setting on the edge of the little village of Mortehoe, with wonderful views along the north Devon coast and access to the Coast Path and lovely Rockham Bay. This is a big site: the statics sit on level ground near the entrance, around a central grassy area with outdoor play equipment; campers and tourers can choose to stay anywhere in an extensive area of undulating clifftop ground – there are all sorts of nooks and crannies in which you can set up a 'private' camp. Facilities are good: there's a big toilet block, with family/disabled facilities, washing-up area, laundry, well-stocked shop and dog-walking field. BBQs are allowed (raised off the ground). This is a real family site: no single sex groups of more than three are allowed, nor large groups (six adults max). Note that camping pitches cannot be reserved.

Extensive camping pitches (not marked); 24 s/c static caravans for hire (4–8 people). **Rates** *camping* £13 (low)–17 (high) 2 adults, £2–3 child (2–15), under 2 free, statics £225 (low)–525 (high) pw. **Credit** MC, V. **Amenities** disabled facilities, DIY laundry, shop, parking, outdoor playground, walking distance to beach.

MODERATE

Wheel Farm Country Cottages ★★

Berry Down, Combe Martin, Devon EX34 0NT; ☎ 01271 882100; www. wheelfarmcottages.co.uk. Off A3123 south of Combe Martin.

A peaceful spot in rolling countryside above Combe Martin, 3 km from the sea and within easy reach of the National Park, Ilfracombe and Barnstaple. A range of 17th-century granite farm buildings and a watermill have been sympathetically converted into comfortable family accommodation (unusually there is some single accommodation, ideal for a 'lone' grandparent). Millwheel has its own garden, while the other cottages have outdoor seating areas, and the whole is set within seven hilly acres of beautiful grounds, with woodland areas, ponds, tennis court, play area and nature trail. Wheel Farm is ring-fenced by an organic farm, and wildlife planting predominates plus there's a huge field for ball games. The indoor swimming pool adjoins a real suntrap terrace. And if you can't face stirring yourself you can use the handy local meals service.

10 s/c cottages, 1–6 people. **Rates** *£250 (low)–1190 (high) pw.* **Credit** *MC, V.* **Amenities** *babysitting, cot (free), mini gym, parking, indoor pool, sauna, cottage kitchen meals service,*

laundry room, no dogs,
tennis court. **In cottage** cooker/
microwave, fridge/freezer, dishwasher, shower/bath, TV/DVD.

EXPENSIVE

Woolacombe Bay Hotel ★ ★ ★

Woolacombe, Devon EX34 7BN;
☎ 01271 870388; www.woolacombe-
bay-hotel.co.uk. Centre of
Woolacombe, off B3343. Bus from
Barnstaple, Ilfracombe.

A huge and rather grand
Edwardian hotel sitting within
its own grounds in the heart of
Woolacombe, with easy access
to 4.8 km of sandy beach.
Woolacombe gets extremely
crowded in the high season, but
the hotel feels cut off from the
hustle and bustle. It's extremely
well set up for family groups of
all shapes and sizes, with a range
of accommodation possibilities:
children can share their parents'
room, have an adjoining room or
separate room next door. There
are children's suppers for 14 years
and under and a summer activity
programme, with a morning
crèche for under fives and excellent options for older children:
squash, golf (the hotel has a nine-
hole course), horse riding and
surf lessons. The extensive lawned
area in front provides a lovely
venue for afternoon tea and is
where you'll find one of the outdoor pools, wooden outdoor
adventure playground and tennis
court: and all around is the wonderful sound of the surf crashing
onto the sands of Woolacombe
Bay. A very relaxed place to stay
for families of all ages.

56 doubles/family suites. **Rates** £385
(low)–728 (high) pppw dinner/B&B;
£70–385 (child/children's supper) pw.
Credit AmEx, MC, V. **Amenities**
babysitting, bar, crèche, children's
club, cot (free), disabled access possible, gym, laundry service, parking,
2 outdoor pools, indoor pool, restaurant, spa. **In room** Internet access,
shower/bath, TV/video.

INSIDER TIP ▶▶

Woolacombe Bay Hotel also has
a large number of self-catering
flats, apartments and mews
suites available, sleeping 4–8
people; the apartments have their
own outdoor pool. All are within
walking distance of the hotel and
can use the hotel facilities. Prices
range from £180 (low)–1,550
(high) per week.

6 & 10 Nautilus ★ ★

Golf Links Road, Westward Ho!,
Devon EX39 1SY; ☎ 01491 826757;
www.devonholidays4u.co.uk. Off
Beach Road in Westward Ho!. Bus
from Barnstaple, Bideford.

Something a little different for
this part of north Devon, which
may appeal to those looking for
contemporary accommodation:
two stunning award-winning
architect-designed apartments in
a new development bang on the
beach at Westward Ho! These
two identical apartments are next
to each other and so ideal for
two families; accommodation is
open plan, with the living area –
plus balcony – on the second
floor to make the most of wonderful views over the beach.
Everything about these apartments is high quality; accommodation is spacious, and family
games, DVDs, videos and books

Nautilus Westward Ho!

supplied. The owners also have three properties in Lynton and Lynmouth.

2 s/c apartments, 4 people + cot. **Rates** *£610 (low)–995 (high) per apartment.* **Credit** *MC, V.* **Amenities** *cot (free), parking, cooker/microwave, fridge/freezer, dishwasher, washing machine/drier, shower/bath, TV/DVD, telephone, no pets.*

FAMILY-FRIENDLY DINING

INEXPENSIVE

Mother Meldrum's Tearoom and Restaurant ★★★

Lee Road, Lynton, Devon EX35 6JH; 📞 *01598 753667. In the Valley of Rocks just west of Lynton, near the cricket pitch.*

Treat the children to tea or an early supper in the company of witches! Mother Meldrum featured in the novel *Lorna Doone* (p. 55) and is thought to be based on a witch, Aggie Norman, who lived in the Valley of Rocks in the 19th century. Today you can enjoy Ragged Jack rock cakes, Witch's Fingers or a bowl of Witch's Spell ('wibble wobble' jelly and ice cream) in this really family-friendly tearoom and garden, which stays open late in holiday times for early suppers; children's meals come complete with orange or blackcurrant squash. Enjoy a Rock Climber's Special (£5.35), Walker's Warmer (£3.40) or a range of omelettes, sandwiches and salads. Cakes and desserts are all homemade (£1.25–2.50) and delicious. Remember to make a wish at the Wishing Tree in the sheltered garden 'near where pixies young and witches old once lived' – and see if you can spot the odd flowerpot man around the garden!

Open *10am–5.30pm (later in holidays) end Mar–end Oct, winter weekends (depending on weather).* **Main**

course £3.50–5.35. **Amenities** *high-chair, disabled access, reservations accepted, parking (paying car park nearby), local Exmoor ponies and goats, dogs welcome, safe walled garden.*

The Quay Café ★ ★ ★ GREEN

Fremington Quay, Fremington, Barnstaple, Devon EX31 2NH; ☏ 01271 378783; www.fremington quay.co.uk. Signed off the B3233 Bideford–Barnstaple road – best accessed by bike on the Tarka Trail.

Reward yourself with a bite to eat at this award-winning café if you've put in some effort – by cycling along the Tarka Trail (p. 54). The café is in a renovated railway station overlooking the beautiful Taw estuary, by the RSPB reserve. The menu is based on fresh local vegetables, game and fish – bass and mullet caught by Instow fishermen, mussels from the Taw and Torridge, salad from Tapeley Park organic gardens – with daily specials and baguettes (local cheeses, £4.95), salads, West country wines, beers and ciders, plus excellent cream teas with organic cream and homemade jam, as well as a tempting display of cakes. Wall panels tell the fascinating story of the quay – linked by train to Barnstaple in 1840, and the busiest port between Bristol and Land's End in the 19th century. Upstairs in the old signal box you'll learn more about the local flora and fauna on Home Farm Marsh, home to the Tarka Trail (see p. 54).

Open *9.30am–5.30pm summer, 10.30am–4.30pm winter; closed Mon Nov–Mar.* **Main course** *£4.95–8.50.*

Credit *MC, V.* **Amenities** *children's menu, highchair, disabled access, limited parking, bike racks.*

MODERATE

The Hunter's Inn ★

Heddon Valley, Parracombe, Devon EX31 4PY; ☏ 01598 763230; www. thehuntersinn.net. Best accessed from the A399 at Kentisbury or the A39 just north of Parracombe (west Exmoor).

The Hunter's Inn has an enviable position, nestling in a clearing in the wooded Heddon Valley in a very remote part of western Exmoor. There are easy walks to the craggy cove at Heddon's Mouth, complete with tales of smugglers – it's one of very few landing places on this inhospitable coast. New owners in early 2006 have renovated much of the building, introduced a new menu and brought back the peacocks and peahens that have been associated with the inn for years. Food is locally sourced wherever possible, with fish from Clovelly and beef from just up the road at Trentishoe. Children have their own menu or smaller portions of adult dishes such as a 4oz ribeye steak, mushroom and spinach lasagne or tagliatelle with broccoli and smoked haddock (£5) – and a fantastic range of local ice creams. All the food is homemade and the owners – who have young children – understand the importance of giving children 'real' food.

Open *10am–11pm 365 days a year.* **Main course** *£5–8.95 (bar), £8.75–11.95 (restaurant).* **Credit**

Hunter's Inn, Parracombe

MC, V. **Amenities** *children's menu, portions of main courses, highchair, disabled access, reservations accepted, parking, large landscaped garden with peacocks, walks to cove.* **Accommodation** *11 rooms including 2 family rooms, from £40 double/twin, £20 child (4–14) sharing, £25 child adjoining room.*

Lowtrow Cross Inn ★ ★ FIND

Upton, Nr Wivelicombe, Taunton, Somerset TA4 2DB; 📞 *01398 371220. On the B3190 northeast of Bampton (Brendon Hills, eastern Exmoor National Park)*

It's hard to find a good, traditional, country pub where the dedicated family room feels just as good as sitting in the bar area. So often families with young children get shoved into some unappealing side room – so the Lowtrow Cross Inn is a real find. Originally a working farm, dating from the 17th century, this warm, welcoming inn has got it right when it comes to families.

They don't supply highchairs, but the family room is spacious and relaxed, and you still feel that you're part of the pub. Older well-behaved children (around 10 years and above) are allowed in a seating area just off the bar. Unusually for Exmoor, too, the pub isn't stuffed full of hunting memorabilia but has a good traditional atmosphere, with beams, low ceilings, open fires, and a good-sized garden. The food is excellent: salmon fillet (£10.95), mixed chilli beans and rice (£8.95), fillet steak (£13.95); children can choose sausage and chips, ham, egg and chips, and good local ice cream. Puddings are homemade and delicious.

Open 12pm–2.30pm, 6pm–11pm Wed–Sat, 12pm–3pm, 7pm–10.30pm Sun, 6pm–11pm Mon–Tues (open lunchtime Bank Holiday Mons). **Main course** *£7.25–13.95.* **Credit** *MC, V.* **Amenities** *children's menu,*

The Duddings

reservations accepted, parking, garden, large family room just off main bar area.

INSIDER TIP 〉〉
Pulham's Mill (📞 01398 371114) is within spitting distance of Wimbleball Lake and Brompton Regis. Dating back to the 11th century this ancient mill used to grind locally grown wheat, but today welcomes visitors to its craft shop and excellent tearoom; Sunday lunches a speciality. If you have very young children keep a close eye on them – the craft shop and tearoom are stuffed with all sorts of temptations for little fingers! Best to sit outside in the pretty garden by the stream.

The Sands Café Bar ★★★

Saunton Sands, nr Braunton, Devon EX33 1LQ; 📞 *01271 891288; www.sauntonsands.com. By the beach car park at Saunton Sands, off*

Try These Too!

- **Duddings Country Cottages:** A group of converted farm buildings in the grounds of a thatched 16th-century longhouse. Duddings, Timberscombe, Dunster, Somerset TA24 7JB; 📞 *01643 841123; www.duddings.co.uk.*
- **The Buttery:** Housed in part of Lorna Doone Farm in a pretty spot. Good for a simple lunch and walk along the river. Malmsmead, Devon EX35 6NU; 📞 *01598 74106.*
- **The Exmoor Forest Inn:** Comfortable and friendly with the atmosphere of a traditional Exmoor hotel and a good amount of space. Simonsbath, Somerset TA24 7SH; 📞 *01643 831341; www. exmoorforestinn.co.uk.*

Keeping It Local – Farmers' Markets & Farm Shops

Barnstaple Pannier Market, Tue, Fri, Sat
Barton Farm Shop, Woolsery, Bideford; ☎ *01237 431690*
Besshill Farm Shop, Arlington; ☎ *01237 850311*
Bideford Pannier Market, Tue, Sat
Bratton Fleming Farmers' Market, Village Hall, 4th Sat
Braunton Farmers' Market, Parish Hall, 4th Sat
Combe Martin Farmers' Market, Village Hall, 3rd Sat
Dulverton Farmers' Market, every other Fri
Hartland Farmers' Market, Parish Hall, 1st Sun Apr–Oct
Heanton Farmers' Market, Wrafton, Parish Hall, 2nd Sat
Ilfracombe Farmers' Market, Lantern Centre, High Street, 2nd and 4th Sats
Lynton Farmers' Market, Town Hall, 1st Sat

B3231 Braunton–Croyde. Bus from Barnstaple, Croyde.

At last – a beach café that has dishes on both lunch and dinner menus that every child will eat: plain spaghetti with cheese, as well as spaghetti bolognaise, and children's minute steak and fries (£4.25–5.95)! This lovely upstairs café bar has a big outside decking area with views towards Saunton Sands, a good 5 km of sandy beach and dunes. The needs of young families have been properly considered: dinner is served from 6pm, enabling families to come straight off the beach (there are showers below the café). Sandwiches are served from 10am–6pm (including down-to-earth cheese and pickle, or ham and mustard); lunch and dinner menus are quite similar, with the addition of evening specials such as chargrilled tiger prawns (£8.95), pan-seared sea bream (£12.95) and roasted chicken breast with bubble and squeak (£10.95). There's also 'mussel mounds' (try Somerset mussels – in cider and onion). It's a relief to find a trendy beach café bar that still has its feet firmly on the ground and in such a fabulous spot.

*Open 9.30am–9.30pm Feb–Oct; phone for winter opening. **Main course** £4.50–14.50 (lunch), £5.95–14.50 (dinner). **Credit** AmEx, MC, V. **Amenities** half portions available some dishes, highchair, disabled access, reservations accepted, parking, on beach, outside seating on balcony.*

> **INSIDER TIP**
>
> Take a step back in time and treat the family to something different – a ride in a purpose-built open wagon, drawn by Shire horses! **West Ilkerton Farm Horsedrawn Tours** (☎ *01598 752310; www.westilkerton.co.uk*) will give you a wonderful drive over Exmoor, with a chance to handle and drive the horses. Suitable for all ages, including wheelchair users; picnics and cream teas also on offer.

5 Devon's Heartland

DEVON'S HEARTLAND

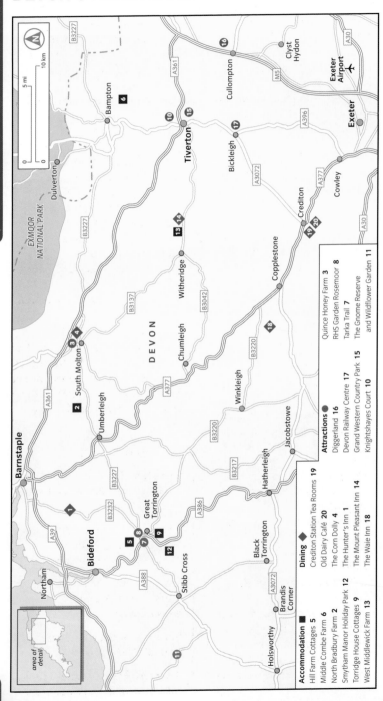

Accommodation ■
Hill Farm Cottages **5**
Middle Combe Farm **6**
North Bradbury Farm **2**
Smytham Manor Holiday Park **12**
Torridge House Cottages **9**
West Middlewick Farm **13**

Dining ◆
Crediton Station Tea Rooms **19**
Old Dairy Café **20**
The Corn Dolly **4**
The Hunter's Inn **1**
The Mount Pleasant Inn **14**
The Waie Inn **18**

Attractions ●
Diggerland **16**
Devon Railway Centre **17**
Grand Western Country Park **15**
Knightshayes Court **10**
Quince Honey Farm **3**
RHS Garden Rosemoor **8**
Tarka Trail **7**
The Gnome Reserve
and Wildflower Garden **11**

I t's fair to say that Devon's heartland wouldn't be most families' choice of holiday destination. There's no coastline – although the North Devon coast is easily accessible from the more northerly parts of the area – no wild moorland areas to explore and no really big centres of population other than Tiverton on the eastern edge. Look at any map of Devon and you'll soon see that other than the North Devon link road that links Tiverton with Barnstaple those roads that wend their way through the middle of the county (such as the A377 Exeter–Barnstaple) are long, winding and tortuous. So why would anyone go there? Well, if you want a taste of 'real' Devon – that part of the county pretty much untouched by tourism, still the domain of the farming community, with small remote villages, traditional market towns such as Crediton, South Molton and Hatherleigh, excellent pubs (with a reliable year-round local trade) – you'll enjoy exploring Devon's heartland. Once off the main routes you won't get anywhere quickly – there are miles of narrow hedged lanes – and you'll need a good map. Tourist attractions are few and far between, and accommodation possibilities quite limited – but holiday in this part of the county and you'll certainly avoid the crowds, even at the height of the tourist season.

VISITOR INFORMATION

Visit **www.devonshireheartland. co.uk** for up-to-date information on accommodation, eating out and attractions. The area is partly covered by the free guide **Essential Devon** (*www.essential devon.com*), and by some of North Devon's free papers: **North Devon & Exmoor Towns & Villages guide** (*www. northdevon.com*), **Scene North Devon holiday guide** (*www. northdevongazette.co.uk*) and the **Tarka Country Visitor.** Tiverton TIC is an excellent source of information, and there are local guides to towns such as Great Torrington, South Molton and Crediton, available from specific TICs. You'll need several

OS Explorer maps: 113 Okehampton, 114 Exeter & the Exe Valley, 127 South Molton & Chumleigh, and small sections of 112 Launceston & Holsworthy and 126 Clovelly & Hartland.

Information Centres

Crediton, The Old Town Hall, High Street; ☎ *01363 772006; www.crediton.co.uk*

Great Torrington, Castle Hill, South Street; ☎ *01805 626140; www.great-torrington.com*

Holsworthy, The Square; ☎ *01409 254185; www. holsworthy.co.uk*

South Molton, East Street; ☎ *01769 574122*

Tiverton, Phoenix Lane; ☎ *01884 255827; www.essentialdevon.com*

Orientation

Devon's heartland is huge, stretching south from the Somerset–Devon border on the M5 to just north of Exeter; the northern boundary runs west along the southern fringes of Exmoor, then parallel to the A361 North Devon link road to Barnstaple, taking in South Molton, before curving south-west via Great Torrington and Holsworthy to the Cornish border. The southern edge stretches all the way down to the A30 as it curves round the northern edge of Dartmoor and crosses West Devon.

Getting Around

You will need a car, and must be prepared for relatively long journey times to cover short distances if going off the main routes. The A361 cuts right across Devon's heartland from east to west but is a poor introduction; all other A roads are in places narrow and twisting, passing through few settlements. Don't do exploring unless you really enjoy driving! To get a real feel for the area try one of the east–west roads – A3072 Bickleigh–Crediton, B3042 Tiverton–Chawleigh, B3227 South Molton–Umberleigh – where you will find fantastic views and little traffic (other than tractors). Bus connections along the major routes are quite good; pick up a copy of **Tiverton & District Transport Information** from the TIC, or

Traveline *0871 200 2233; www. traveline.org.uk*. Main line trains run through Tiverton Parkway (near the M5, east of the town) and onto Exeter; the Tarka Line runs from Exeter northwest parallel to the A377, calling at Crediton and then a line of remote stations such as Copplestone, Eggesford and Umberleigh before reaching Barnstaple.

Child-Friendly Events & Entertainment

Mid Devon Show

Tiverton, late July.
www.middevon.co.uk

The area's largest annual show, held near Tiverton, is a traditional agricultural show, with livestock, heavy horses, carriage driving, craft and food stalls, and children's events. The event was sadly cancelled in 2007 due to water-logged conditions – a real blow to the local agricultural community.

South Molton Old English Fayre

Mid June, South Molton. 01769 574122

The tradition of holding fairs in South Molton dates from the 16th century when Elizabeth I granted a charter to the town, permitting two fairs, one in June, and a sheep fair in August. The tradition lives on, with the crowning of the queen, a floral dance in the square, craft stalls, music and dancing, a fair lunch and children's tea.

WHAT TO SEE & DO

Children's Top 10 Attractions

❶ **Blowing** funny glass shapes at Dartington Crystal. See below.

❷ **Counting** fairies in a wild-flower garden. See p. 71.

❸ **Driving** a dumper truck and scaring dad! See p. 70.

❹ **Cuddling** baby rabbits, guinea pigs and ducklings at Torridge House. See p. 76.

❺ **Leading** mum and dad round the garden trail at Rosemoor. See p. 73.

❻ **Cycling** along the Tarka Trail for ice cream at the organic café at Yarde. See p. 74.

❼ **Riding** on a narrow-gauge steam train, and stopping for a picnic by the River Exe. See p. 71.

❽ **Staying up** late to watch badgers in their natural habitat. See p. 70.

❾ **Drifting** along the Grand Western Canal in a horse-drawn barge. See p. 74.

❿ **Camping** in the middle of nowhere – at Nomansland! See p. 75.

Towns & Villages

Great Torrington

There's plenty to do in and around the historic little town of Great Torrington, which sits on the hills above the valley of the River Torridge and the old Torrington Station (Tarka Trail, p. 74). The 'Cavalier town' is famed for the Battle of Great Torrington, which marked the end of Royalist resistance in the West Country in 1646. Learn all about it at **Torrington 1646** (next to the TIC, main car park), complete with costumed characters and weaponry displays (☎ *01805 626146; www.torrington-1646.co.uk*). Cavalier beer is brewed in the town and sold throughout north Devon. Torrington has a Victorian pannier market on Thursdays and Saturdays and the excellent **Plough Arts Centre** on Fore Street, where there is a good café (☎ *01805 624624; www.plough-arts.org*). On the edge of town **Dartington Crystal** provides good wet-day fun with handcasting and glass blowing (free for children – ☎ *01805 626242; www.dartington.co.uk*); just down the A386 at Little Torrington the **Pots 'n' Paints** ceramics painting studio provides a couple of hours of fun for children and adults (☎ *01805 625577; www.glebefarmhouse.co.uk/pottery*). Torrington swimming pool is on School Lane (☎ *01805 623085; www.leisure-centre.com*). The Royal Horticultural Society's (RHS) wonderful **Rosemoor Garden** is just south of the town (p. 73), and **Torrington Common**, a large open space with playground above the Torridge valley, is a great spot for picnics and flying kites.

Tiverton

Mid Devon's largest town is situated on the Rivers Exe and Lowman; the name originates from 'Twy-Ford' (two fords crossing the rivers). Tiverton isn't the prettiest of Devon's towns, but a visit to the TIC is essential – and will prove that Tiverton is more interesting than it may at first appear! One of the town's best features is the **Grand Western Canal Country Park,** perfect for feeding ducks and gentle walks and cycle rides (p. 74), and where you can hire a rowing boat or self-drive day boat, or take a leisurely ride on the *Tivertonian,* a traditional horse-drawn barge (*℡ 01884 253345; www.horse boat.co.uk*). **Tiverton Castle** dates from the 12th century and is open on certain days of the week from Easter to late October (*℡ 01884 253200; www.tiverton castle.co.uk*), and **Tiverton Museum of Mid Devon Life** on Beck's Square runs fun events and activities for children during school holidays (*℡ 01884 256295; www.tivertonmuseum.org.uk*). And if you do nothing else in Tiverton go for tea at the **Four and Twenty Blackbirds** in Gold Street, a lovely traditional tea shop near the clock tower (*℡ 01884 257055*).

INSIDER TIP »

Something for wildlife watchers: **Devon Badger Watch** (*℡ 01398 351506; www.devonbadger watch.co.uk*), just 8 km north of Tiverton, runs badger watching evenings from April to October (minimum age seven). Get really close to badgers and enjoy seeing them in their natural habitat, both above and below ground, from the comfort of a purpose-built hide.

Fun Days Out

Diggerland ★ ★ AGES 5 AND OVER

Veerbeer Manor, Cullompton, Devon EX15 2PE; ℡ 08700 344437; www. diggerland.com. On B3181 Willand–Cullompton just off M5 Junction 27 Bus from Exeter, Taunton, Tiverton.

The whole idea of 'Diggerland' has intrigued me for many years! It's an extraordinary place: a rather tired outdoor adventure playground (huge towers, slides, swings and so on) leads to the 'main event', where you can pick up a model duck with a digger, play skittles with a digger, dig holes in Devon's red soil, go on a Land Rover safari, drive a JCB or a dumper truck, go on the Diggerland train. There are mini diggers for younger children, and certain rides are limited by age or height, but there's huge variety here for children (and adults) to get their teeth into! If you're feeling brave you can take a ride on the crazy Spin Dizzy or Sky Shuttle. At £12.50 per person over three years old it's not a cheap family outing, but it's certainly unusual with a high staff-to-visitor ratio – and you will have a huge amount of original fun. There's also indoor fun for wet days, including computer games.

Open *10am–5pm weekends, bank holidays, school holidays.* **Admission** *£12.50 per person, under 3 free.* **Credit** *MC, V.* **Amenities** *café, disabled access, parking, picnic area, shop, unlimited rides.*

The Gnome Reserve and Widlflower Garden ★

AGES UP TO 12

West Putford, near Bradworthy, Devon EX22 7XE ☎ *01409 241435; www.gnomereserve.co.uk. Follow signs off the A386 Barnstaple–Torrington, A39 from Kilkhampton or Buck's Cross.*

Gnome Reserve, West Putford

It's hard knowing quite how to describe the Gnome Reserve, tucked away down long, narrow lanes in the depths of the countryside. Perhaps the best way of describing it is to remember that a few years ago it was featured in a book about country eccentrics. Your first task is to don a gnome hat so as to 'blend in' with the inhabitants, then it's off into the gnomes' woodland home. They're involved in every conceivable occupation – fishing (of course), feasting, abseiling, playing football, the gnome orchestra, mining, on the beach…there's even a bust commemorating Seigfried, the first inhabitant in 1979. There's also a really lovely wildflower garden to explore via a level path (said by the RHS to be one of the best in the country, with 250 labelled species), with a clever quiz for children – counting fairies, looking out for certain plants – that's entered into a monthly draw. Cream teas and cakes are served undercover by the house, or you can eat a picnic in the gardens. Only recommended for eccentric teenagers, obviously – but fun for adults and younger children.

Open *10am–6pm end Mar–end Oct.* **Admission** *£2.75 adult, £2.25 child (3–16), under 3 free, £2.50 OAP/'recycled teenagers'.* **Amenities** *café, disabled access possible (wildflower garden), parking, picnic area, shop.*

Devon Railway Centre ★★★

FIND **ALL AGES**

The Station, Bickleigh, near Tiverton, Devon EX16 8RG; ☎ *01884 855671; www.devonrailwaycentre.co.uk. Off the A396 Exeter–Tiverton at Bickleigh.*

An excellent day out for all members of the family, from the under 10s (who can drive their own train, Toby) to the over 60s who can wallow in steamy nostalgia! Cadeleigh station closed in 1963, and was for many years used as a road maintenance depot. Restoration began in the early 1990s – the signal box is currently being rebuilt – and it now houses the largest collection of narrow gauge exhibits in the southwest. There's tons of railway memorabilia and two great half-mile train rides through a wildlife conservation site – we were taken there by Ivor, built in 1944 for industrial work and now in honourable 'retirement'. Hop off the train at Riverside Halt and enjoy your picnic on the banks of the Exe – keep an eye out for herons and otters. Three railway carriages house an incredible collection of 14 different model railway layouts – trains start running at the press of a button, and clever 'I Spy' and 'Can you see?' games keep children interested. Reasonably priced refreshments are served in the original station building – and new for 2007 is a model village (phase 2 for 2008). A great day out.

Open 10.30am–5pm Easter holidays, May bank holiday–end Sept, Oct weekends + half-term, Christmas specials. Admission £5.60 adult, £4.60 child 3–15, under 3 free, £4.80 OAP, £17.30 family. Credit MC, V. Amenities café, disabled access to part of site, parking, riverside picnic area, shop, outdoor play area.

Animal Attractions

Quince Honey Farm ★
AGES 6 AND OVER

North Road, South Molton, Devon EX36 3AZ; ☏ 01769 572401; www.quincehoney.co.uk. On the B3226 Barnstaple road in South Molton.

Did you know that honey bees were unknown in North America until taken there by settlers in 1622? And that they reached Australia by ship in the same way? The bees travelled in log hives and were allowed to fly; the ship only sailed slowly so the bees used the ship as their 'landmark'. Everything you've ever wanted to know about bees and honey production is covered at this working honey farm and – depending on the time of year – you can watch the honey being filtered and bottled. Wild honey bee sites have been recreated in the form of a chimney, dovecote and so on, and at the press of a button you can reveal the mass of bees working inside. Candles, beeswax polish and skin and hair care products are also manufactured at the farm, and on sale in the shop – where you can taste the different sorts of honey produced. In August all 1,500 hives are moved to Exmoor where the bees benefit from feeding on heather.

Open 9am–6pm Apr–end Sept, 9am–5pm Oct; shop only 9am–5pm Mon–Sat winter. Admission £4 adult, £3 child (5–16), under 5 free, £3.50 OAP. Credit MC, V. Amenities café, disabled access to café and shop only, parking, picnic area, shop.

Gardens

Knightshayes Court ★
ALL AGES

Bolham, Tiverton, Devon EX16 7RQ; ☏ 01884 254665; www.nationaltrust.org.uk. Signed off A396 just north of Tiverton.

This beautiful late Victorian country house, started in 1869, was built for the Heathcoat-Amory family at a 'suitable' distance from their textile mills in nearby Tiverton, and stands proudly in glorious gardens and parkland with distant views of the factory chimneys. The house and gardens are now in the care of the National Trust, and whereas children are often uninterested in country house interiors, the gardens and grounds are just brilliant for exploration! There are formal gardens near the house, a beautiful water lily pond and topiary fox and hounds running along a yew hedge; stone steps lead into the woodland garden, unbelievably beautiful in spring, with tiny paths weaving through great swathes of flowers. The newly restored – and enormous – walled kitchen garden is packed with all manner of culinary and herbaceous plants; much of what is on offer in the café is grown here. Picnics are not allowed in the gardens, but there are acres of parkland to enjoy, and endless good picnic spots. Pushchairs and baby slings are available for loan, and there's a children's garden trail.

Open 11am–5pm mid Mar–early Nov daily. *Admission* £5.90, child £3, members free. *Credit* MC, V. *Amenities* café, disabled access possible, parking, picnic areas, woodland walks, children's trail.

RHS Garden Rosemoor ★★

Great Torrington, Devon EX38 8PH; ☏ *01805 624067; www.rhs.org.uk/ rosemoor. 1 km south of Great Torrington on A3124. Bus from Barnstaple, Bideford.*

Rosemoor is, quite simply, gorgeous. This wonderful RHS garden nestles in the valley of the River Torridge surrounded by beautiful woodlands. It's a perfect place to drift around, with all sorts of different gardens linked by paths and arches, and lots of secret corners for children to explore. A tunnel leads under the road to access the original garden at Rosemoor, Lady Anne's Garden, a plantsman's garden started in the 1950s. On this side of the road you will also find less formal garden areas and the folly, and the lovely Wisteria tearoom. The estate was originally bought by Lady Anne's parents in 1923 as a fishing lodge. Rosemoor has a special children's garden trail, and a dedicated family weekend in August.

Open 10am–6pm Apr–Sept, 10am–5pm Oct–Mar. *Admission* £6 adult, £2 child (6–16), under 6 free, RHS members free. *Credit* MC, V. *Amenities* café, restaurant, disabled access, picnic area, parking.

Knightshayes Court

For Active Families

Tarka Trail AGES 5 AND OVER

The Tarka Trail can be accessed at the old Torrington Station (built in 1871; the last revenue earning train ran in November 1982), just below the town, and you can either follow the old railway line north towards Bideford or south to Meeth, beyond which the trail follows footpaths and country lanes towards Okehampton and Dartmoor. If you go south you'll ride along the quietest part of the trail, through unspoilt countryside, with a chance for a bite to eat at the excellent **organic café** at Yarde (☎ *01237 423655*); cycle north towards Bideford (turn round at the old Bideford station, where there's a café and visitor centre) and you'll ride along smooth tarmac by the River Torridge, passing the birthplace of Henry Williamson's Tarka en route (Williamson lived in the area for many years, and published *Tarka the Otter* in 1927). Both routes are level, easy and fun, without any road crossings.

Torrington Station to Meeth 16 km; Torrington to Bideford station 8 km. **Cycle hire** *Torridge Cycle Hire, Station Yard, Torrington;* ☎ *01805 622633*

Grand Western Country Park
AGES 5 AND OVER

This is a fantastic easy cycle ride through some of Mid Devon's prettiest countryside: along the banks of the old Grand Western Canal, begun in 1810 as part of a grand scheme to link the English

Grand Western Canal

and Bristol Channels via Exeter and Bristol. Only the Tiverton–Taunton stretch was ever completed, and was last used in the 1920s. The towpath is wide and level and the scenery glorious; there are bridges to cross and to pass under: look out for water lilies, yellow flags, mallard, heron, kingfisher and moorhen. If you can organise it start from Sampford Peverell or Halberton and follow the canal all the way to the Tiverton Canal Basin, where there are two very good cafés – the floating Barge Canal Shop and the thatched 16th-century Canal Tearooms – and lots of information on the history of the canal. On your way you'll probably see a colourful canal boat pushing smoothly through the water, towed by a heavy horse; you can join a trip from the canal basin.

Sampford Peverell to Tiverton Canal Basin 8 km. **Cycle hire** *Abbotshood Cycle Hire, Halberton;* ☎ *01884 820728; www.abbotshoodcycle hire.co.uk*

FAMILY-FRIENDLY ACCOMMODATION

INEXPENSIVE

West Middlewick Farm ★

Nomansland, Tiverton, Devon EX16 8NP; ☎ 01884 861235; www.west middlewick.co.uk. Just west of Nomansland on B3137. Bus from Exeter, Tiverton, Barnstaple.

A traditional Mid Devon dairy farm with two camping areas – a small paddock by the toilet block and a lovely four-acre field with wonderful views. Nomansland sits on a ridge of land running east to west across the county, with views of Exmoor one way and Dartmoor the other – a good striking-off point for both! Although the farm is apparently in the middle of nowhere there's easy access via the B3137 to Tiverton or South Molton. The farm has been welcoming campers since 1933, and the family have farmed in the area for generations. It's all very relaxed and down to earth – the camping field is accessed though the farmyard – children can watch the herd being milked in the old parlour (bring wellies), and there are calves and lambs to be fed. There's no playground or games room – just a big grassy area in the middle of the site for children to enjoy. A real bonus for grandparents: there's a lovely B&B suite (on two floors), with a comfortable sitting room and views to the moors – so that extended family groups can be accommodated in the campsite and the house.

25 caravan pitches, unlimited tents. **Rates** £7 (low)–9 (high) per caravan/ tent/2 adults per night, £2 child. **Amenities** disabled access, family shower room, laundry, parking, dogs on leads.

INSIDER TIP ❯

Although Devon's heartland has no coast, you can still spend your holiday on the water – on a traditional narrowboat on the Grand Western Canal. The navigable part of the canal is only 18 km long – there are no locks – so you can only cruise for a short distance, but can base your holiday 'far from the madding crowd' on this tranquil water. The narrowboat sleeps four; for details contact **Mid Devon Hire Boats & Moorings** (☎ *01884 252178; www.middevonhireboats.co.uk*)

MODERATE

Hill Farm Cottages ★★

Weare Trees Hill, Great Torrington, Devon EX38 7EZ; ☎ 01805 622432; www.hillfarmcottages.co.uk. On the Wear Gifford road just north of Great Torrington.

There's a real sense of intimacy as you walk under the archway and through the gate into Hill Farm Cottages – a lovely safe place for families with children up to around 11 years old. The converted cottages, some with views over Great Torrington Common, nestle closely together round the old farmyard, now filled with flowers and shrubs. The cottages are set in six acres of land, with chickens, ducks, rabbits, sheep, goats, ponies and donkeys to visit along with feeding and egg collecting. There's an outdoor mini adventure play area and Wendy House, and lots of open grassy space for flying kites and ball games. A real bonus is the indoor swimming pool, and a great indoor games room with table tennis, mini football table, pool table, table skittles, play farm, play construction site, children's toyshop and numerous other toys. The cottages are conveniently situated just outside Great Torrington, and also close to the pretty village of Weare Gifford.

5 s/c cottages, 4–6 people. **Rates** *£320 (low)–790 (high) pw.* **Amenities** *babysitting, cot (free), disabled access to one cottage, extra bed (free), parking, indoor pool, farm animals, games/play room, laundry room, adventure play area.* **In cottage** *fridge/freezer, cooker/microwave, shower/bath, TV/video.*

Torridge House Cottages
★★★ FIND

Little Torrington, Devon EX38 8PS; ☎ *01805 622542; www.torridge house.co.uk. Opposite the church in Little Torrington, signed off A386 south of Great Torrington.*

If your children like small animals and you're looking for a really personal 'hands-on' experience with pets this is the place for your family! The owners have been welcoming visitors to their cottages for 20 years, and clearly get a real kick out of sharing both their home and their numerous pets. A huge flock of ducks, geese and chickens greet you on arrival; there are pigs and piglets (fed by willing dads), lambs to feed, eggs to collect,

and chickens to put to bed. And best of all there's a large room with wall-to-wall hutches and pens around a safe 'animal table', on which children are allowed to pet guinea pigs, baby rabbits, ducklings and so on (all animal activity is supervised). Guests can get as involved as they wish, and can help with feeding and cleaning out. On top of the animal attractions there's an enclosed outdoor swimming pool, plenty of outdoor play equipment and a games room. Wonderfully laid back and relaxed, and a chance to handle more pets than your child has ever dreamt of!

9 s/c cottages, 2–8 people. **Rates** *£306 (low)–1,345 (high).* **Credit** *MC, V.* **Amenities** *babysitting, cot (free), disabled access possible in some cottages, DIY laundry room, parking, outdoor pool, chef-cooked ready freezer meals, Internet access in main house.* **In cottage** *cooker/microwave, fridge/freezer, dishwasher/washing machine/tumble dryer (some cottages), fridge/freezer, TV/DVD/video.*

North Bradbury Farm ★★★
FIND

Chittlehampton, Umberleigh, Devon EX37 9RE; ☎ *01769 572661; www. northbradburyfarm.co.uk. Off B3277 South Molton–Umberleigh, east of Chittlehampton.*

North Bradbury's motto is 'Arrive as guests – leave as friends', and because there are just two cottages converted from a 17th-century barn (the Cider Barn and Stables, which can be taken together – there is an interconnecting door) a holiday here would suit those families looking for something rather more personal than is usual with a larger holiday 'complex'. North Bradbury is a working farm where you can get involved with feeding and animal care if you wish – children can have rides on Pudding the pony. Every eventuality is provided for: cream tea on arrival, cake service, freezer meals, big drying and utility room, welly boots, and baby carriers. There's a small farm shop (Jacob sheep rugs for sale), farm walk and colouring books, enclosed gardens with decking and BBQ, tree house, sandpit, paddling pool, ride-on toys...this place is excellent value with facilities punching above its weight. The old shippen (cattle shed) has been converted into a lovely dining room, and here excellent dinners are served on request (charge per head) with unlimited wine. Brilliant for an extended family or for two families holidaying together.

2 s/c cottages, 2–10 people. **Rates** *£340 (low)–1,100 (high); discount if properties taken together £765 (low)–1,600 (high).* **Amenities** *babysitting, baby monitors, cot (free), laundry, parking, home-cooked restaurant meals in medieval-themed dining room.*

FAMILY-FRIENDLY DINING

`INEXPENSIVE`

Crediton Station Tea Rooms ★★

Crediton, Devon EX17 5BY; ☎ *01363 777766. Signed off A3777 east end of Crediton.*

Crediton Station Tearooms

Thoughts of *A Brief Encounter* abound in this wood-panelled platform tearoom – the building dates from 1847. Trains still run from Exeter–Barnstaple along this line (Tarka Line), which opened in May 1851 under the Exeter and Crediton Railway Company: the North Devon Railway extended the line from Barnstaple to Crediton later on in that year. Baskets of toys and games (and the occasional train) will keep youngsters amused; older family members will be fascinated by the excellent exhibition of train memorabilia celebrating 150 years of the Exeter–Barnstaple railway. There are wonderful old photographs documenting the history of the station, from World War II photos of evacuees to the stories of individual railway workers. Food is very reasonably priced, with a good choice of breakfasts: Fireman's Feast, Traveller's Treat, Controller's Nosh (£4). Puddings are homemade and traditional:

junket, apple pie, spotted Dick and custard (£2). It's a quiet, relaxing, rural spot, with none of the hustle and bustle associated with mainline stations: perfect for a straightforward cup of tea and a satisfying slab of delicious home-made cake.

Open *9am–4pm Mon–Fri, 9am–3pm Sat.* **Main course** *£3–4.* **Credit** *MC, V.* **Amenities** *highchair, toy box, disabled access, parking.*

The Corn Dolly ★ ★ ★ FIND

115a East Street, South Molton, Devon EX36 3DB; ☎ 01769 574249. On the B3227 in the centre of South Molton.

Welcome to the most perfect teashop in Devon! Simple wooden tables, bone china, corn dollies hanging from every beam and a fabulous display of tempting cakes create a real 'old farmhouse kitchen' ambience. Children have a great choice between a Tigger Tea (beans on toast), Humpty Dumpty Tea (boiled egg and soldiers), Little Bo Peep Tea (scone and jam, jelly and ice cream) and Little Jack Horner (Marmite soldiers and cake – £2.75–3.25, including a drink). Adults are recommended the Corn Dolly teacake – a good 15 cm in diameter! – or the lightest, tastiest, warm cheese scone ever. And then there are wonderful salads and sandwiches, the Corn Dolly breakfast, Gamekeeper's Tea, Seafarer's Tea or A Queen's Ransom (crumpets and Stilton) – or strawberry pavlova. There's something in this award-winning teashop to tempt every member of the

family – the only difficulty is trying to decide what to eat next!

Open *9.30am–5pm Mon–Wed, Fri, Sat; 8.30am–5pm Thurs, 11am–5pm Fri.* **Main course** *£4.95–7.45.* **Credit** *MC, V.* **Amenities** *children's menu, highchair, disabled access possible (small step), reservations accepted, gift/craft shop.*

INSIDER TIP »

When you're in South Molton check out **Griffin's Yard,** North Road (☎ *01769 572372*) – a fantastic organic and natural foods emporium, selling a huge selection of high quality foods, organic wines, fruit, vegetables, ecological household products and natural remedies. Very family friendly – and also has a café and crafts gallery.

MODERATE

The Mountpleasant Inn ★ ★ ★ FIND

Nomansland, Tiverton, Devon EX16 8NN; ☎ 01884 860271. On the B3137 Tiverton–Witheridge. Bus from Tiverton, Barnstaple.

A bright, bustling, friendly, family-run pub that welcomes everyone – especially other families! Set in the very heart of the county it's well worth the effort of getting to this popular inn dating from the 18th century when it was an ostler's house (where horses were changed when a coach came through the village). The restaurant is situated in the old blacksmith's forge. It's one of those 'real' local pubs where you could sit at the bar with a pint for a chat – or equally well take the family for a really good meal. The children's menu (£3.95 – sausage and mash, steak and chips, cheddar pasta) includes a carton of juice and a chocolate treat; adults will enjoy generous helpings of steak and kidney pie (£8.50), salmon fillet (£9.95) or spinach and feta pie (£8.50). Puddings are made locally and extremely tempting. It's spacious and the pub consists of several linked rooms. You'll want to go back again and again.

Open *11.30am–11pm Mon–Sat, 12pm–10.30pm Sun.* **Main course** *£8.50–14.95.* **Credit** *MC, V.* **Amenities** *children's menu, highchair, beer garden, disabled access possible, reservations accepted, parking.*

Old Dairy Café ★★★

Devonshire Traditional Breed Centre, Downes, Crediton, Devon EX17 3PL; ☎ 01363 772430; www.dtbcentre. co.uk. 1 km east of Crediton on A377. Bus from Exeter, Barnstaple.

A brilliant place for a family lunch or tea with lots of extras thrown in. The family room is full of toys and games; there's an excellent farm shop selling a wide variety of local produce; and all sorts of different rare breed fowl and bantams, ducks and geese to look at, some with fluffy topknots, others with baggy 'trousers' and feathery feet! The poultry live in beautifully maintained grassy pens, and it's fun to see just how many different shapes and sizes there are – and to watch the ducks splashing around in the pond. The Old Dairy Café serves an excellent range of home-cooked food, from jacket potatoes (£4.25) to daily specials: turkey and ham pie (£7.25), lamb chops (£7.25), mushroom stroganoff (£6.45) and a variety of salads. The farm's own Ruby Red beef features on the menu; Sunday lunches are a speciality, and healthy options are highlighted. Look out for special Teddy Bear picnic days for the under fives in the summer; plans for 2008 include a pets' corner.

Try These Too!

- **Smytham Manor Holiday Park**: A lovely peaceful campsite in the extensive grounds of Smytham Manor, set in a sheltered valley. Little Torrington, Devon EX20 8PU; ☎ *01805 622110; www.smytham. co.uk*.
- **Middle Combe Farm**: An idyllic 16th-century semi-fortified thatched hall house set in a 200 acre organic working farm. Uplowman, Tiverton, Devon EX16 7QQ; ☎ *01647 434063; www. helpfulholidays.com.*
- **The Hunter's Inn**: Dating back to the 17th century with an atmosphere of an old country inn. Newton Tracey, Barnstaple, Devon EX31 3PL; ☎ *01271 858339*.

Keeping It Local – Farmers' Markets & Farm Shops

Crediton Farmers' Market, Town Square, 1st Sat

Cullompton Farmers' Market, Station car park, 2nd Sat

Culm Valley Farm Shop, Cullompton; 📞 *01884 38513*

Fiona's Farm Fayre, Winkleigh; 📞 *01837 83382*

Fishleigh Farmhouse Foods, Umberleigh; 📞 *01769 560242*

Griffin's Yard, North Road, South Molton; 📞 *01769 574284/572372*

Halberton Court Farm Shop, Halberton, Tiverton; 📞 *01884 821458*

Holsworthy Pannier Market, The Square, Wed

Little Turberfield Farm Shop, Sampford Peverell; 📞 *01884 820908*

Lizzy's Larder, Milton Damerel, Holsworthy; 📞 *01409 261440*

South Molton Farmers' Market, Pannier Market, 4th Sat

Tiverton Farmers' Market, Pannier Market, 3rd Wed

Toogood's Farm Shop & Deli, Tiverton; 📞 *01884 243421*

Wildwood Farm Shop, West Anstey, South Molton; 📞 *01398 341222*

*Open 9.30am–5pm Tues–Fri, 10.30am–4.30pm Sat/Sun/bank holidays. **Main course** £4.95–7.25. **Credit** AmEx, MC, V. **Amenities** half portions available, highchair, outside seating, disabled access, family room, reservations accepted, rare breed poultry.*

The Waie Inn ★★ FIND

Zeal Monachorum, Crediton, Devon EX17 6DF; 📞 01363 82348; www.waieinn.co.uk. Signed off the A377 at Lapford; pub is at the bottom of the village.

Rural Mid Devon is the last place in the world you would expect to find a pub like The Waie Inn. I've never come across anything like it. The Waie Inn has fun facilities on a par with many 'official' attractions: an indoor swimming pool, skittle alleys, squash courts, huge indoor play area (£3.50 charge for children, with café and outside seating area), and four acres of landscaped grounds, with outdoor play equipment, animals to meet, five-a-side football pitch, fishing, zipwire, camping and much, much more! Originally a working farm, the building has over the last few years grown to incorporate various farm buildings; the most recent extension houses the very impressive indoor play area. As you'd expect in an agricultural area food is reasonably priced and traditional. There's also some great puddings, too: meringue glace, knickerbocker glory, banana split. The pub and facilities are open all day – but if you're after a traditional Devon pub look elsewhere!

*Open 7.30am–late daily. **Main course** £3.60–11.90. **Credit** MC, V. **Amenities** children's menu, highchair, disabled access, reservations accepted, parking, huge amount of indoor and outdoor activities, camping, 11 letting bedrooms, including family suites.*

6 Dartmoor & West Devon

DARTMOOR & WEST DEVON

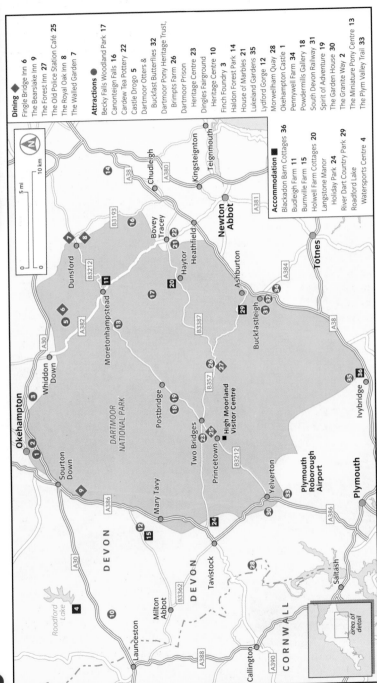

Dartmoor, the largest area of wild country in southern Britain, comes as something of a surprise to those who think of Devon as a 'soft' landscape of rolling green fields and picturesque thatched cottages – or who race past it en route to a Cornish holiday. Dartmoor National Park covers 953 square km, part of a vast raised granite plateau rising to 621 m at its highest point, High Willhays, in the northwest corner near Okehampton. In times of bad weather it can be a forbidding place. But there is a less harsh side to the moor: millions of years ago the granite plateau was tilted so that most of the rivers flow south. Where the small moorland streams hit the softer rocks at the granite edge they cut deep valleys, now thickly wooded – the Teign gorge at Castle Drogo, the Dart below Dr Blackall's Drive, the Avon and the Erme — which provide wonderful opportunities for those who don't want to tackle the high moor. Equally the beautiful Tamar Valley, where West Devon meets Cornwall, is altogether a gentler place, a designated AONB where the balmy climate for years supported market gardening and flower growing.

Those who get to know Dartmoor usually fall in love with its rolling heather-covered hills, craggy granite tors, steep-sided wooded valleys, patches of ancient oak woodland, sparkling rivers, peace and quiet – and an incredible feeling of space. It's an ideal destination for families who don't want to spend day after day on the beach, and who enjoy straightforward family activities: going for picnics, walking, cycling, exploring prehistoric sites, scrambling over the tors. Having said that, both the South Devon and North Cornish coasts can be reached after a bit of a drive, giving the best of both worlds. You won't find amusement arcades or discos here: but you will find wide open spaces, welcoming country pubs, and a range of interesting holiday accommodation, from B&B in a moorland hotel to beautiful self-catering cottages on a Victorian farm in the shadow of Haytor.

VISITOR INFORMATION

If you want to know anything about Dartmoor – how the tors were formed, where the ponies come from, even what the weather is going to do next – go to one of the many information centres (see p. 84). The biggest is the Dartmoor National Park Authority's **High Moorland Visitor Centre** in the old Duchy hotel building in Princetown. A permanent exhibition details Dartmoor's history and contemporary life, with good interactive displays for children. Check out too the Tamar Valley AONB Service at Cotehele Quay (p. 92; ☎ *01579 351681; www.tamar valley.org.uk*). You'll need good maps: OS Explorer OL28 for Dartmoor, and for the part of West Devon covered in this chapter Explorers 112 (Holsworthy & Launceston) and 108 Lower Tamar Valley & Plymouth.

DNPA, Parke, Bovey Tracey
(📞 *01626 832093; www.dartmoor-npa.gov.uk*; see also *www.virtuallydartmoor.org.uk*)

High Moorland Visitor Centre,
Princetown; 📞 *01822 890414/0845 3454975*

Information Centres

Haytor, lower car park; 📞 *01364 661520*

Newbridge, riverside car park; 📞 *01364 631303*

Postbridge, car park on B3212; 📞 *01822 880272*

TICs

Okehampton, White Hart Courtyard; 📞 *01837 53020; www.okehamptondevon.co.uk*

Tavistock, Bedford Square; 📞 *01822 612938; www.tavistock-devon.co.uk*

Community information centres

Ashburton, by car park; 📞 *01364 653426; www.ashburton.org/infocentre*

Bovey Tracey, lower car park; 📞 *01626 832047; www.boveytracey.gov.uk*

Buckfastleigh, Valiant Soldier; 📞 *01364 644522; www.buckfastleigh.org*

Ivybridge, Global Travel; 📞 *01752 897035*

Moretonhampstead, The Square; 📞 *01647 440043*

Orientation

Moretonhampstead – 'gateway to the high moor' – lies about 20 km west of Exeter. Dartmoor is bordered by the A38 (Ashburton, Ivybridge) to the south, the A30 to the north (Okehampton), and the A386 (Tavistock) to the west. Two roads cross the moor from east to west: the B3212 and B3357, crossing at Two Bridges. There is very remote land to north and south of Two Bridges, only accessible on foot. The softer eastern and southern fringes of the moor are threaded with a tangle of narrow lanes winding through small walled fields, wooded river valleys and pretty villages and hamlets. The Tamar Valley AONB lies to the west of the moor and adjoins Cornwall: the Tamar forms the boundary.

Getting Around

A car is essential for getting around Dartmoor and the Tamar Valley. There are various ongoing initiatives to encourage the use of local transport, such as the Dartmoor Sunday Rover Ticket which gives unlimited travel on Dartmoor's bus and train

Lustleigh May Pole

network (☎ Traveline *0871 200 2233; www.traveline.org.uk*), the Transmoor Bus from Exeter to Plymouth (weekends only) and the Dartmoor Freewheeler bus, which will carry you and your bike for free (Sundays Easter–Oct). Information centres will provide information on local bus services.

Child-Friendly Events & Entertainment

Lustleigh May Day
Follow the May Queen as she travels around the village under a floral bower, and watch her coronation on the famous May Day rock. A really traditional event, with Morris dancers, Maypole dancing, fun and games in the orchard and cream teas in the village hall.

2pm, first Sat in May, Lustleigh village, off A382 between Bovey Tracey and Moretonhampstead. Free.

The Contemporary Craft Fair
One of the most prestigious craft events in the UK, with an impressive line up of craftspeople from the Southwest. Loads to watch and enjoy: demonstrations, master classes, workshops for all ages, pottery, basket making, wire sculpting and much, much more. Plus there's a children's craft tent, full of inspiring activities!

Early June. Mill Marsh Park, Bovey Tracey (off A382); www.craftsat boveytracey.co.uk

Dartmoor Folk Festival
This friendly traditional festival was started by local musician Bob Cann in 1978. Lots to appeal to the whole family: Dartmoor Fayre, song and music sessions, crafts, dance displays, pub sessions and children's entertainers and events.

Early Aug (after Sidmouth Folk Week, p. 23). South Zeal, nr Okehampton; ☎ 01837 840102; www.dartmoor folkfestival.co.uk

Dartmoor ponies

WHAT TO SEE & DO

Children's Top 10 Attractions

❶ Helping to feed lambs, calves and pigs at **Burnville Farm**. See p. 100.

❷ Scrambling along the rocky River Lyd in search of the Devil's Cauldron at **Lydford Gorge**. See p. 89.

❸ Getting close to miniature ponies at Moretonhampstead's **Miniature Pony Centre**. See p. 92.

❹ Cycling along the **Granite Way** past Dartmoor's highest tors. See p. 94.

❺ Canoeing on the **River Tamar** in a Canadian canoe. See p. 92.

❻ Riding on a steam train along the **Primrose Line** from Buckfastleigh station. See p. 94.

❼ Sailing, windsurfing and kayaking at **Roadford Reservoir**. See p. 97.

❽ Exploring the spooky ruins of **Okehampton Castle**. See p. 88.

❾ Paddling in the West Dart river at Hexworthy Bridge. See p. 102.

❿ Dressing up in Victorian clothes and taking a carriage ride at **Morwellham Quay**. See p. 91.

Towns & Villages

Ashburton ★

This ancient stannary (tin mine) town is the largest in the National Park and has a good range of independent shops, a museum, open-air swimming pool and several good cafés and places to eat – try **Café Green Ginger** (East Street; ☎ 01364 653939), which has a delightful walled garden, or get takeaway pizza from the **Olive Pizzeria** (☎ 01364 654492). If you're in need of outdoor clothing or advice on kitting the family out for Dartmoor **Trailventure** (North Street; ☎ 01364 652522) will be happy to help.

Bovey Tracey ★

Known as 'the Gateway to the Moor' Bovey Tracey is home to the Dartmoor National Park Authority (p. 83). There are several possibilities for families (ideal for a wet day): the **House of Marbles** (☎ 01626 835285; www.houseofmarbles.com) has the largest collection of marbles in the world, and the biggest marble run in Britain. See glass being blown and look round the Bovey Pottery Museum. Nearby is the **Cardew Pottery** (☎ 01626 832172; www.craftsatcardew.co.uk), where you can paint pottery ornaments watch pottery being made, and explore the lake and woodlands. The **Devon Guild of Craftsmen** (☎ 01626 832223; www.crafts.org.uk), which displays the work of local craftspeople, has a lovely terrace café – or get takeaway pizza from **The Pizza Box,** Fore Street (☎ 01626 833900; www.thepizzabox.net). A few kilometres to the west **Becky Falls Woodland Park** (☎ 01647 221259; www.beckyfalls.com) is an ideal place for the children to let off steam. The falls were first opened to the public in 1903, and today have a variety of woodland trails (gentle to rugged, with boulder scrambling)

FUN FACT ≫ **Spooky Formations** ≪

Dartmoor is famous for its extraordinary granite formations known as 'tors'. One of the best for scrambling is Hound Tor, said to represent a pack of hounds frozen in mid flight. Nearby on Hayne Down stands Bowerman's Nose, a 12 m high granite column inside which it is believed the 11th-century hunter Bowerman is trapped for eternity, sent there by a coven of witches whom he once disturbed. And just over the down is sad Jay's Grave where lies the body of Kitty Jay, who was betrayed and committed suicide after the son of a local landowner refused to marry her. To this day there are always fresh flowers on her grave, placed there – some say – by a ghostly hand...

and a petting zoo with miniature ponies, lambs, rabbits, goats and guinea pigs. Other attractions include travelling musicians and medieval players, and a Victorian flea circus!

Okehampton ★

A workaday town which is full of surprises and has great choices for children. For one thing it has a real **castle** (English Heritage; ✆ *01837 52844*), built soon after the Norman Conquest of 1066. The extensive ruins are great fun to explore – especially with an audio tour – with picnic spots and walks by the West Okement river. Take a look at the **Museum of Dartmoor Life,** with interactive displays (✆ *01837 52295*, by the information centre), or have a milkshake at the **Panache Café Bar** in Red Lion Yard (✆ *01837 54234*). Just round the corner is the fully licensed New **Carlton cinema** (✆ *01837 658586; www. merlincinemas.co.uk*). You can hire bikes and spin along the **Granite Way** (p. 94), jump on the **Dartmoor Railway** (✆ *01837 55637*) and take a trip to Meldon station, close to Dartmoor's highest tors, or go for a swim at **Parklands Leisure Centre** in Simmons Park. A couple of miles to the east is **Finch Foundry** (National Trust; ✆ *01837 840046*) at Sticklepath, a 19th-century water-powered forge with waterwheels and noisy hammers, which used to produce all manner of agricultural and mining tools. A little further afield at Drewsteignton can be found **Castle Drogo** (National Trust; ✆ *01647 433306*) the 'youngest' castle in the country, built 1911–31 as a private house. Children love exploring the house and garden; there's a family event every day in the school holidays plus children's play area, quiz, trail and activity pack.

Princetown ★

A visit to Princetown is a must. This tough little town sits almost 427 m above sea level, and even in summer is often shrouded in mist. But it's a fascinating place, founded by Sir Thomas Tyrwhitt in the late 18th century and home to the infamous **Dartmoor Prison** (and excellent museum, p. 89) and the **High Moorland Visitor Centre** (✆ *01822 890414*). There are cafés and pubs, and easy walks along the old Princetown railway line. A few miles east along the B3212 is **Powdermills Gallery** (✆ *01822 880263; www.powder mills.com*). Where the buildings of an old gunpowder factory have been converted to a number of different uses, one housing an excellent gallery where the work of more than 30 Dartmoor craftspeople is on sale. Access land leads to the factory ruins; panels on the gallery walls reveal its history. Cream teas are served here on summer weekends.

Tavistock ★

Dartmoor's grandest market town, below the western edge of the moor. Pick up a town trail from the information centre. Don't miss the **Original Pasty House** (West Street), and look round the famous **Pannier Market** – a real treasure trove. Enjoy a picnic in the **Meadows,** situated between the River Tavy and the canal, or stop for a snack at **Dukes Coffee House** (Pannier Market Arcade). Go for a swim at the **Meadowlands Centre,** just next to **The Wharf** cinema and theatre (📞 *01822 611166).* **Morwellham Quay** (p. 91) lies a few miles to the southwest, and **Lydford Gorge** (National Trust; 📞 *01822 820320)* can be found off the A396 to the north. Children love this place (not suitable for the very young) – there's a play area and special children's activity days. A short walk through pretty oak woodland is followed by an exciting scramble along the banks of the River Lyd, complete with whirlpools and waterfalls, culminating in the mysterious Devil's Cauldron.

Fun Days Out

Canonteign Falls ★ ALL AGES

Christow, Devon EX6 7NT; 📞 01647 252434; www.canonteignfalls.com. On the B3193 5 km north of the Chudleigh Knighton/Teign Valley exit off the A38.

Take a trip to the top of England's highest waterfall, 67 m above the Teign Valley; choose a trail to suit the make-up of your party. Paths wind up through ancient woodland – via the Secret Garden and Victorian Fern Garden – past a series of cascades to Buzzard's View, with fabulous views. The less energetic (and those with buggies) can follow Grandad's Way around the lakes and wetlands, and play Pooh sticks in the feeder streams. Excellent playground areas keep children amused while adults relax by the lakeside, or learn more about the history and wildlife of this beautiful spot in the lower barn.

*Open 10am–6pm early Mar–early Nov and during winter school holidays; closed Christmas. **Admission** £5.75 adult, £4.25 child (5–16), under 5 free, £4.75 OAP, £18.50 family. **Credit** AmEx, MC, V. **Amenities** café and kiosk, disabled access (not to bottom of falls), parking, baby carriers available, play areas, mini assault course, dogs (on leads), 80-acre picnic area, shop.*

Dartmoor Prison Heritage Centre ★ ★ FIND AGES 5 AND UP

HMP Dartmoor, Princetown, near Yelverton, Devon PL20 6RR; 📞 01822 892130; www.dartmoor-prison.co. uk. On the B3357 on the northern edge of Princetown Transmoor. Bus service weekends Plymouth–Exeter; daytime buses from Yelverton/Tavistock

This fascinating little museum doesn't look particularly interesting from the outside, but is a bit like Doctor Who's Tardis: step inside and you'll be amazed! The museum documents the history of the prison from 1809, when the first prisoners, captured during the war with France, were

Picnics, Paddling & Pastimes

One of the main draws of somewhere like Dartmoor is the fact that so much family entertainment is free. What could be better than packing up a picnic, finding a grassy spot by a sparkling river, and letting the children do what children like doing best – play with water! Take notice of posters which ask you not to enter certain areas of some rivers, for example where salmon spawn – and be careful not to damage riverbanks or dislodge rocks in the river. Do not let your children enter the water if rivers are running high. Swimming is possible in deep pools at places such as **Newbridge** on the Dart and on the upper Teign.

Scrambling over granite boulders is another favourite pastime – particularly good at spots such as **Bonehill Rocks** near Widecombe, or at **Horsham Steps** on the River Bovey near Lustleigh. There are ancient oak woodlands to explore at **Wistman's Wood** near Two Bridges, **Blackator Copse** near Meldon Reservoir, and at **Piles Copse** in the lower Erme Valley. Or why not find an open windy spot – quite easy on Dartmoor! – and have a go at kite flying?

Show the children how people used to live on Dartmoor! The Bronze Age settlement at **Grimspound**, a stone enclosure once surrounding 24 huts, sits on the edge of Hameldon 8 km southwest of Moretonhampstead and dates from around 1300BC. One hut circle has been partially restored – you can see the curved porch. The remains of the medieval village just below **Hound Tor**, where several houses are grouped together – and which was probably abandoned around the time of the Black Death in the 14th century – are also fun to visit. Children will also enjoy playing around the lovely medieval clapper bridges at **Postbridge** and **Dartmeet**.

marched there from Plymouth. Today Dartmoor is a category C prison, holding over 600 inmates. The museum is stuffed with bits and pieces relating to life behind bars: old newspaper cuttings, photos, gruesome leg irons, models carved out of meat bones, a flogging frame and cat o' nine tails last used in 1947, even a string of knotted sheets found recently from a foiled escape attempt. Look for the knife made out of matchsticks, or get your child's photo taken for 'prison records'! An excellent DVD, in which prisoners talk about their lives in the prison today, is an added bonus.

Open *9.30am–12.30pm, 1.30pm–4.30pm, Mon–Sat; 9.30am–12.30pm, 1.30pm–4pm Sun; closed Christmas Day and Boxing Day.* ***Admission*** *£2 adult, £1 child (18 and under), under 5 free, £1 OAP.* ***Credit*** *MC, V.* ***Amenities*** *disabled access (upstairs only), parking, shop.*

Dingles Fairground Heritage Centre ★★ AGES 5 AND UP

Lifton, Devon PL16 0AT; ☎ 01566 783425; www.fairground-heritage. co.uk. Follow signs off the A30 from

Dingles Fairground Heritage Centre

Roadford Lake junction (between Okehampton and Launceston).

A great place for grandparents to take grandchildren for a spot of nostalgia. You're immediately assaulted by the sounds and smells of steam engines and the topsy-turvy world of the fairground – 'gallopers', penny-slot machines, switchbacks, the Wall of Death, Wild West shows – accompanied by cheerful tunes from traditional fairground organs. This extraordinary collection of industrial and farm steam engines, vintage vehicles and fabulous fairground memorabilia is a real surprise. Children will particularly enjoy the wacky mirrors – such simple entertainment! – and the huge Rodeo Switchback, built in the 1880s, with its collection of bizarre, garishly coloured creatures.

Open 10.30am–5.30pm Thurs–Mon (closed Tue/Wed), end Mar–end Oct. ***Admission*** £6 adult, £4.50 child (4–16), under 3 /OAP free, £19.50

family. **Credit** *MC, V.* **Amenities** *café, disabled access, parking, picnic area, shop, some fairground rides (phone in advance to check).*

INSIDER TIP ▸▸

Take an apple with you to Dingles Steam Village and watch it pass through the amazing apple peeler, which deals with 3,000 apples an hour!

Morwellham Quay ★★★
ALL AGES

Nr Tavistock, Devon PL19 8JL; 📞 *01822 832766;* **www.morwellham-quay.co.uk.** *About 6 km southwest of Tavistock; follow signs off the A390 between Tavistock and Callington.*

This is a very individual place. In the mid-19th century, when the Cornish mining industry was at its height, Morwellham was one of the busiest ports in the country. The docks, quays, limekilns, mills, workshops, cottages – around 300 people lived here – and tramways have all survived remarkably well. It's wonderfully atmospheric, and easy to imagine you're back in 1860 – ably assisted by staff dressed in period costume! Take a ride into the old copper mine, explore the restored village, board the *Garlandstone* – an old Tamar ketch – take a carriage ride, visit the Victorian farmyard, take a stroll through the nature reserve – or dress up in Victorian clothes! Don't miss the village schoolroom and shop, and follow the children round one of the informative trails. In 2006 Cornish and Devon

Mining Heritage was designated a World Heritage Site (p. 133) by Unesco, to which the Tamar Valley – and Morwellham – forms the eastern gateway. Plans are afoot for a new visitor orientation centre and an extensive network of footpaths, bridleways and cycleways. Whether your interest is in industrial history, the grand age of sail, Victorian cottage gardens or simply having an ice cream on the banks of the River Tamar, you will have a fabulous time.

Open *10am–5.30pm daily end Mar–end Oct; 10am–4.30pm daily end Oct–end Mar; closed Christmas/ New Year's Day.* **Admission** *£8.90 adult (inc copper mine train ride), £6 child (5–16), under 5 free, £7.80 OAP, £19.50 family.* **Credit** *MC, V.* **Amenities** *café, disabled access, parking, picnic area, pub Fri/Sat evenings, shop, carriage rides, special events/activities throughout year.*

> **INSIDER TIP**
>
> Take the family on a three-hour canoe trip from Morwellham down-river to historic Cotehele Quay, with a stop-off at Calstock. Learn how to paddle on the beautiful Tamar river with **Canoe Tamar** (📞 *0845 430 1208; www.canoe tamar.co.uk*). Canoes are safe and stable – perfect for family outings – and instruction is given. Daily trips Jun–Sept.

Animal Attractions

Pennywell Farm ★★★
ALL AGES

Buckfastleigh, Devon TQ11 0LT; 📞 01364 642023; www.pennywell farm.co.uk. Follow signs off the A38 2 km south of Buckfastleigh.

Set aside a whole day for Pennywell Farm, the first place in the country to promote real 'hands-on' interaction with animals. The owners' enthusiasm is evident at every turn! A new specially designed barn (opened in 2007) enables children to mingle with lambs, goats, rabbits, guinea pigs, chinchillas, chickens...and the world-famous Pennywell miniature pigs. A fantastic choice of activities includes everything from cuddling a lop-eared rabbit, feeding a lamb and listening to nursery rhymes to pony rides, a mini-beast safari, pond dipping and 'duck trials'. Every 30 minutes a ringing bell announces a new activity – rounding up the ducks at bedtime looked good fun! Add in gravity go-karts, trampolines, cider tasting, an indoor theatre, a willow maze and fabulous views and you can see why Pennywell has scooped a number of impressive awards over the years.

Open *10am–5pm early Feb–end Oct.* **Admission** *£9.50 adult, £6.90 child (3–16), under 3 free, £8.50 OAP.* **Credit** *AmEx, MC, V.* **Amenities** *café and kiosk, disabled access, parking, picnic area, shop, new activity every 30 minutes.*

The Miniature Pony Centre
★★ **AGES UP TO 10**

Moretonhampstead, Devon TQ13 8RG; 📞 01647 432400; www. miniatureponycentre.com. About 3 km west of Moretonhampstead on the B3212. Transmoor bus service weekends Plymouth–Exeter.

Come rain or shine this is a great place for younger children. There

Miniature Pony Centre, Moretonhampstead

are excellent adventure play areas (indoors and outside), a toddlers' playground, lakeside picnic area and nature trails, and a fantastic range of 'miniature' animals: Shetland ponies, Mediterranean donkeys, sheep and lambs, pigs and pygmy goats. Visitors can wander through the miniature pony paddock, or into the open barn, and get really close to the animals. The pony rides are really popular, and each rider receives a rosette. Every child gets a free spotter guide and activity book to fill in, as well as the chance to join in with a number of other activities: lamb feeding, grooming a pony, or watching a birds of prey display.

Open 10.30am–4.30pm late Mar–end Oct, 10am–5pm Jul/Aug. **Admission** £6.50 adult, £5.50 child (3–16), under 3 free, £5 OAP, £22 family. **Credit** AmEx, MC, V. **Amenities** café, disabled access, parking, picnic area, shop, free dog kennels.

Dartmoor Otters & Buckfast Butterflies ★★ ALL AGES

The Station, Buckfastleigh, Devon TQ11 0DZ; ☏ 01364 642916; www. ottersandbutterflies.co.uk. Just off the A38 at Buckfastleigh; follow signs for town then turn left. Bus service from Exeter, Ashburton, Plymouth, Newton Abbot, Totnes, Paignton.

At Buckfastleigh several attractions are available on the same site (all-day combined tickets available). A wall of heat hits you as you enter the butterfly house – it's like walking into a tropical forest! Children love this place: there are vividly coloured butterflies, pretty little birds flitting through bowers of exotic flowers and banana trees, and terrapins wallowing in pools and waterfalls. Back in the open air take a look around the otter sanctuary, where these irrepressible creatures can be seen playing in open-air pens and pools. The otters are fed

Out & About on Dartmoor

Climbing A great way to exercise older kids, climbing is a sport that's within reach of everyone, regardless of size, shape or age! Get close to Dartmoor's granite and take part in a real family activity. Information centres will have details on qualified providers.

Cycling The Dartmoor Freewheeler bus service – which will carry your family and your bikes – operates in spring and summer (☎*01822 890414; www.dartmoor-npa.gov.uk*).

Horse Riding One of the best ways to get a real feel for the moor is to go exploring at a civilised pace: on horseback. Some of the following offer day rides, or evening pub rides in summer: **Babeny Farm Riding Stables,** Poundsgate (☎ *01364 631296*); **Cholwell Riding Stables,** Mary Tavy (☎ *01822 810256*); **Dartmoor Riding,** Shilstone Rocks Stud, Widecombe-in-the-Moor (☎ *01364 621281; www.dartmoor-riding. com*); **Skaigh Stables,** Belstone (☎ *01837 840917* (day), *840429* (eve); *www.skaighstables.co.uk*); **Dartmoor Riding Centre,** Cheston, near South Brent (☎ *01364 73266*).

Letterboxing A moorland treasure hunt! Letterboxes are hidden all over the moor, each containing a rubber stamp and visitor's book. Working out clues and finding them is great fun for all the family

three times a day, and can be viewed swimming underwater.

Open 11am–3pm daily Feb/Mar/Nov otters only; 10am–5.30pm Apr–end Oct otters and butterflies. **Admission** £6.50 adult, £4.95 child, £5.95 OAP, under 3 free, £19.50 family. **Credit** AmEx, MC, V. **Amenities** snack bar, disabled access, parking, picnic area, shop.

South Devon Railway ★★
ALL AGES

☎ 0845 345 1420; www.southdevon railway.org.

The South Devon Railway runs steam trains on the 'Primrose Line' from Buckfastleigh to Totnes along the beautiful valley of the River Dart. Trains run several times a day (phone for times). If you have any time left

why not hop on the vintage bus – no extra charge – that runs into Buckfastleigh and also to Buckfast Abbey.

Open 10am–5pm late Mar–end Oct, plus Christmas specials. **Admission** £9 adult return, £5.40 child (5–14), £8.10 OAP, £26 family. **Credit** MC, V. **Amenities** café, disabled access, parking, picnic area, museum, workshop, model railway, model railway and gift shop, riverside walk, maze, children's play area.

For Active Families

The Granite Way AGES 5 AND UP
This easy cycle ride is great fun for all the family, with different options depending on the makeup of your party. The route (part of Route 27 Devon Coast to Coast) follows the old London

☎ *01364 73414* – a free booklet is available from information centres).

Swimming Outdoor pools (summer only) at Moretonhampstead, Chagford, Ashburton and Bovey Tracey.

Walking Enjoying Dartmoor on foot doesn't necessarily involve tramping off across the high moor into the mist, loaded down by a huge rucksack (though the Two Moors Way long-distance trail starts at Ivybridge and runs across the county for 164 km to Lynmouth on the north coast). There are lots of opportunities for short, easy walks – you can follow marked trails around the shores of the Teign Valley reservoirs, bump along the old railway line from Princetown to Fogginator Quarry, take the pushchair through the nature reserve at Stover Country Park near Bovey Tracey (☎ *01626 835236; www.devon.gov.uk*) or spot kingfishers along the River Teign below Castle Drogo (p. 88). The DNPA offers a full programme of guided walks, some aimed specifically at families, throughout the year. Details may be found in the **Visitor Guide,** available in all information centres, along with books on family walks (and those suitable for pushchairs). Another option is to join a **Dartmoor Nature Tour** to find out about the moor's wildlife (☎ *0785 8421 148; www.dartmoornaturetours.co.uk*).

and South Western Railway line (closed to commercial traffic in 1968) around the northwest corner of Dartmoor. Pass Dartmoor's highest point – High Willhays (621 m) – and Meldon reservoir, cross 45-m high Meldon viaduct (visitor centre and café in a former buffet carriage), and have a cream tea at Sourton village hall (summer weekend afternoons). The railway line is barred beyond Southerly Halt, where there is a picnic site. Keen cyclists – and those with older children – can continue on past the Bearslake Inn (p. 103) and via quiet (and hilly) country lanes through Bridestowe to rejoin the old railway line and on to historic Lydford with its castle and beautiful gorge.

Okehampton station to Lydford 17.7 km. **Cycle hire** *YHA, Okehampton station* ☎ *01837 53916; Dartmoor Railway, Okehampton station* ☎ *01837 55330; Devon Cycle Hire, Sourton Down* ☎ *01837 861141/ 01822 615014; www.devoncycle hire.co.uk.*

The Plym Valley Trail
AGES 5 AND UP

A bumpy start from Clearbrook on Dartmoor's western edge leads cyclists onto the former South Devon and Tavistock Railway line, opened in 1859. For families it's a lovely way of accessing beautiful woodlands at Plym Bridge, with relics of the industrial past (and good picnic spots by the river): slate quarries, workers' cottages, a small lead/silver mine, a canal and three railway lines, and

The Dartmoor Pony

Drive across Dartmoor any day of the year and you'll see ponies – they're one of the moor's biggest attractions, and a pony is the symbol of Dartmoor National Park. Most of the ponies are not true Dartmoor ponies but cross-breeds, often with a bit of Shetland pony in the mix. Don't try to approach the ponies; never stroke or feed them. Apart from the fact you may get bitten or kicked (these ponies are wild) it is dangerous for the ponies to become too familiar with people and cars. The **Dartmoor Pony Heritage Trust** (*www.dhpt.co.uk*), based at **Brimpts Farm**, near Dartmeet (*01364 631450; www.brimptsfarm.co.uk*), is a charity dedicated to the preservation of the indigenous Dartmoor Pony, now officially recognised as an endangered species. Visit the ponies – you can even adopt one – or go on a guided walk across the moor, with a pony carrying your lunch! There are also walking trails around the farm and through the 19th-century tin-mining area, which can be nicely rounded off with a cream tea in the farmhouse.

beautiful wildflowers in spring. There's one fairly dark tunnel to negotiate en route (but it doesn't last for long). There's also a stretch along narrow lanes at Bickleigh and a steep descent; younger children should dismount. A fun extension leads under the A38 on the edge of Plymouth and along the banks of the Plym estuary to the National Trust's magnificent 18th-century Saltram House, a good spot for a rest before the return journey.

Clearbrook to Coypool 11 km; optional 5 km there-and-back extension to Saltram House. **Cycle hire** *Tavistock Cycles, Tavistock ☎ 01822 617630; Dartmoor Cycle Hire, Tavistock ☎ 01822 618178; www. dartmoorcycles.co.uk*

> **INSIDER TIP** ›
> There are good – and shorter – cycle trails suitable for all abilities

through **Haldon Forest Park** (☎ *01392 834251; www.haldon forestpark.org.uk*), signed off the A38 between Exeter and the eastern edge of the National Park, plus an adventure playground, refreshments, and even showers. A number of specially designed walking trails have also been laid through the forest – a Play Trail, Butterfly Trail and Sensory Trail – with all sorts of interesting bits and pieces along the way to encourage children to keep going. Bikes are available on site from **Forest Cycle Hire** (☎ *01392 833768; www.devoncyclehire.co.uk*).

Spirit of Adventure
AGES 8 AND UP

Powdermills, Near Postbridge, Yelverton, Devon PL20 6SP; ☎ 01822 88077; www.spirit-of-adventure. com. On the B3212 between Two Bridges and Postbridge. Transmoor bus service weekends Plymouth– Exeter; daytime buses from

Yelverton/Tavistock to Princetown, then year-round service to Bellever.

Kayaking, canoeing, rock climbing, abseiling, gorge scrambling, orienteering, mountain biking, hill walking... Dartmoor has so many activities on offer! Wander past Haytor Rocks on a dry day and you're almost bound to see climbers working their way to the top of the crag. Tempted? If you or your children feel like being a bit adventurous but don't know where to start – and want to be in safe hands – book a day out with qualified instructors from Spirit of Adventure. Try a rock-climbing adventure day – suitable for total beginners – or learn to paddle a canoe or kayak. And if you want to go that little bit further the company runs family adventure weekends (or weeks), based at Power Mills Bunkhouse in the heart of the moor. I can guarantee that learning how to steer a Canadian canoe with your child, or building a raft together, can be a life-changing experience!

INSIDER TIP

For a really active day when every member of the family – whatever the age range – will be kept happy and occupied go to the River Dart Adventures at Holne Park (p. 98). It's open to day visitors (£6.50 per person, under five free, £24 family) from 10am until dusk on weekends and school holidays.

INSIDER TIP

Walking on Dartmoor with the family doesn't have to be a daunting prospect. If you're not too confident in your map-reading

skills, and want to know more about GPS (Global Positioning System) book the family on a day out with Compassworks (01566 783236; www.compassworks. co.uk), who specialise in teaching navigation skills. You'll all have a lot of fun – and be less likely to get lost in the future!

FAMILY-FRIENDLY ACCOMMODATION

INEXPENSIVE

Roadford Lake Watersports Centre ★★

Lower Goodacre, Broadwoodwidger, Lifton, Devon PL16 0JL; 01409 211507; www.swlakestrust.org.uk. Follow signs from the A30 between Okehampton and Launceston.

If you have active children who want to try their hand at a variety of water sports why not take the family camping at Roadford Lake, a few kilometres off the A30 near the Devon–Cornwall border. This peaceful spot comes alive on bright and breezy days when local sailors and windsurfers take to the water in dinghies, canoes and windsurfers. Call in advance to arrange for some tuition, from novice to advanced level – or join the children (over eight) on a Wet and Active day when you can try out three different watery activities. It's a very relaxed place to while away the hours: the lakeside campsite has lovely views over the lake and towards Dartmoor, and on the opposite shore lunch or a cream tea can be enjoyed at the Lakeside restaurant.

*38 lakeside camping pitches, £5 per night adult, £3 per night child 5–14, under 5 free, £13 per night family (4). **Credit** MC, V. **Amenities** BBQ area, lakeside restaurant (daily 10am–4pm, longer hours in summer), visitor centre and play area, walking trails, sailing, windsurfing, canoeing, kayaking, rowing (phone in advance), angling (advance booking recommended).*

River Dart Country Park
★★★ GREEN

Holne Park, Ashburton, Devon TQ13 7NP; ☎01364 652511; www.river dart.co.uk. On the Dartmeet road; follow signs from the A38 Pear Tree Cross junction west of Ashburton on the Princetown road.

River Dart Pirate Ship

It's hard knowing quite where to start when trying to cover everything that's good for families at the River Dart Country Park. For a start there's the setting, in the grounds of Holne Park House. There's a huge amount of space – 90 acres of woodland and parkland – allowing for spacious pitches within the extensive camping fields. Everything you need is on site: a new bar and café for 2007, swimming pool, tennis courts, woodland walks and cycle rides. There's an extraordinary amount of adventure play equipment hidden away amongst the trees: a sandy beach play area (great for toddlers), play lake, multi-deck pirate ship, zip wire, swings and slides, all operated under River Dart Adventures. On top of these are some Daredevil Activities (available high season only), high ropes course, canoeing and indoor climbing wall. Families tend to come back over and over again,

and it's easy to see why! The owners have recently installed their own hydro-electric power generator on the River Dart.

*120 electric hook-ups + 130 camping pitches 1 Apr–30 Sept. **Rates** £10.50 (low)–22 (high) 2 people. £5–6.50 extra person. 4 s/c cottages: 6–10 people. **Rates** £275 (low)–925 (high). Cot free. Extra bed (charge). B&B available in main house: 10 rooms inc some family rooms, £60–125. **Credit** MC, V. **Amenities** Café/restaurant/ bar, takeaway meals, disabled access, parking, extensive woodland and parkland, DIY laundry, shop, swimming pool, tennis courts, fishing, games room, free access to River Dart Adventures, cycling, dogs on leads, wealth of wildlife.*

MODERATE

Budleigh Farm ★★

Moretonhampstead, Devon TQ13 8SB; ☎ 01647 440835; www.budleigh farm.co.uk. On the A382 about 1 km south of Moretonhampstead, 10 km north of Bovey Tracey.

This delightful working farm lies in the pretty Wray valley on Dartmoor's eastern edge. The thatched farmhouse dates back 500 years, and the Victorian granite outbuildings – built for W.H. Smith of stationery empire fame – have been tastefully converted into seven well-appointed self-catering cottages. Accommodation is flexible: the double bed in the Granary is accessed via a wooden ladder! Each cottage has a different feel, according to its original use: stable, granary, or linney. Children can roam freely around the farm (except for the shooting range); there is a stream to play in, and plenty of space to kick a football. Each cottage has somewhere to sit outside and enjoy the peace of the countryside, interrupted only by the cawing of rooks and the gentle baaing of sheep. Three cottages share an extensive garden. An added bonus is the heated outdoor swimming pool, accessed without intruding on the owners' privacy.

7 s/c cottages: 2–6 people. **Rates** *£165 (low)–530 (high).* **Credit** *MC, V.* **Amenities** *Disabled access to one 2-person property, cot (free), extra bed available, DIY laundry, parking, outdoor heated swimming pool (May–Sept), table tennis room, public telephone, Internet access (in office), target shooting and archery (additional charge), dogs welcome in some cottages.* **In cottage** *fridge/freezer, cooker/microwave, shower and/or bath, TV/video.*

Blackadon Barn Cottages ★★

Ivybridge, Devon PL21 0HB; 📞 *01752 897034; www.blackadonbarns.co. uk. Follow signs to Wrangaton off*

A38 between Ivybridge and South Brent, then signs to Moorhaven Village; follow main drive then turn right up narrow lane. About 2.5 km from Ivybridge station.

If you're torn between holidaying on the moor or coast why not go for the best of both worlds? This idyllic corner of southwest Dartmoor feels far away from anywhere yet is just 10 minutes from the A38, and a mere 30 minutes from the South Devon coast (the sea is visible from the farm). The original farmyard buildings have been tastefully converted into a number of well-equipped cottages round the cobbled yard. The perfect location for a family holiday with something to suit all ages: Dartmoor is on the doorstep, the coast not too far away, and Plymouth and Exeter easily reached. The owners provide a number of car-free options for visitors, making the most of public transport. The farm backs onto the open moor, providing excellent walking opportunities; swimming in the Avon river near Shipley Bridge is popular. The farm has its own water supply, vegetables are home-grown and recycling encouraged. Blackadon has its own Wealth of Wildlife folder, produced in association with DNPA (p. 84). Children can help feed the ducks, chickens and goat.

6 s/c cottages: 2–10+ people. **Rates** *£225 (low)–1375 (high).* **Credit** *MC, V.* **Amenities** *babysitting, cot free, disabled access, extra bed available (charge), visitors' laundry, all cottages non-smoking, parking, outdoor play area, special rates for local swimming pools and golf course.* **In cottage** fridge/freezer, cooker/microwave, washing machine/drier, shower and/or bath (or both), TV/DVD/satellite.

EXPENSIVE

Burnville Farm ★★★ FIND

Brentor, Tavistock, Devon PL19 0NE; ☎ 01822 820236 (B&B), ☎01647 433593 (cottages); www.burnville. co.uk. 3.2 km southwest of Lydford, just off the A386 Tavistock–A30 (Okehampton).

This beautiful place, tucked away in rolling farmland just off the moor near historic Lydford in West Devon, is a real find. Four fantastic individual properties, each in its own extensive grounds set up for family groups: the Coach House, for example, has a TV room and play room as well as the main sitting room. Two properties have indoor swimming pools, and there's a lovely enclosed outdoor pool for hot days. Guests can use the tennis court and wander through the walled vegetable garden. Children can row on the pond, ride off on mountain bikes, and feed lambs, calves, pigs and chickens. New for 2008 is a games room and gym. There is a tremendous sense of freedom and space at Burnville, and many families return year after year. The elegant late Georgian farmhouse has fantastic views towards Dartmoor and Brentor church, and offers bed and breakfast in sumptuous surroundings, with full use of the main drawing room and dining room. A place that's hard to leave!

*4 s/c 'cottages', 6–11 people. **Rates** £299 (low)–2307 (high). **Credit** MC, V. **Amenities** babysitting, cot free, extra bed free, gym, parking, dogs welcome, swimming pools, tennis court, badminton court, games room, delicious evening meals available in own house or main. **In cottage** fridge/freezer, cooker/microwave, dishwasher, washing machine/tumble drier, woodburner, bath/shower, Internet access, TV/DVD/video.*

Holwell Farm Cottages ★★

Widecombe in the Moor, Devon TQ13 7TT; ☎ 01364 631453; www. holwelldartmoor.co.uk. From Bovey

Try These Too!

- **Langstone Manor Holiday Park.** Down to earth and unpretentious establishment in an unspoilt and peaceful corner. Moortown, Tavistock, Devon PL19 9JZ; ☎ 01822 613371; www. langstone-manor.co.uk
- **The Walled Garden.** A real find in the pretty cob-and-thatch village of Dunsford. Church Cottage, Dunsford, Devon EX6 7AA; ☎ 01647 253338; www.churchcottagedunsford.co.uk
- **Fingle Bridge Inn.** Sits on the banks of the River Teign in the shadow of Prestonbury Iron Age Camp. Drewsteignton, Devon EX6 6PW; ☎ 01647 281287; www.finglebridge.co.uk

Holwell Farm Cottages

Tracey take the B3387 towards Widecombe; turn left at Hemsworthy Gate, and left again down the drive after 1 km.

For a little bit of self-catering luxury look no further than Holwell Farm, set in a sheltered position in the heart of open moorland, surrounded by some of Dartmoor's most famous tors: it's hard to see Holwell until you actually get there. The beautifully appointed cottages have been converted from Victorian granite barns, originally constructed as a 'model farm' in the early 1900s. Holwell 'grows' out of the rugged Dartmoor landscape, and the peace and quiet is almost tangible. The cottages have been furnished and fitted out to the highest possible standard, with slate floors and solid oak furniture, and comforting range cookers on which to lean. Children will enjoy exploring the 400 plus acres of farm and open moorland; plus egg collecting, pigs and piglets, Dartmoor ponies and foals – the farm is also a

Dartmoor Pony stud – falconry, horse riding, climbing, canoeing, fishing, walking, Wealth of Wildlife folder – the list of things to do here is almost endless.

4 s/c cottages, and 1 detached house: 6–12 people. **Rates** *£600 (low)–2200 (high).* **Credit** *MC, V.* **Amenities** *babysitting, cot free, disabled access (1 cottage), extra bed available (charge), parking, dogs welcome, special rates for health and beauty treatment, fly fishing, falconry locally, horse riding.* **In cottage** *fridge, range cooker and microwave, dishwasher, woodburner (wood supplied), shower and/or bath (or both), TV/DVD/satellite, pre-ordered shopping, ready meal and wine cellar service, 5 stars (Visit Britain).*

FAMILY-FRIENDLY DINING

INEXPENSIVE

The Old Police Station Café ★★

Tavistock Road, Princetown, Near Yelverton, Devon PL20 6QF; ☎ *01822 890407. On the B3357 in the centre of Princetown, by village green.*

This bustling, bright, no-non-sense family-run café – in the old police station building – serves a good range of tradi-tional, well-priced meals, ideal for families. There is much on the menu to tempt even the pickiest child, most of it home-made. Waitress service is quick, friendly and efficient; the exten-sive menu ranges from all-day breakfasts and baguettes to homemade fish pie (£5.25) and fish, chips and mushy peas (£5.75). Children will be tempted by the Devon cream tea or knickerbocker glory (£2.95) and a range of puddings. Guidebooks and gifts are on sale, and there's outside seating for sunny days; takeaways available. The owners plan to take over another big café site in Princetown, Lord's, which should open in 2008.

Open 9am–6pm Apr–Oct, 9am–5pm winter; closed Christmas Day. **Main course** £4.75–6.95. **Credit** AmEx, MC, V. **Amenities** highchair, disabled access possible, reservations accepted, parking.

MODERATE

The Forest Inn ★★

Hexworthy, Devon PL20 6SD; ☎ 01364 631211; www.theforest inn.co.uk. Signed off the B3357 between Ashburton and Two Bridges.

'Hooves, muddy paws, boots wel-come!' The Forest Inn's motto is spot on – step inside this com-fortable, homely establishment and you'll have no choice but to sit back and relax. The old moor-land hotel positively welcomes families (and especially dogs!): under 14s are not allowed in the immediate bar area (with open fires and comfy Chesterfields) but there is a large dining area plus a bright and cheery family room, and seating in the courtyard out-side. Food is homemade and locally sourced, with beef from

Keeping It Local – Farmer's Markets & Farm Shops

Bovey Tracey Produce Market, Union Square, 2nd and 4th Sat
Dean Court Farm Shop, nr Buckfastleigh ☎ 01364 642199
Ivybridge Farmer's Market, Glanvilles Mill car park, 3rd Sat
Lifton Strawberry Fields, Lifton, ☎ 01566 784605; www.lifton strawberryfields.co.uk
Moorlands Farm Shop, Whiddon Down, nr Okehampton ☎ 01647 213666; www.moorlandsfarmshop.co.uk
Moretonhampstead Country Market & Craft Fair, Parish Hall, every Tues
Okehampton Farmer's Market, St James' Chapel Square, 3rd Sat
Tavistock Farmer's Market, Bedford Square, 2nd and 4th Sat
Tavistock Pannier Market, Bedford Square, Tues–Sat
Ullacombe Farm Shop, nr Bovey Tracey ☎ 01364 661341
Widecombe-in-the-Moor Village Market, Church House. 4th Sat

Brimpts Farm just up the road. Children have smaller portions of 'real' meals – pork steak (£11.25) and cheese, tomato and basil pasty (£6.95) and a range of tempting puddings (£3.50). The inn offers family accommodation – light, airy rooms with moorland views. This is the perfect base for walking, cycling, riding, canoeing – or pottering down to Hexworthy Bridge and watching your children play in the West Dart river.

Open 11.30am–2.30pm, 6pm–11pm daily; also summer weekend afternoons. Main course £6.95–11.25. Credit MC, V. Amenities board games, books, highchair, family room, disabled access, reservations accepted, parking, stables, Duchy of Cornwall fishing permits, dogs welcome. Accommodation 10 rooms, some en suite (2 family), from £60 double/twin. Extra bed/no cots. TV in most rooms.

The Royal Oak Inn ★★

Dunsford, Devon EX6 7DA; ☎ 01647 252256; www.royaloakd.com. In the centre of the village, by the church, off the B3212, 8 km east of Moretonhampstead. Bus from Exeter and Moretonhampstead; Transmoor bus service weekends Plymouth–Exeter.

Younger children will be captivated by the Royal Oak's menagerie! Walk through the pretty flower-filled courtyard and into the extensive gardens (lovely views) to find rabbits, guinea pigs, goats, chickens, even Megan and Milo, miniature Shetland ponies. Look out for Scrumpy Jack, a huge black Flemish giant rabbit, probably the biggest you've ever seen! The Royal Oak welcomes families of all ages and offers a good range of homemade food: Devon rarebit (£5.50), stilton, leek and walnut pie (£7.95), beef and stilton pie (£7.95). There's a children's menu, and excellent fish 'n' chips (£5.50) on Tuesday nights (eat in or takeaway). The building dates from the 1870s; fire destroyed the original traditional cob-and-thatch working farm and inn, and the kitchen is in what was once the milking parlour. Accommodation is in a converted cob barn off the courtyard, with en suite double and twin rooms: a couple of the larger ones can take extra beds.

Open 12pm–2.30pm (not Mon except Bank Hols), 6.30pm–11pm Tues–Sat (7pm–9pm Mon, 7pm–10.30pm Sun). Main course £5.95–9.95. Credit MC, V. Amenities children's menu, board games, pool table, highchair, reservations accepted, parking, pets' area in courtyard and garden. Accommodation 5 rooms, some adaptable for families, from £60 double/twin. Extra bed £15 child, £20 adult.

INSIDER TIP ▶

Going out for a cream tea is obligatory when staying on Dartmoor. Manaton and Sourton village halls serve teas on summer weekends, and there are two good cafés at Widecombe in the Moor. If you'd prefer to take your family (and your cream tea) to the banks of a moorland stream Postbridge village shop will supply you with a handy takeaway version.

The Bearslake Inn ★★★

Lake, Near Sourton, Devon EX20 4HQ; ☎ 01837 861334; www.bearslakeinn.com. On the A386, 3.2 km south of the A30 (Okehampton). Bus from Okehampton and Tavistock.

One of west Devon's best-kept secrets! This carefully restored thatched 13th-century longhouse houses one of the best pubs in the area, with a cosy bar, several attractive family rooms, a 32-cover restaurant and a huge garden with wonderful moorland views. It's on the Granite Way cycle route; all the families I met had arrived by bike. There's a great choice of excellent home-made food, sourced locally. Children can have smaller portions of adult dishes – West Country lamb chops (£12.95), blue cheese chicken (£11.95), seared fillet of salmon (£11.75), roasted bell peppers (£10.95) – or choose something from the extensive lunchtime menu: baguettes, ploughman's, sausage and mash, salads. The beautifully yet simply furnished beamed bedrooms are tucked up under the thatch, some accessed up steps from the garden. The spacious family rooms are more like suites, with the second bedroom area accessed through an archway.

Open *11am–3pm, 6pm–11pm Mon–Sat, 12pm–4pm Sun.* **Main** *course* £6.95–12.95. **Credit** *MC, V.* **Amenities** *children's menu, high-chair, disabled access, reservations accepted, restaurant, parking, on Granite Way cycle route Okehampton–Lydford, extensive garden with stream (parental supervision required).* **Accommodation** *6 double/twin en suite rooms (3 family), from £70 double/twin. Extra bed/cot. All with TV, some DVD.*

INSIDER TIP »

Look out for the National Park's Ranger Ralph Club events, which take place throughout the year and are specifically for children. You can meet Dartmoor ponies at Brimpts Farm (p. 96), build homes for pixies from natural materials found in the woods, or spend the day messing around with paints – all with a Dartmoor theme. *01626 831080; www.dartmoor-npa.gov.uk.*

INSIDER TIP »

Apart from those attached to National Trust properties, and those open during the spring and summer under the National Gardens scheme, the Dartmoor and West Devon area has another couple of very special gardens to visit. The Garden House at Buckland Monachorum near Tavistock (* 01822 854769; www.thegardenhouse.org.uk*) is a wonderfully informal garden, with twisting paths, archways, bridges (even a tower), a beautiful walled garden, activity sheets for children and delicious food in the 18th-century vicarage. Lukesland Gardens near Ivybridge (* 01752 691749; www.lukesland.co.uk*) has pools and waterfalls, flowering trees and shrubs, children's trails and special children's events at half-terms and school holidays.

The Bearslake Inn, near Sourton

7 South Devon

SOUTH DEVON

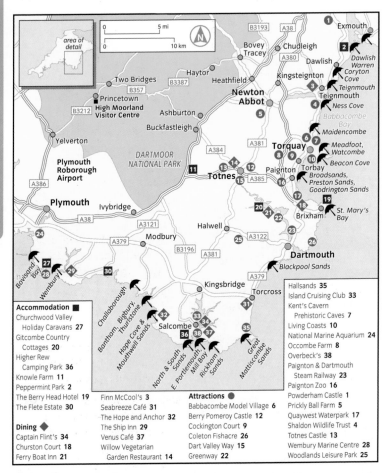

Accommodation ■
Churchwood Valley
  Holiday Caravans **27**
Gitcombe Country
  Cottages **20**
Higher Rew
  Camping Park **36**
Knowle Farm **11**
Peppermint Park **2**
The Berry Head Hotel **19**
The Flete Estate **30**

Dining ◆
Captain Flint's **34**
Churston Court **18**
Ferry Boat Inn **21**

Finn McCool's **3**
Seabreeze Café **31**
The Hope and Anchor **32**
The Ship Inn **29**
Venus Café **37**
Willow Vegetarian
  Garden Restaurant **14**

Attractions ●
Babbacombe Model Village **6**
Berry Pomeroy Castle **12**
Cockington Court **9**
Coleton Fishacre **26**
Dart Valley Way **15**
Greenway **22**

Hallsands **35**
Island Cruising Club **33**
Kent's Cavern
  Prehistoric Caves **7**
Living Coasts **10**
National Marine Aquarium **24**
Occombe Farm **8**
Overbeck's **38**
Paignton & Dartmouth
  Steam Railway **23**
Paignton Zoo **16**
Powderham Castle **1**
Prickly Ball Farm **5**
Quaywest Waterpark **17**
Shaldon Wildlife Trust **4**
Totnes Castle **13**
Wembury Marine Centre **28**
Woodlands Leisure Park **25**

South Devon is the most popular part of the county in terms of family holidays – and the most crowded in the summer months. It's not hard to see why: much of South Devon – which stretches from the Exe estuary all the way west to Plymouth – is a designated Area of Outstanding Natural Beauty (AONB) (℘ *01803 861384; www.southdevonaonb.org.uk*): 337 square km of beautiful and often unspoiled coastline, estuaries and countryside, from Berry Head in Brixham to Jennycliff in Plymouth. There's something for everyone here: rugged cliffs, sandy coves, peaceful countryside, rolling hills, pretty villages, flower-filled hedgebanks and the tucked-away estuaries of the Dart, Avon, Erme and Yealm. You can choose to stay far off the beaten track or in a bustling seaside town such as Teignmouth, or in cosmopolitan Torquay; you can walk along the Coast Path to find secluded sandy beaches around Prawle Point (Devon's most southerly point, where the rocks date back more than 400 million years), or get involved in the rough and tumble of sailing or windsurfing in the Salcombe estuary. There are historic towns such as Totnes and Dartmouth, lush gardens and historic castles to visit, boat trips to take...and for those who want a taste of city life, Plymouth – Devon's largest city – is right on the doorstep.

VISITOR INFORMATION

The local paper the **Herald Express** produces free brochures: **What's On Torbay** (*www.whatsontorbay.co.uk*) and **What's on South Hams** (*www.whatsonsouthhams.co.uk*); the brochure and website *www.englishriviera.co.uk* cover Torquay, Paignton and Brixham, and *www.holidaytorbay.co.uk* looks at attractions in that area. The **South Devon Holiday & Short Breaks Guide** (*www.visitsouthdevon.co.uk*) is a good source of information on the eastern part of South Devon. Visit *www.somewhere-special.com* for details on the South Hams (between Torbay and Plymouth); see also *www.southdevon.org.uk*. For Plymouth see *www.visitplymouth.co.uk*.

Information Centres

Brixham, The Old Market House, The Quay; 01803 214885; www.torbay.gov.uk

Dartmouth, The Engine House, Mayor's Avenue; 01803 834224; www.discoverdartmouth.com

Dawlish, The Lawn; 01626 215665; www.southdevon.org.uk

Kingsbridge, The Quay; 01548 853195; www.kingsbridgeinfo.co.uk

Modbury, 5 Modbury Court; 01548 830159; www.modburydevoninfo.co.uk

Newton Abbot, 6 Bridge House, Courtenay Street; 01626 215667; www.teignbridge.co.uk

Paignton, The Esplanade; 0870 707 0010; www.torbay.gov.uk

Plymouth, Mayflower Centre, Barbican; 01752 306330; www.plymouthcity.co.uk

Salcombe, Council Hall, Market Street; 01548 843927; www.salcombeinformation.co.uk

Shaldon Car Park, Ness Drive; 01626 873723; www.teignbridge.co.uk

Teignmouth, The Den, Sea Front; 01626 215666; www.southdevon.org.uk

Torquay, Vaughan Parade; 0870 707 0010; www.torbay.gov.uk

Totnes, Town Mill, Coronation Road; 01803 863168; www.totnesinformation.co.uk

Orientation

The area denoted as South Devon in this guidebook stretches from the Exe estuary south along the coast to Torbay, then via Start Bay, Prawle Point and Bigbury Bay to Plymouth. The northern boundary runs along the A38 between Exeter and Plymouth.

Getting Around

This area boasts a good network of A roads, and is one of the best connected parts of Devon, largely on account of its two major centres of population – Torbay and Plymouth – and a good number of sizeable towns: Teignmouth, Totnes, Dartmouth and Kingsbridge. The main railway line runs from Exeter via Teignmouth and Newton Abbot to Totnes, then along the southern edge of Dartmoor to Plymouth. There are reasonably good bus connections: call Traveline for all public transport routes and timetable enquiries (📞 *0871 200 2233; www. traveline.org.uk*).

South Devon's river estuaries are crossed by car ferries over the Dart (Kingswear–Dartmouth), and between Plymouth's Devonport and Torpoint. Passenger ferries cross the Teign, Dart, Salcombe estuary, Avon and Yealm (ask in TICs). **River Link** in Dartmouth operates an excellent Round Robin trip: a circular tour of Totnes, Dartmouth and Paignton by river, steam train and River Link bus (📞 *01803 834488; www.riverlink.co.uk*). For boat trips in Torbay and the River Dart – including the Brixham and Torquay ferries – 📞 *01803 844010*.

Child-Friendly Events & Entertainment

Dartmouth Royal Regatta

This famous week-long event has been held since 1822: a wonderful mix of sailing and rowing races, fête, funfair, street market, children's fancy dress, crab-fishing competitions, with a huge fireworks display on the last night, and much, much more.
End Aug 📞 *01803 834224; www. dartmouthregatta.co.uk*

Plymouth Summer Festival

An ongoing event held all over the city throughout the summer months; music, dance, family-friendly events from seashore safaris to bug hunts and boat trips, with the British Fireworks Championship and the finish of the Fastnet Sailing Race in mid-August.
Jun, Jul, Aug 📞 *01752 306330; www. plymouthsummerfestival.com*

Salcombe Town Regatta

Everything that can float goes out on the water! Plus all sorts of other events, and a fireworks display.
Mid Aug 📞 *01548 843927*

WHAT TO SEE & DO

Children's Top 10 Attractions

❶ Sipping a Shiver-me-Timbers cocktail at Captain Flint's in Salcombe. See p. 123.

❷ Helping to feed African penguins at Living Coasts. See p. 115.

❸ Trying to keep your balance in a dinghy in the Salcombe estuary. See p. 118.

❹ Following the wildlife trail at Occombe Farm. See p. 114.

❺ Exploring rockpools on Wembury beach. See p. 119.

❻ Taking giant steps at Babbacombe Model Village. See p. 112.

❼ Ghost-spotting at Berry Pomeroy castle. See p. 112.

❽ Sleeping in a hidden log cabin in the Churchwood Valley. See p. 119.

❾ Swimming in the clear blue water off Blackpool Sands. See p. 116.

❿ Climbing to the top of Smeaton's Tower. See p. 110.

Towns & Villages

Dartmouth & Salcombe

The beautiful coastline between Dartmouth and Salcombe includes Devon's most southerly land, Prawle Point, plus sheltered beaches, good pubs and cafés, and some great gardens and attractions. A short walk out of historic Dartmouth is the late 14th-century **castle** (and Castle Tea Rooms), at the mouth of the Dart (✆ *01803 833588; www. english-heritage.org.uk*). On the Kingswear side of the river is the National Trust's house and garden at **Coleton Fishacre,** which descends to a small beach (family activity packs, children's quiz/trail; ✆ *01803 752466; www. nationaltrust.org.uk*), the **steam railway** to Paignton (p. 111) and, a little upstream, the lovely woodland garden at **Greenway,** once Agatha Christie's home (✆ *01803 842382; www.national trust.org.uk*).

Salcombe has ferries to safe beaches on the estuary: East Portlemouth, Mill Bay, North and South Sands; fishing trips, boat hire and sailing with the **ICC** (p. 118); quirky collections of curios and beautiful gardens at **Overbeck's** (children's quiz/trail; ✆ *01548 842893; www. nationaltrust.org.uk*); fantastic **Salcombe Dairy ice cream,** and one of the famous 'green' **Venus Cafés** at East Portlemouth (also at Blackpool Sands, Bigbury and Tolcarne Beach in Newquay; *www.venuscompany.co.uk*) where you can buy excellent food, beach gear, organic food and the Venus dolphin box, full of puzzles and ideas for fun things to do on the beach.

Plymouth

From the A38 en route for Cornwall you could be forgiven

Plymouth Sutton Harbour

for thinking that there's little point in venturing into Plymouth. But aim for the Barbican and you'll rethink your opinion of this historic city, famed for its naval connections and for Sir Francis Drake playing bowls on Plymouth Hoe. The first impressive building you come across is the **National Marine Aquarium,** Britain's biggest aquarium, with more than 3,000 marine animals and masses of interactive activities for children, plus holiday workshops – open evenings during August (✆ *01752 220084; www. national-aquarium.co.uk*). Next stop is the Mayflower Steps, from where the Pilgrim Fathers sailed to New England in 1620, and the TIC. The Barbican on Sutton Harbour is the oldest part of the city – Plymouth was heavily bombed in the war – and the narrow cobbled streets are packed with cafés, restaurants and interesting shops: **Forsyth & Brown's chocolate shop, the Plymouth Gin Distillery**

(✆ *01752 665292; www.plymouth gin.com*), **Barbican Pannier Market** (all-day breakfasts and children's meals – £1.99) and **The House that Jack Built,** a veritable treasure trove. Look out for Cap'n Jasper's, where you can buy a mug of tea for 40p and a half yard of hot dog. There are boat trips round the docks and naval ships, to the Yealm or up the Tamar, with **Sound Cruising** (✆ *01752 408590; www.sound cruising.com*) and **Tamar Cruising** (✆ *01752 822105; www.tamar cruising.com*), and water taxi trips to Mountbatten (✆ *01752 408590; www.mountbattenferry. com.* Plymouth's historic Hoe is a short walk from the Barbican, with fantastic views across Plymouth Sound to the **Rame peninsula** (p. 137), striped 22-m-high **Smeaton's Tower** (93 steps to the top! ✆ *01752 304774; www.plymouth.gov.uk/museums*), a sensory garden and the wonderful art deco **Tinside Lido** pool (✆ *0870 300 0042*), recently restored and open all day in the summer holidays (weather permitting).

Totnes

Historic Totnes is situated at the lowest crossing point of the River Dart, and the first stone bridge was built in the early 13th century. By Tudor times Totnes was Devon's second most important port, heavily involved in the woollen industry, and exporting tin and granite from Dartmoor.

The English Riviera

The towns of Torquay, Paignton and Brixham have collectively been christened 'the English Riviera'. It's an area unlike anywhere else in Devon: big, bustling, crowded. If you can face it there's a lot on offer for visitors (see also **Occombe Farm** p. 114, **Living Coasts** p. 115, **Kents Cavern** p. 113, **Babbacombe Model Village** p. 112), and on a hot summer's day the area around Torquay harbour does feel almost Mediterranean. The three towns are all quite different: Brixham is still a fishing port, with seafood stalls on the harbourside, a replica of Sir Francis Drake's ship *Golden Hind*, ghost walks on summer evenings (okay for buggies; 📞 01803 857761), and **Berry Head Country Park** (📞 01803 883262); Paignton, in the centre of the bay, has a long, popular beach with pier (📞 01803 522139; *www.paigntonpier.co.uk*), beach huts, amusements and crowds, **Quaywest Waterpark** at Goodrington Sands (📞 01803 550034; *www.quaywest.co.uk*), the excellent **Paignton Zoo Environmental Park** (p. 116), and the **Paignton and Dartmouth Steam Railway** (📞 01803 555872; *www.paigntonsteamrailway.co.uk*). Take a trip on one of the best train rides in the country, along the coast of Torbay before cutting inland to pick up the Dart estuary: an easy way to visit Kingswear and Dartmouth. The coastline at Torquay is a little more sophisticated, with some expensive hotels, lovely beaches – and palm trees! Here you can have fun for free at **Cockington Court** (📞 01803 606035; *www.countryside-trust.org.uk*), with its historic manor house, parkland walks, special events, craft workshops, carriage rides, café and Ark play area. Visit **Bygones** Victorian street (📞 01803 326108) in St Marychurch, take a trip round the bay with **Torbay and Brixham Belle Cruises** (📞 01803 293797/852707), have fun at **Waves leisure pool** (📞 01803 299992), or at the **Rainbow Fun House** in Torwood Road (📞 01803 296926; *www.rainbowfunhouse.co.uk*).

Today you can get a good view over the old town from the battlements of the **Norman castle** (📞 01803 864406; *www.english-heritage.org.uk*); jump on the **South Devon Railway** to Buckfastleigh; cycle down the **Dart Valley Way** (p. 118); take a river trip down the Dart to Dartmouth (p. 108); go swimming at the **Totnes Pavilion** (📞 01803 862992); buy excellent local cheeses at **Ticklemore Cheese Shop** (📞 01803 865926); have fun throwing pots at **China Blue** on Station Road (📞 01803 860906; *www.china-blue.co.uk*); or go to the Elizabethan market (Tuesdays in summer). Totnes still has many fine 15th- and 16th-century buildings: don't miss the wonderful **Anne of Cleves** teashop in the High Street (📞 01803 863186). A few miles down the A386 towards Dartmouth is **Woodlands Leisure Park**

(📞 *01803 712598; www.woodlands park.com*), a good all-weather day out for active children.

Fun Days Out

Berry Pomeroy Castle ★★
AGES 5 AND UP

Berry Pomeroy, Near Totnes, Devon TQ9 6NJ; 📞 01803 866618; www. english-heritage.org.uk. Signed off A385 4 km east of Totnes.

A brilliant place for children – a 'real' castle, with towers, battlements, walkways, spiral staircases and hidey-holes. The substantial 'ruins' of Berry Pomeroy castle are tucked away in a steep wooded valley – you have no idea it's there until you're suddenly faced with the massive late 15th-century gatehouse. An audio tour leads visitors through the castle and grounds, giving detailed information on the castle's history: the Elizabethan mansion, the shell of which stands proudly within the outer defences, was enlarged around 1600 and was the most spectacular house in Devon. It was abandoned in 1700, and became the subject of all sorts of legends, folklore – and, of course, ghostly hauntings. The Castle Teashop overlooks the gatehouse, and there are signed woodland walks (steep paths) through the valley of the Gatcombe Brook below. A really fun (and educational) place for children.

Open *10am–5pm Apr, May, Jun, Sept; 10am–4pm Jul, Aug, Oct.* **Admission** *£3.60 adult, £1.80 child (under 16), £2.70 OAP.* **Credit** *MC, V.*

Berry Pomeroy Castle, near Totnes

Amenities *café, disabled access grounds/ground floor, parking, picnic area, audio tour, shop.*

Babbacombe Model Village
★★ **AGES 3 AND UP**

Hampton Avenue, Torquay, Devon TQ1 3LA; 📞 01803 315173; www. model-village.co.uk. Signed throughout Torquay, bus from Torquay Harbour, Brixham, Paignton, Exeter, Teignmouth, Dawlish.

Britain's biggest model village extends over four acres of beautifully landscaped gardens in the heart of Babbacombe. Much of the village is on a steep slope, requiring effort from those with buggies! Every imaginable scene is played out in miniature, from a medieval settlement through the ages to the construction site for the London 2012 Olympics; there's a farm, garden centre, quarry, train, castle, even a cottage on fire, with fire engines and fireman in action. See if you can spot the monster in the pond at

Babbacombe Model Village

the bottom of the site! There's a fun quest for the whole family, with clues and riddles, and a trail for children, spotting various lettered characters. Indoor attractions include a model railway and fantastic model circus, with cutaway big top and caravans and moving figures. The 4D cinema shows animated films (far too scary for young children). Allow about two hours for your visit – and if you're visiting during the summer take a trip to the village at night when the whole site is beautifully illuminated.

Open All year from 10am mid Feb–mid Oct, otherwise 11am; last admission varies from 3.30pm–9.30pm depending on season. *Admission* £7.90 adult, £5.50 child (3–14), under 3 free, £6.90 OAP, £24.90 family. *Credit* MC, V. *Amenities* café, disabled access (but steep paths), parking (paying), picnic area, shop, 4D cinema.

Kents Cavern Prehistoric Caves ★ ★ AGES 5 AND UP

Ilsham Road, Torquay, Devon TQ1 2JF; ☎ 01803 215136; www.kents-cavern.co.uk. Signed throughout Torquay, bus from Torquay harbour.

These award-winning and extraordinary caves have been attracting visitors for more than 125 years (excellent for wet days – but understandably crowded). The caves are fascinating both in terms of their geological significance (magnificent stalactites and stalagmites – the rocks date back 385 million years) and human interest (hand axes from 450,000 years ago have been found). The ½ km route takes around 45 minutes to complete, with an exhibition in the first chamber and cameos of some of the characters who may have lived here, plus genuine artefacts. Children's activities take place all year, especially through the summer holidays, when they can join Cavog the caveman on an archaeological dig – and there's a woodland adventure trail where they can have a go at cave art and tribal face painting. A new feature for 2007 in July and August was the Cavern Ghost Show, an evening of scary fun and spooky entertainment for all the family.

Open 10am–4pm Mar–Oct (4.30pm Jul/Aug) for regular tours; 4 daily tours Nov–Feb. Admission £7 adult, £5.50 child (3–15), under 3 free, £6.50 OAP, £23.50 family. Credit MC, V. Amenities café, disabled access (not caves), parking, picnic area, shop, woodland trail, ghost shows.

Powderham Castle ★ ★ ★
ALL AGES

Kenton, Devon EX6 8JQ; 01626 890243; www.powderham.co.uk. On A379 to Dawlish, 10 minutes from M5 junction 30. Bus from Exeter, Newton Abbot, Torquay. Bike from Exeter along canal. Ferry from Exmouth to Starcross.

For a really good, varied, interesting and fun day out for all the family go to Powderham Castle, in beautiful gardens and parkland on the Exe estuary. A real sense of history is cleverly combined with a genuine family-friendly feel – a notice on the drive asks visitors to 'Take care – grandchildren playing'! There's masses to do, both inside the house and in the grounds: newly restored Victorian kitchen, tractor and trailer rides, Secret Garden (donkey, goats, guinea pigs, chickens and so on), and Courtenay Fort adventure playground for under 12s.

During the summer holidays you can have a go at archery, and watch birds of prey displays. There are acres of space to explore, with picnic areas by the lake and in the Secret Garden. And to make even more of your day, why not get to Powderham by bike (p. 36)?

Open 10am–5.30pm Sun–Fri early Apr–end Oct. Admission £7.95 adult, £5.95 child (5–14), under 5 free, £7.50 OAP, £22.45 family. Credit MC, V. Amenities café, disabled access (not upstairs in castle), parking, picnic areas, shop, outdoor play area, animals, archery, falconry, special events.

Animal Attractions

Occombe Farm ★ ★ **ALL AGES**

Paignton, Devon TQ3 1RN; 01803 520022; www.occombe.org.uk. Signed off A380 at Five Lanes, west of Paignton. Bus from Paignton. Torquay.

Occombe Farm is described as a 'demonstration' organic farm – the land hasn't been drained or fertilised since World War II – with the aim of connecting people with food, farming and the countryside. It certainly works in this wonderful combination of excellent farm shop, café, with bakery and nature trails and special events. There's wine tasting, a family nature quiz, craft corner, 'meet the sheep', bat bonanza, spider hunt and so on – plus easily accessible farm animals. There's a farmyard trail and two nature trails – 1.8 km and 1 km. Wildlife cameras beam photographs back to the education centre, plus there's a children's letterboxing trail, bird ID sheet, wildflower spotter sheet, and audio trail. In the paddocks you can get close to Ruby Red cattle – a traditional Devon breed – and rare breed pigs and sheep; farmers' markets are held on alternate Saturdays.

Open *9.30am–5pm Mon, 9am–5pm Tue–Sat, 10am–4pm Sun. **Admission** free. **Credit** MC, V. **Amenities** café, disabled access, parking, picnic area, shop, nature trails, farm animals.*

Living Coasts ★ ★ ★ ALL AGES
FIND

Torquay Harbourside, Beacon Quay, Torquay, Devon TQ1 2BG; ☎ 01803 202470; www.livingcoasts.org.uk. Signed from all over Torquay. Bus from Torbay, Totnes, Exeter. Ferry from Exmouth, Paignton, Brixham.

Just off Torquay's busy harbour lies the old Beacon Quay, now completely transformed and home to this superb coastal zoo. Your trip starts up long sloping walkways inside the building, with fascinating information panels (children can follow Pat the Penguin and his friends), to emerge by an underwater chamber where puffins dive. You're then out into the open in a world of rocks, beaches, pools and waves, with penguins, cormorants, avocets, kittiwakes and seals, all living in fantastic recreated habitats under the open sky inside a huge aviary – as if you've been invited into their natural environment. And all this with the sounds and smells of the ocean, and a backdrop of deep blue sea and sky. There's a free children's trail, feeding sessions and talks throughout the day, and back inside the buildings loads of interactive fun for children – and a fantastic shop and café, with outside seating overlooking the harbour. A wonderful day out.

Living Coasts, Torquary Harbourside

Hedgehog Hospital ‹‹

Take a trip to the **Hedgehog Hospital** at **Prickly Ball Farm,** just outside Newton Abbot (☎ *01626 362319; www.pricklyballfarm.co.uk*). The hospital cares for and rehabilitates wild hedgehogs; you can see hedgehogs from around the world, and help feed them if you arrive early enough. The farm has a good pets' corner, big barn with larger animals, children's play area and café.

Open 10am–4.30pm or 6pm daily (varies throughout year). ***Admission*** £6.75 adult, £4.70 child (3–15), under 3 free, £5.25 OAP, £20.50 family. ***Credit*** MC, V. ***Amenities*** café, disabled access, picnic area, restaurant, shop.

INSIDER TIP ›

Living Coasts comes under the same umbrella as Newquay Zoo (p. 173) and Paignton Zoo Environmental Park (☎ 01803 697500; www.paigntonzoo.org. uk): part of the Whitley Wildlife Conservation Trust, an education and conservation charity dedicated to protecting our global wildlife heritage. Buy a saver ticket at either Living Coasts or Paignton Zoo and visit both attractions. Both offer the chance to 'be a keeper for a day' (minimum age 15) and offer adoption schemes, plus events for children in holiday times.

Best Beaches

Bantham, near Kingsbridge
Very popular and lovely big sandy beach, rock pools, sand dunes. Surfing. Car park.

Beacon Cove, Torbay Small quiet pebbled cove with rock pools close to harbour.

Bigbury Acres of golden sand at low tide, perfect for families, rock pools, Burgh Island. Café, car park.

Blackpool Sands, near Dartmouth
Idyllic enclosed sandy cove with background of conifers. Not huge; very popular and very busy in summer. Café, car park.

Bovisand Bay, near Plymouth Sheltered sandy bay with cliffs; large expanse of sand at low tide. Popular with families. Café, car park.

Broadsands, Paignton Unspoilt red sand Torbay beach (no amusement arcades). Café, car park.

Challaborough Good sandy family beach, rock pools, very crowded in summer; big campsites behind beach.

Coryton Cove, Dawlish Small secluded sandy cove in Dawlish. Café, car park.

Dawlish Warren 3.2 km of golden sand and dunes, popular with families. Children's rides and amusements at one end. Parking.

East Portlemouth Three unspoilt sandy beaches on estuary, accessible by ferry from Salcombe. Café.

Goodrington Sands, Paignton Long sandy beach, rock pools, popular. Café, car park.

Thurlstone Warren Point Beach

Great Mattiscombe Sands
Beautiful sandy beach, rock pools, near Start Point. Parking by lighthouse and along walk.

Hope Cove & Mouthwell Sands Sheltered sandy coves, rock pools, safe swimming. Café, car park.

Maidencombe, Torquay Small cove with sand and shingle beach, safe swimming. Café, car park.

Meadfoot, Torquay Shingle beach beneath cliffs; quieter than some Torbay beaches. Café, car park.

Mill Bay, Salcombe Lovely small sheltered sandy bay on estuary; safe swimming. Car park, ferry from Salcombe.

Ness Cove, Shaldon Accessed via original smugglers' tunnel; sandy, sheltered, popular. Café.

Preston Sands Popular red sand family beach in Paignton,
rock pools. Very busy. Pier, café, car park.

Rickham Sands, nr Prawle Point Beautiful sandy beach, rock pools, long walk from car park but worth it.

Salcombe North & South Sands Two popular sandy beaches on edge of Salcombe. Café, car park, ferry to South Sands from town centre.

St Mary's Bay, Brixham Sand and shingle beach, steep access but quiet and secluded.

Teignmouth Red sandy beach, popular, with all amenities. Pier.

Thurlstone Beautiful National Trust beach, sandy, popular with families. Café, car park.

Watcombe Beach, Torquay Beautiful quiet sandy cove; steep access.

Wembury Fabulous rock pools (p. 119); small, rocky beach with sand at low tide. Café, parking.

For Active Families

Island Cruising Club
AGES 5 AND UP

Island Street, Salcombe, Devon TQ8 8DP; 📞 *01548 531176; www.icc-salcombe.co.uk*

Salcombe's Island Cruising Club is a sailing club with a difference. HQ is on *Egremont*, a nicely unsmart and characterful old Mersey ferry moored a little upriver from Salcombe in a peaceful spot. There's nothing remotely snooty about the club – it's been in existence since 1951, and provides a range of sailing courses and holidays for every age and level of ability. If you're on holiday your children can spend the day at the club (alone if 8 or over, with you if 5–7 years) messing about in boats and having fun; minimum age for staying on board without a parent is 10. The club runs RYA dinghy and keelboat courses for children and adults, and powerboat and yacht cruising opportunities for adults. If you've never tried sailing before but always fancied a go, the ICC is the ideal place to start.

Dart Valley Way Cycle Route
AGES 8 AND UP

There's a lovely there-and-back cycle route along the Dart Valley south of Totnes, following part of the Dart Valley Way. It's mainly off road, but there are some hilly sections – including a steep climb through woodland near Asprington – so it is not recommended for the very young. It's the perfect way of escaping the hustle and bustle of Totnes: soon after passing through The Plains (once an area of tidal marsh, now smart apartments and riverside pubs) at the bottom of town you're on your undulating way through the peaceful parkland and meadows of the Sharpham estate (renowned for wine and cheeses; *www.sharpham.com*), overlooking the River Dart. You can go as far as you like, but if everyone's coping OK push your bikes uphill then spin down quiet lanes into the pretty village of Ashprington and The Durant Arms (an inn since 1725). And if you can't make it quite that far stop off at the Sharpham estate café for a break.

Totnes to Ashprington 5.6 km. **Cycle hire** *Hot Pursuit, Totnes Industrial Estate;* 📞 *01803 865174; www.hotpursuit-cycles.co.uk; B.R. Trott, Warland Garage;* 📞 *01803 862493.*

FAMILY-FRIENDLY ACCOMMODATION

INEXPENSIVE

Higher Rew Camping & Touring Caravan Park ★

Higher Rew, Malborough, Kingsbridge, Devon TQ7 3BW; 📞 *01548 842681; www.higherrew.co.uk. 1.6 km inland from South Sands beach, Salcombe.*

Although sunny Salcombe (p. 109) gets fantastically busy in holiday periods it's perfectly possible to stay nearby and dip into town as you please. There's a good, peaceful campsite 1.6 km from South Sands at Higher Rew. Having a safe sandy beach just down the road is a huge bonus – there's a watersports centre (01548 843451; www. southsandssailing.com), plus a ferry into Salcombe, from where you can catch another to the beaches on the East Portlemouth side of the estuary (and Venus Café p. 109). The campsite (beautifully situated up a quiet lane with lovely views across the valley) is an easy walk away from one of the prettiest beaches in the area – Soar Mill Cove – with access to the Coast Path. On site there's a play barn, tennis court and covered play area for under 11s, and masses of space for flying kites and having outdoor fun.

90 camping pitches. **Rates** *£5–12 per night, £1 child 2–16 high and mid season, under 2 free.* **Credit** *MC, V.* **Amenities** *disabled access, parking, shop, laundry, dogs welcome.*

INSIDER TIP
Just by the entrance to Peppermint Park (p.124) you'll find **Ryder's Hot Bread Shop** (bakery and takeaway), where mouth-watering pasties, scones, cakes, filled rolls and all manner of treats are baked. There are takeaway cream teas, a deli counter, and outside seating.

MODERATE

Churchwood Valley Holiday Cabins ★ ★ ★ GREEN

Wembury Bay, Plymouth, Devon PL9 0DZ; 01752 862382; www. churchwoodvalley.com. Follow signs for Langdon Court Hotel from Elburton (A379 Plymouth–Kingsbridge); then signs for Churchwood Valley).

Just 11 km from Plymouth City Centre (a lovely water taxi ride from nearby Mountbatten to the Barbican p. 110) Churchwood Valley is a wildlife paradise, ideal for those looking for straightforward reasonably priced, secluded accommodation within walking distance of sand and rock pools at Wembury. It's hard to believe there are so many cabins on site – all are concealed by trees and shrubs, dotted along a labyrinth of 'drives' on the valley slopes. Apart from lovely tangled woodland the site has extensive meadows in which to walk. There's an excellent shop and huge information room, with masses of books and wildlife information, plus a fun pack for children. The cabins range from pretty simple (children sleeping on a sofabed in the lounge, and prices to match) to more sophisticated, with two bedrooms, washing machines and dishwashers: all have outdoor seating areas, some have small enclosed gardens; most are accessed up a short flight of steps. Each feels very private – and decidedly special.

52 wooden cabins, 2–6 people. **Rates** *£240–750.* **Credit** *MC, V.* **Amenities** *cot (charge), disabled access possible to some cabins but hilly site, DIY laundry, parking, dogs welcome; dog-sitting service.* **In cabin** *fridge/freezer, microwave/cooker, shower and/or bath, TV.*

INSIDER TIP
Most children (and many adults!) like nothing better than exploring rock pools – but it's good to learn a bit about what you're looking for. The **Wembury Marine Centre**

(📞 01752 862538; *www.wembury marinecentre.org.uk*) near Churchwood Valley offers a range of events during the summer, including guided rock pool rambles. This stretch of coast is a Marine Conservation Area on account of the wide range of habitats (and flora and fauna) present.

Knowle Farm ★ ★ ★ GREEN

Rattery, near Totnes, Devon TQ10 9JY; 📞 01364 73914; www.knowle-farm.co.uk. Take the Rattery turning off the A30 between Buckfastleigh and Ivybridge, then the next right (before the village) down a dead-end lane.

A long, deep Devon lane leads to Knowle Farm, tucked away in a valley just off the A38 (only 30 minutes from Plymouth, Exeter or the South Devon beaches). This is a wonderful place for younger (and especially pre-school age) children. Although not a working farm there are friendly animals everywhere – chickens and ducks outside the door every morning, sheep and pigs, a peacock, rabbits, donkeys, and Pete, a Dartmoor pony. The parking area is separate from the cottages – converted barns – so children can roam safely; the cottages are comfortably furnished and well equipped. There's a good indoor soft play area and outdoor play area for little children, plus an outside wooden adventure play unit, tennis court, table tennis and pool table, and a huge indoor swimming pool (1–1.5 m deep) with outside seating (swimming lessons available if required), plus 44 acres of farm and woodland to explore. Not surprisingly many families forget about the car once they've settled in – their children are happy to stay put!

Knowle Farm near Totnes

6 s/c cottages: 2–8 people + cot(s).
Rates £190 (low)–1,055 (high).
Amenities babysitting, cot fee, disabled access (partial, 2 cottages), special rates at Fitness First (gym), in Totnes, parking, indoor pool (swimming lessons available). **In cottage** fridge, cooker and microwave, dishwasher, washing machine/tumble dryer, woodburner, bath/shower, wireless Internet access, TV/DVD.

The Flete Estate ★ ★

Haye Farm, Holbeton, Plymouth, Devon PL8 1JZ; ☎ 01752 830234; *www.flete.co.uk*. Directions for individual properties available; estate 16 km east of Plymouth.

One of the most special and more secluded parts of the South Devon coast is the area around the beautiful Erme river and estuary, 16 km east of Plymouth. It's a fantastic spot: the Flete estate owns 5000 acres of land and has six delightful self-catering cottages and houses available for rent, each in a stunning location, far off the beaten track. Three are terraced coastguards' cottages, a stone's throw from the sea near the mouth of the Erme, each with two sitting rooms, shared garden and games' room, and the wonderful private beach at Mothecombe (the car park only opens to the public on limited days, so the beach is often almost deserted) a few minutes' walk away. At the other end of the scale is elegant Efford House, set in its own grounds, and used as a location in the 1995 film 'Sense and Sensibility'. The estate owns three gently sloping sandy beaches, perfect for beach games and building sandcastles.

6 s/c cottages/houses, 5–12 people.
Rates £600–2,150. **Amenities** babysitting, cot (free), parking.
In cottage cooker/microwave, fridge/freezer, dishwasher, washing machine/drier, TV/DVD.

EXPENSIVE

Gitcombe Country Cottages
★ ★

Near Cornworthy, Totnes, Devon TQ9 7HH; ☎ 01803 712678; *www.gitcombe.co.uk*. Between Totnes and Dartmouth off A381; detailed directions needed.

The first thing that strikes you as you approach Gitcombe – down the long private drive between thick Devon hedges – is the incredible view of Dartmoor across rolling countryside. The next thing that hits you is the house itself, tucked away in a sheltered valley with all the feel of a small country estate. A range of big barns and cottages – including the original 17th-century farmhouse – near the Georgian farmhouse have been sympathetically restored to provide top-quality holiday accommodation in 14 acres of hilly gardens, meadows and woodland. Some properties are 'upside down' to take advantage of the views; all but one have log burners (free logs) and some have mezzanine play areas. There's two fantastic swimming pools (decking and outside seating), a tennis court, a soft play area for the under fives and a wonderful hand-carved wooden children's playground. It's all rather grand and feels extremely special.

8 s/c barns/cottages, 2–8 people. **Rates** *£449–2,533.* **Amenities** *babysitting, cot (free), parking, indoor and outdoor swimming pool, hot tub, sauna/steam room, soft play area, games room, tennis court, boules court.* **In cottage** *cooker/microwave, fridge/freezer, dishwasher, washing machine/tumble drier, shower/bath, TV/DVD/Sky/Satellite TV.*

FAMILY-FRIENDLY DINING

INEXPENSIVE

Willow Vegetarian Garden Restaurant ★ ★ ★ FIND GREEN

87 High Street, Totnes, Devon TQ9 5PB; 📞 *01803 862605. Top of Totnes High Street in The Narrows.*

Totnes has long been known as the 'alternative' capital of Devon, and it's a fun place to look around, with all kinds of interesting independent shops and eating places (p. 110). Willow is a long-established licensed vegetarian and vegan restaurant, which is genuinely family friendly – from babies upwards – and the food consistently delicious! Around 60% of the ingredients used are organic, and all dishes homemade using local ingredients. It's a lovely, warm place, with wooden floors and tables and local artists' work on the walls: there are two main rooms, and the back one – with children's toys and books – leads into the pretty flower-filled walled garden. Wednesday evening is Indian night, and there's live music on Friday evenings. Another great place to corrupt committed carnivores!

Open *10am–5pm Mon–Thurs, Sat; 9am–5pm Fri; 7pm–10.30pm Wed, Fri, Sat.* **Main course** *£7.50–8.40 (evenings).* **Amenities** *half portions available, highchair, walled garden, disabled access, live music some eves, reservations, children's toys.*

Seabreeze Café ★ ★

Torcross, Kingsbridge, Devon TQ7 2TQ; 📞 *01548 580697; www.seabreezebreaks.com. On Torcross seafront. Bus from Dartmouth, Kingsbridge.*

This is a whitewashed thatched cottage with bright blue shutters – cane chairs, tables and cream-coloured shades – overlooking Start Bay...a real find in this tucked-away corner of the South Hams. Food is organic, fairtrade and locally sourced wherever

FUN FACT ⟫ **Remains of Hallsands** ◀

A few kilometres south along the coast from Torcross lie the remains of the old fishing village of **Hallsands.** In January 1917 the village was almost totally destroyed by a huge storm, perhaps as a result of dredging work off the coast at the turn of the century, when tonnes of shingle were taken for Royal Navy building work at Devonport in Plymouth. A viewing platform on the coast path above the site gives a glimpse of what remains, and you can have tea in the lovely garden at Trout's on the clifftop.

possible; enjoy breakfast overlooking the sea (children's £4.50 – orange juice, bacon, tea, scrambled eggs on toast with the crusts cut off), an excellent cream tea, homemade cakes, sandwiches (delicious croque monsieur £5) and paninis, local ice cream, fabulous sundaes (£3.50) and an intriguing range of milkshakes (13 flavours) and smoothies. Kite-surfing, kite buggying (minimum age 15) kayaking, bicycle hire and B&B are also available (£60–120 per room per night).

Open *10am–5pm (high), 10am–4.30pm (low), early Mar–mid Nov, plus Christmas/New Year.* **Main course** *£4–6.50.* **Credit** *MC, V.* **Amenities** *highchair, reservations, on beach.*

Finn McCool's ★★

25 Regent Street, Teignmouth, Devon TQ14 8SX; ☎ 01626 774040. On Teignmouth seafront.

A classier fish and chip shop than the norm: blue-and-white checked tablecloths, comfortable chairs, tables laid with blue napkins and side plates, and outside seating with smart blue sunshades overlooking the sea at the end of Teignmouth's long promenade. Finn McCool's is a relaxed place to take the family for traditional reasonably priced fish and chips, and if you don't feel like perching on a wall with a takeaway you can eat inside in very pleasant surroundings. Children can choose fish cakes, cod, fish bits or sausages (£3); those not wanting fish and chips can have smoked mackerel salad or veggie sausages. In the evenings the

inside menu is more sophisticated, but still reasonable, with local fish a speciality.

Open *11am–3pm, 5–9.30pm Mon–Sat, 12pm–3pm, 5pm–9pm Sun.* **Main course** *£4.50–5.95 (daytime), £6.95–10.95 (evenings).* **Amenities** *children's menu, highchair, disabled access, reservations.*

> **INSIDER TIP ▶**
>
> When in Teignmouth don't miss the excellent play area on The Den (separate areas for different ages, 18 months–15 years), and the adventure golf and fun and games on the pier. Take the ferry to Shaldon from the River Beach to the **Shaldon Wildlife Trust's** lovely collection of rare and endangered animals on Ness Drive, near the tunnel leading to The Ness beach (☎ 01626 872234; *www.shaldonwildlife trust.org.uk*), open every day.

MODERATE

Captain Flint's ★★★

82 Fore Street, Salcombe, Devon TQ8 8BY; ☎ 01548 842357. In main street at the bottom of the town (no parking).

Walk through Salcombe's main street any early summer evening and you'll come across a queue of excited children (and their parents) clamouring to get inside Captain Flint's. It's the perfect place for families; the menu is bright and original, with everything linked to R. L. Stevenson's *Treasure Island*: pirates and parrots and adventures on the high seas. Choose from pizza, pasta or salads, delighting in such names as Captain Smollett (pizza with spicy tomatoes, peppers, corn, mushrooms, onion,

Try These Too!

- **Peppermint Park:** A peaceful oasis in a bustling holiday centre. Warren Road, Dawlish Warren, Devon EX7 0PQ; *01626 863436; www.peppermintpark.co.uk*.
- **The Berry Head Hotel:** Very 'English' hotel situated in an elegant early 19th-century house. Berry Head Road, Brixham, Devon TQ5 9AJ; *01803 853225; www.berryheadhotel.com*.
- **The Ship Inn:** A spacious and characterful pub in a lovely setting on the creekside in the pretty village of Noss Mayo. Noss Mayo, Devon PL8 1EW; *01752 872387; www.nossmayo.com*.

spicy cream, cheese – £6.95). Young Mutineers have their own dishes and cocktails (Pretty Polly, Shiver-me-Timbers) and there's a great choice of ice cream specials (£3.95) with local ice cream. Be warned: you can't book a table, and closing time depends on the length of the queue – but turnaround is quick and you shouldn't have to wait too long. A treat for the whole family.

Open 5.30pm every day in school holidays; 6.30pm term-time, Easter–end Oct. Closing time depends on demand – get there early! **Main course** £5.75–11.50. Credit MC, V. **Amenities** children's dishes and cocktails, highchair, disabled access.

Ferry Boat Inn ★★

Dittisham, Devon TQ6 0EX; 01803 722368. On the River Dart quay at Dittisham, south-east of Totnes.

A traditional cosy low-beamed cheerful pub with a great atmosphere and a huge picture window overlooking the Dart river opposite the wooded gardens of Greenway. It gets very crowded – not only with people but on account of the mass of nautical

bits and pieces! – but there are a few tables outside and the shingly bucket-and-spade beach and quay to sit on (good crabbing spot). In the evening children under 14 are allowed in one area of the pub up to 9pm (with children's books and games). Local fish is a speciality – crab cakes (£9.95), whitebait (£7.50), fish pie (£10.50) and shell-on prawns (£6.50 half pint, £13 pint). The building dates back 300 years.

Open 12pm–11pm all year. **Main course** £5.50–9.95 (lunch), £7.50–15.95 (evenings). **Credit** MC, V. **Amenities** half portions available, live music sessions, reservations accepted, on quay/beach.

The Hope and Anchor ★★

Hope Cove, Kingsbridge, Devon TQ7 3HQ; 01548 561294; www.hopeandanchor.co.uk. Hope Cove is signed off the A381 Kingsbridge–Salcombe. Bus from Kingsbridge.

The bright, friendly Hope and Anchor is in the oldest part of Hope Cove – Inner Hope – where pretty thatched cottages cluster round the slipway. You can soak up the sun from the extensive outside seating areas – fabulous views – while the children play on the sandy beach opposite. The food is excellent, portions generous (shareable with younger children) and local fish available such as grilled lemon sole (£9.95), fisherman's pie (£9.95) and Salcombe crab salad (£11.25). Children are well catered for (£4.25) and although the pub gets understandably crowded it accommodates all manner of different groups – families included – very comfortably. Ask for a colouring book to keep younger members occupied.

Open *8am–midnight 365 days a year.* **Main course** *£8.95–13.95.* **Credit** *AmEx, MC, V.* **Amenities** *children's menu, highchair, beach opposite, disabled access, reservations accepted, parking (pay & display) in village, decking area and garden, masses of outside tables, easy access to sandy* beach. **Accommodation** *11 rooms, including 3 family (3–5 people).* **Rates** *£30–45 pppn, £15 child 10–16, under 3 free. All with sea views.*

EXPENSIVE

Churston Court ★ ★

Churston, Brixham, Devon TQ5 0JE; 📞 *01803 842186; www.churston court.co.uk. Signed off A3022 Paignton–Brixham.*

The little village of Churston Ferrers sits high up on the Downs between Paignton and Brixham, a welcome break after the urban mass of Torquay and Paignton. The Churston Court is next to the parish church, and a visit to this huge Grade I listed inn is an extraordinary experience (masses for children to marvel at – and no doubt the odd ghost!). It's a historic gem, originally a Saxon manor and once the haunt of sea captains and smugglers. Huge inglenook fireplaces, flagstone

Brixham Harbour

Keeping It Local – Farmers' Markets & Farm Shops

Dartmouth Farmers' Market, Market Square, 2nd Sat
Dawlish Farmers' Market, The Lawn, every 2nd Fri
Kingsbridge Farmers' Market, Town Square, 1st Sat
Kitley, Yealmpton; ☏ *01752 880925*
Newton Abbot Farmers' Market, Courtenay Street, Tue
Occombe Farm Shop/Farmers' Market, Preston, Paignton; ☏ *01803 520022*
Plymouth Farmers' Market, Armada Way, 2nd and 4th Sat
Riverford Farm Foods, Staverton, Totnes; ☏ *01803 762523;* also at Yealmpton; ☏ *01752 880925*
Saltash Farmers' Market, Reagle Street, 4th Sat
Stokeley Farm Shop, Stokenham, Kingsbridge; ☏ *01548 581010*
Totnes Farmers' Market, Civic Hall, last Sat
Waye Barton Farm, Littlehempston, Totnes; ☏ *01803 813051*

floors, oak panelling, original portraits, weaponry and the odd suit of armour fill every room (and there are lots of them!). Great for exploring and for a good meal, with fresh fish from Brixham's daily catch, and a popular carvery. Evening meals are served from 6.30pm, for example: rack of lamb (£19.95), breast of chicken (£14.95) and sweet potato and pumpkin Thai curry (£13.50). Outside there's a terraced area and a large lawn with tables: children are asked (very nicely) to behave.

Open *10am–11.30pm daily.* ***Main course*** *£7.95–9.95 (lunch), £13.50–19.95 (evenings).* ***Credit*** *AmEx, MC, V.* ***Amenities*** *half portions available, highchair, disabled access, reservations, parking.* ***Accommodation*** *20 double/twin rooms, £65–110 per room per night).*

8 Southeast Cornwall

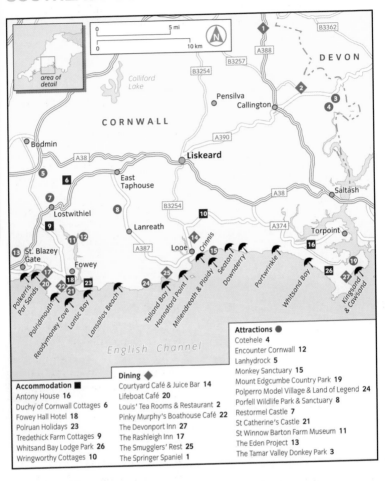

Attractions ●
Cotehele 4
Encounter Cornwall 12
Lanhydrock 5
Monkey Sanctuary 15
Mount Edgcumbe Country Park 19
Polperro Model Village & Land of Legend 24
Porfell Wildlife Park & Sanctuary 8
Restormel Castle 7
St Catherine's Castle 21
St Winnow Barton Farm Museum 11
The Eden Project 13
The Tamar Valley Donkey Park 3

Dining ◆
Courtyard Café & Juice Bar 14
Lifeboat Café 20
Louis' Tea Rooms & Restaurant 2
Pinky Murphy's Boathouse Café 22
The Devonport Inn 27
The Rashleigh Inn 17
The Smugglers' Rest 25
The Springer Spaniel 1

Accommodation ■
Antony House 16
Duchy of Cornwall Cottages 6
Fowey Hall Hotel 18
Polruan Holidays 23
Tredethick Farm Cottages 9
Whitsand Bay Lodge Park 26
Wringworthy Cottages 10

Southeast Cornwall is often described as the 'forgotten corner' of the county. It's the most easily accessed (and most often ignored) part, lying just over the Tamar Bridge from Devon, but it's true that the majority of visitors speed on along the A38 to Bodmin, St Austell and points west. In terms of visitor numbers it's much quieter than many other parts of Cornwall, with a few 'honeypot' exceptions: Fowey, Looe and Polperro. Southeast Cornwall has few 'artificial' tourist attractions – other than the ground-breaking Eden Project – but can offer the visitor a wealth of historic fishing villages: Looe is the county's second-largest fishing port – steeped in tales of smuggling. There are safe, sheltered bathing beaches and isolated coves cover more than 64 km of coastline, including the 4.8-km-long sandy beach at Whitsand Bay; magnificent country houses to visit, from medieval Cotehele on the Tamar to Victorian Lanhydrock near Bodmin; boat trips to Plymouth and along the coast; the ancient capital of Cornwall at Lostwithiel (of which Sir John Betjeman said 'There is history in every stone...'); plus sailing and canoeing on the Fowey river.

VISITOR INFORMATION

Visit *www.secta.org.uk* (the website of the **South East Cornwall Tourist Association**) for information on accommodation, eating out and things to do. The official **Visit South East Cornwall** brochure and website (*www.southeastcornwall.co.uk*) is another good source. Two maps cover the area: OS Explorers 107 St Austell & Liskeard, and 108 Lower Tamar Valley & Plymouth.

Information Centres

Fowey, South Street; ☎ *01726 833616; www.fowey.co.uk*

Looe, The Guildhall, East Looe; ☎ *01503 262072; www.caradon. gov.uk*

Lostwithiel, The Community Centre; ☎ *01208 872207; www. lostwithieltic.org.uk*

Orientation

Southeast Cornwall is easy to define: the eastern boundary is the Tamar river and the border with Devon; the northern the southern edge of Bodmin Moor. For the purposes of this guide the area extends west to the far side of Gribbin Head beyond Fowey, and north to include the Eden Project near St Blazey. The A38 crosses the Tamar at Plymouth and continues west via Liskeard and Bodmin; Liskeard stands on the A390 between Callington and St Austell. In the south the A387 runs from Torpoint west via Looe to Polperro.

Getting Around

Road links are pretty good in this part of Cornwall although, once again, turn off the main roads and you'll be plunged into a world of narrow lanes and few signposts! The main access from the east is via the A38 over the Tamar Bridge; a picturesque alternative is to take the Torpoint Ferry from Stonehouse in Plymouth (☎ *01752 361577; www.torpointferry.org.uk*). The mainline railway runs from Plymouth over the Tamar to Liskeard, Lostwithiel and onto Bodmin Parkway. The picturesque Looe Valley Line links Liskeard to Looe, a good way to avoid the traffic and trials of parking in Looe (though the car park at West Looe is vast); you can stop off for a picnic by the river at St Keyne (☎ *08457 484950; www.nationalrail.co.uk*).

For information on bus and train timetables ask in the local TIC or ☎ Traveline *0871 200 2233; www.traveline.org.uk*.

Child-Friendly Events & Entertainment

Fowey Royal Regatta & Carnival Week

A week of activities on and off the water: sailing and raft races, children's entertainment, flora dance, carnival, 'giant pasty ceremony', bands, gig racing, visiting ships, fireworks. One of the best local regattas in the country. *3rd week Aug.* ☎ *01726 832245; www.foweyroyalregatta.co.uk*

WHAT TO SEE & DO

Children's Top 10 Attractions

❶ **Canoeing** along the upper reaches of the Fowey river from Lerryn. See p. 138.

❷ **Wandering** through subtropical forest at the Eden Project. See p. 131.

❸ **Riding** a donkey at the Tamar Valley Donkey Park. See p. 134.

❹ **Learning** to sail at Fowey. See p. 131.

❺ **Spotting** woolly monkeys at the Monkey Sanctuary. See p. 136.

❻ **Playing** Pooh sticks at Lanhydrock. See p. 135.

❼ **Puffing up** the cliff path after a day on the beach at Lantic Bay. See p. 136.

❽ **Cycling** through the grand surroundings of Mount Edgcumbe Country Park. See p. 137.

❾ **Going** all colourful at Pinky Murphy's! See p. 142.

❿ **Feeding** pygmy goats and lambs at Tredethick Farm. See p. 140.

Towns & Villages

Fowey

This delightful old Cornish port – beloved of the novelist Daphne du Maurier – is all narrow streets, characterful pubs and cafés, steps and alleyways and a picturesque harbour, extremely busy in the high season! Every 15 minutes the town bus drives from the main car park down steep lanes to St Fimbarrus church (where the Saints' Way walk sets off for Padstow on the north coast) in the town centre (good for the elderly or very young – it's a tough climb). There are endless places to eat and drink – look out for **The Other Place** ice cream parlour just below Varco's Corner (Treleaven's ice cream) – and masses of ways to take to the water: the Mevagsissey ferry (*www.mevagissey-ferries.co.uk*), **Odyssey River Trips** (☎ *07792 625908*) and **Fowey River Steamers** (☎ *01208 833278*), self-drive motor boats (☎ *07989 991115*), **Fowey Kayak Hire** (☎ *01726 833627/833019; www. foweykayakhire.co.uk*), **Fowey River Canoe Expeditions** (under eights free – ☎ *01726 833627*), coastal trips with

Fowey Marine Adventures
(📞 01726 832300; www.fma.
fowey.com) – sailing instruction
from Fowey Maritime Centre
(📞 01726 833924; www.fowey
maritimecentre.com) – the TIC
has more information. Take a
water taxi across to smaller,
quieter **Polruan**, from where you
can follow Hall's Walk upriver
and return on the **Bodinnick
ferry**; or spend the day at sheltered **Readymoney Cove** to the
south of town. Just above stands
St Catherine's Castle (www.
english-heritage.org.uk), a small
artillery fort, part of Henry VIII's
south coast defences. There's not
a huge amount to see, but the
views are stunning. Back in town
visit the **Marine Aquarium** on
the Town Quay, or go for a
swim in the outdoor pool at the
Community Leisure Centre
(📞 01726 832908).

Lostwithiel

It's all too easy to miss Lostwithiel
as you shoot past on the A390 –
but it's a good place to spend a
morning, or to break your journey. This ancient town is today
nicely off the beaten track, but
was once the busiest town on the
south coast (exporting tin) and
the county capital from around
1270; the Stannary Parliament
continued until 1752. The grid
of narrow streets leading to the
river is packed with cafés (try
The Duchy Coffee Shop in Fore
Street, a late 17th-century building, or **Muffins** a little further
down the street, with a lovely

garden), individual shops, ancient
buildings – the remains of the
13th-century **Duchy Palace** is in
Quay Street. Explore **Coulson
Park** on the Fowey, or buy homemade pasties from Quay Street –
Lostwithiel Bakery or **Fran's
Pantry** – and make the most of
the picnic tables by Lostwithiel
Bridge. Another good picnic spot
is in the grounds of **Restormel
Castle** (great views), an easy 1.6-
km walk upriver. Originally a
Norman motte-and-bailey construction, the castle was rebuilt by
the Earls of Cornwall in the 13th
century (📞 01208 872687; www.
english-heritage.org.uk). Near the
unspoilt village of **Lerryn**, on a
creek of the Fowey river 4.8 km
south of Lostwithiel, is **St
Winnow Barton Farm Museum**
(📞 01208 873742), a quirky collection of farm implements from a
bygone age, plus a very good café.

Fun Days Out

The Eden Project ★ ★ ★
ALL AGES

Bodelva, St Austell, Cornwall PL24
2SG; 📞 01726 811911; www.eden
project.com. Signed off A30 Bodmin,
A391 St Austell, A390 St Blazey. Eden
branchline bus from St Austell station.

The Eden Project is the last thing
you would expect to find in the
almost lunar landscape of the
'Cornish Alps', the mountainous
heaps of waste generated by centuries of china clay working. The
brainchild of Tim Smit (better
known for unearthing the Lost
Gardens of Heligan p. 180), the
project's aim was to 'create a

Eden Project

spectacular theatre in which to tell the story of human dependence on plants...the eighth wonder of the world' – and that's just what's happened. Two huge biomes (vast conservatories) – humid tropics and warm temperate – plus the outside temperate biome represent the world's climatic zones: you can walk through the equivalent of an Amazonian rainforest. Willow and bamboo play areas are designed to make children think about the part plants play in their lives; peep holes at viewing sites enable small children to get a good view; plus zigzag paths, wooden stepping stones, willow sandpit and tunnels, a food story trail, story-telling area and special children's events. Tasty, wholesome, delicious, locally sourced food is available for children in the cafés and restaurant. It's impossible to sum up the attractions of Eden in a brief paragraph – go and see for yourself!

Open 10am–6pm end Mar–end Oct, 10am–4.30pm rest of year; 9.30am start in summer holidays/Jun half-term. *Admission* £14 adult, £5 child (5–16), under 5 free, £10 OAP, £35 family. Reduced fee if arriving by bike. *Credit* MC, V. *Amenities* café, disabled access, parking, picnic area, restaurant, shop.

FUN FACT **Eden Project**

The Eden Project is stuffed with all kinds of interesting information to fascinate children. Look out for the biggest seed in the world – the coco-de-mer – which comes from the Seychelles, weighs up to 18 kg, and looks like a human bottom! And did you know that Amazonian Indians at one time painted latex from rubber trees on their legs and feet – like Wellington boots?

Cornish Mining World Heritage Site

Many parts of the southwest – the Devon–Cornwall border, Mid Cornwall and the far southwest in particular – are peppered with relics of Cornwall's once lucrative tin-mining industry: engine houses, solitary chimneys, ruined buildings. In 2007 the significance of this heritage in world terms was recognised with the creation of the **Cornwall & West Devon Mining Landscape World Heritage Site**, covering 10 areas across the two counties and a number of specific sites, including Cotehele (see below), Kit Hill (p. 141), Morwellham Quay (p. 91), Geevor (p. 203), Trevarno (p. 206) and Poldark Mine (p. 201). Visit any of these and you'll get a real insight into Cornwall's justifiable pride in its mining heritage. *www.cornish-mining.org.uk*

Cotehele ★ ★ ALL AGES

St Dominick, near Saltash, Cornwall PL12 6TA; ☎ 01579 351346; www. nationaltrust.org.uk. Signed from A390 Callington–Tavistock. Bus from Callington, Tavistock; ferry from Calstock, Plymouth.

There's far more to do and see at this lovely medieval riverside estate than at many National Trust properties. The house was built between 1485 and 1560 for the Edgcumbe family (who later moved to Mount Edgcumbe, p. 137). It is beautifully preserved and on a manageable scale: rooms are small, dark and full of atmosphere – a real step back in time. Beautiful terraced gardens – lots to explore – tumble down the valley side to the old quay, where there is a tearoom in the old Edgcumbe Arms (once a pub), restored buildings with information about the history of the working quay, and the restored

Cotehele Gardens

sailing barge *Shamrock*, built in 1899 and the last working barge on the Tamar. Cotehele is still a working estate, with market gardening, flower growing and small-scale farming. Special events are held throughout the year: wildlife walks, summer fun for children, Easter trails and so on. A few kilometres downriver is Cotehele Mill (separate entry), a restored working watermill and agricultural workshops, open most afternoons mid March–early November.

Open *11am–4.30pm mid Mar–early Nov (house); 10.30am–dusk all year (garden).* **Admission** *£8.40 adult, £4.20 child, £21 family; £5 adult, £2.50 child, £12.50 family (garden and mill); members free.* **Credit** *MC, V.* **Amenities** *disabled access, café, parking, picnic area, restaurant, shop, historic mill and quay, children's quiz/trail.*

INSIDER TIP

Polperro is one of southeast Cornwall's honeypots – the size of the car park is a clear indicator of huge visitor numbers. Although it's only a short walk into the village you can take a ride on a horse-drawn wagon, or on the Polperro 'tram'. At the **Polperro Model Village & Land of Legend** (📞 *01503 272375*) just off the main street there's a reconstruction of the old fishing village (some buildings more than 50 years old), with brightly painted model stone and slate cottages around the harbour and narrow street and alleyways. There's also a small model railway, and moving models and commentary in 'The Land of Legend', where you'll encounter Cornish tin miners, excise men, blacksmiths and witches.

Animal Attractions

The Tamar Valley Donkey Park ★

St Ann's Chapel, Gunnislake, Cornwall PL18 9HW; 📞 *01822 834072; www.donkeypark.com. Signed off A390 Gunnislake–Callington. Bus from Callington, Tavistock.*

Home to 30 donkeys and other rescued animals, the Donkey Park is aimed at younger children. Two of the donkeys – brown Kit and white Bridget (at 48 the oldest resident) – and a herd of pygmy goats are allowed to wander freely through the park – you'll often find them right behind you! A good outdoor playground, as well as guinea pigs, rabbits, and lambs, will keep younger children happy. There's a café and an excellent indoor play area for wet days, complete with slides, tunnels, ball pit, low climbing wall and sand paddock. Every child between 2 and 12 gets a free donkey ride – and if your

Tamar Valley Donkey Park

children are really hooked there's an Adopt-a-Donkey scheme.

Open *10am–5.30pm every day.* **Admission** *£5.50 adult, £5.50 child (includes free donkey ride 2–12), under 2 free, £4.50 OAP.* **Credit** *MC, V.* **Amenities** *café, disabled access, parking, picnic area, shop, adventure playground (indoor and outside).*

Porfell Wildlife Park & Sanctuary ☆ ALL AGES

Trecangate, nr Lanreath, Liskeard, Cornwall PL14 4RE; ☎ *01503 220211; www.porfellanimalland.co.uk. Signed from A390 Liskeard–St Austell.*

Porfell is both a wildlife park and 'retirement home' for animals from zoos and other parks. Some animals take a rather different route to get here – the leopard tortoises, for example, came from Heathrow airport when they arrived in the country with inadequate paperwork! This means that there's a broad spectrum of animals on view, and you're never quite sure what you're going to come across in the labyrinth of pens and cages: meerkat, raccoon, mongoose, ocelot, lynx, owls, porcupines, budgies...there's a small children's farm, with sheep, donkeys, rabbits and guinea pigs, and round the woodland walk you'll see emu, fallow deer, goats and zebra. It's all quite low key and relaxed: the main aim of the sanctuary is to provide the inmates with a peaceful, comfortable life. Daily events enable children to see some of the animals at close quarters.

Open *10am–4pm Feb half-term, weekends to end Mar; 10am–6pm end Mar–end Oct.* **Admission** *£6 adult, £5*

child *(3–13), under 3 free, £5.50 OAP.* **Credit** *MC, V.* **Amenities** *café, disabled access, parking, picnic area, playground, shop, children's quiz.*

Gardens

Lanhydrock ☆ ALL AGES

Lanhydrock, Bodmin, Cornwall PL30 5AD; ☎ *01208 265950; www.national trust.org.uk. Signed from A38 Liskeard–Bodmin, A390 at Lostwithiel. Bus from Padstow, Eden Project (Jun–Aug).*

Magnificent Lanhydrock is one of the most complete 19th-century houses in the country, and although the house is fascinating children may well be more interested in exploring some of the 900 acres of gardens and grounds, with ample opportunities for walks and picnics (plus Pooh sticks from Kathleen Bridge over the River Fowey). It's a beautiful place: acres of rolling parkland, formal gardens near the house (with a miniature thatched cottage to explore), a children's garden trail and craft activities in the courtyard during the summer. There's a very good adventure playground hidden in the trees beyond the picnic area at the end of the car park, and a café in the stableyard. And if you're feeling energetic Restormel Castle is just 2.4 km away, through woods and meadows above the Fowey.

Open *10am–6pm all year (garden).* **Admission** *(gardens and grounds only) £5.30 adult, £2.65 child, members free.* **Credit** *MC, V.* **Amenities** *café, disabled access, parking, picnic area, restaurant, shop, children's trail/quiz.*

Lanhydrock

Southeast Cornwall's famous **Monkey Sanctuary** (📞 *01503 262532; www.monkeysanctuary. org*) is set in a beautiful cliff-top location to the east of Looe, in the wooded grounds of a Victorian house. Apart from the lovely grounds, adventure play area, café and gift shop there are special children's activities and an adopt-a-monkey scheme.

Best Beaches

Crinnis, East Looe Beautiful 1.6-km long sandy beach, great for families. Café, car park.

Downderry Wide sand and shingle beach, rock pools at low tide. East end is for nudists. Café, car park.

Hannaford Point, Looe Long rocky beach, pebbles and sand. Café, car park.

Kingsand & Cawsand Sand and shingle beaches, rock pools. Café, parking.

Lantic Bay, Polruan Glorious sandy beach, steep descent from Coast Path. Decent walk from NT car park.

Lansallos Beach, near Polperro Small sheltered beach 1 km from car park. Steep access, quiet.

Looe Sandy beach, popular with families; very busy in summer. Café, car park.

Millendreath & Plaidy, near Looe Pleasant sandy beaches with rock pools. Parking at Millendreath.

Polkerris Small curved sandy beach. Café, car park uphill walk.

Polridmouth, Fowey Pleasant cove, two sandy beaches joined at low tide. Walk from car park at Menabilly.

Portwrinkle, Crafthole Two sand and shingle beaches, rock pools. Popular with families; steep access. Car park.

Readymoney Cove, Fowey Small sandy cove on estuary; popular with families.

Seaton Grey sand beach popular with families. Very busy in summer. Café, car park.

Talland Bay Two shingle beaches, rock pools. Café, parking.

Whitsand Bay Southeast Cornwall's best and longest beach: 4.8 km of sand. Steep access. Surfing. Car parks.

For Active Families

Mount Edgcumbe Country Park ★ ★ ALL AGES

Cremyll, Torpoint, Cornwall PL10 1JB; ☎ 01752 822236; www.mount edgcumbe.gov.uk. Accessed from Lower Park Gates, Cremyll. Also via Cremyll Ferry from Stonehouse, Plymouth.

This lovely 865-acre country park is open all day, all year round. Mount Edgcumbe House (built in the 1550s, restored after World War II) and Earl's Garden are also open to the public (admission charge), but there's

The Rame Peninsula

The most 'forgotten' corner of Southeast Cornwall is the Rame peninsula, bordered by the rivers Lynher and Tamar, by Plymouth Sound and Whitsand Bay, best accessed by the A374 from Trerulefoot or (from Devon) by the Torpoint ferry (p. 129) or by passenger ferry from Stonehouse to Cremyll (☎ *01752 822105; www.tamarcruising.com*). It's easy to get away from the crowds here, even in the height of the season, and there are some wonderful places to visit: **Mount Edgcumbe House and Country Park** (see above), **Antony House** (18th-century home of the Carew family; ☎ *01752 812191; www.nationaltrust.org. uk*), and the fantastic (and never crowded) beach at **Whitsand Bay** (see above). Wander round the old twin smuggling villages of **Kingsand** and **Cawsand** (*www.crabpot.co.uk*) in the height of the holiday season and you'll see few people. These atmospheric old unspoiled villages – narrow alleys, steep steps, brightly painted cottages squeezed together (very limited access to cars), small, safe beaches – lie on either side of the pre-1844 Devon–Cornwall border – you'll find that many Rame peninsula place names are Old English, not Cornish. Both played an unprecedented role in the smuggling era in Cornwall, helped by proximity to Plymouth and a lucrative market for smuggled goods.

masses to see and do in the park and historic gardens for free (17th–21st centuries), beautifully located on the banks of the Tamar overlooking Devil's Point in Plymouth, Drake's Island and Plymouth Sound. There are historic themed gardens to explore, fountains and geysers, fallow deer to spot, fortifications, cannons and follies to find, and masses of open space to let off steam. In 2007 two new trails were opened: the Landscape Park Trail, a 6.4 km route for walkers through the 18th-century landscaped park, and a multi-use trail for walkers, cyclists, horse riders, buggies, and wheelchairs (a leaflet can be downloaded from the website). The Orangery Restaurant serves morning coffee, light lunches and teas in the beautiful Italian garden.

Open *Pedestrian access all day, all year via Lower Park Gates (small gate unlocked).* **Admission** *free.* **Amenities** *disabled access, picnic area, restaurant (open daily).*

> **INSIDER TIP**
>
> Encounter Cornwall (📞 *01208 871066; www.encounter cornwall.com*), based in Lerryn, provides canoeing, cycling and walking trips suitable for all ages and experience levels. The best way to explore the hidden-away creeks of the Fowey river is by canoe or kayak: try a taster session, or a half-day paddle – suitable for families – or hire canoes if you already know what you're doing.

FAMILY-FRIENDLY ACCOMMODATION

INEXPENSIVE

Polruan Holidays ★ ★

Polruan by Fowey, Cornwall PL23 1QH; 📞 *01726 870263; www. polruanholidays.co.uk. At the top of Polruan village. Bus from Downderry, Looe*

Polruan is one of those small Cornish fishing villages that takes forever to reach along kilometres of narrow hedged lanes – but it's well worth the effort! Situated at the mouth of the Fowey, Polruan has steep narrow streets and characterful cottages, but is much smaller and less 'discovered' than its opposite number, and within striking distance of one of Cornwall's most beautiful beaches at Lantic Bay (p. 136). The campsite is at the top of the village, and looks straight out to sea; although breezy at times the camping area is protected by high shelter hedges. This is a

Polruan campsite

Wringworthy Kids

quiet, clean, tidy, well-maintained family site with big pitches, a good shop, BBQs to borrow, small games 'field', and no bikes. Campers have two small fields; tourers and statics are in a separate area. The delights of Fowey are easily accessed by ferry from Polruan quay.

40 camping pitches, 7 touring pitches, 10 statics. **Rates** *£10 (low)–15.50 (high) per pitch per night 2 people; £165–410 per week statics (4–6 people).* **Amenities** *DIY laundry, shop, dogs on leads.*

MODERATE

Wringworthy Cottages ★ ★

Looe, Cornwall PL13 1PR; ☎ 01503 240685; www.wringworthy.co.uk. On A387 Looe–Widegates.

There's an exceptionally relaxed, friendly, down-to-earth atmosphere at Wringworthy. Although the main house fronts the A387, the cottages (converted farm buildings) and facilities are set in what is almost a two-acre garden,

slightly downhill from the road, with fantastic views over the rolling Cornish countryside. The big purpose-built well-equipped games room (suitable for all ages, from toddlers to early teens) is set apart from the cottages, with an extensive grassy area in front for ball games: younger children have an outdoor play area, and there's a lovely outdoor pool (safely fenced off) for all to enjoy. There's a mix of detached and attached cottages, with parking next to each one, and individual sitting-out areas. Around 9.30am every day children gather to feed the chickens (and collect eggs), rabbits, guinea pigs and Zak and Pepe, the two donkeys. Looe is just a few kilometres down the road, as is the quieter beach at Seaton.

8 s/c cottages, 2–8 people. **Rates** *£150–1,150 per week.* **Credit** *AmEx, MC, V.* **Amenities** *babysitting, cot (free), disabled access some cottages, parking, outdoor pool, animals,* function room. *In cottage* cooker/microwave, fridge/freezer, washing machine (tumble drier available), shower/bath, Internet access, TV/DVD/video/satellite.

EXPENSIVE

Duchy of Cornwall Cottages ★ ★ GREEN (GTBS)

Lamellion Cross, Liskeard, Cornwall PL14 4EE; ☎ 01579 346473; www.duchyofcornwallholidaycottages.co.uk

The Duchy of Cornwall has a number of exclusive individual properties available for rent in Cornwall – barn conversions or restored period houses – plus a contemporary house on Bryher, and the Guard House at the entrance to the Garrison on St Mary's, in the Isles of Scilly (Chapter 12). Restormel Cottage, 1.6 km outside Lostwithiel, with distant views to Restormel castle, is a particularly lovely solid 200-year-old house, said to have been built with stone salvaged from the castle and priory. It's a beautifully peaceful spot, on the edge of woodland (with some lovely walks) yet within easy reach of Lostwithiel, Fowey and the coast. None of the Duchy properties is set up specifically for children, but all are beautifully furnished and equipped, and in stunning locations, with enclosed private gardens.

9 s/c catering cottages/houses, 2–8 people. Rates £300–2,425. Credit MC, V. Amenities cot (free), disabled access (dependent on property), parking. In cottage cooker/microwave, fridge/freezer, washing machine/drier, dishwasher, TV/DVD/video.

Tredethick Farm Cottages ★ ★ ★ FIND

Tredethick, Lostwithiel, Cornwall PL22 0LE; ☎ 01208 873618; www.tredethick.co.uk. 1.6 km southeast of Loswithiel on lane to Lerryn.

A beautifully maintained and extremely high-quality group of converted farm buildings in the heart of the countryside 1.6 km from Lostwithiel and 15–20 minutes from Fowey and the coast. Six cottages are grouped around a flower-filled courtyard and communal garden; one stands in its own grounds at the start of the long, tree-lined drive. Cars are parked away from the cottages so there's masses of space for children to cycle (bikes welcome) and play nearby; plus a lovely indoor pool (accessed by security card and only 1.2 m deep), trampoline, outdoor adventure play area, huge games room – the walls covered with 'thank you' drawings from happy young visitors – and indoor soft play area all kept separate from the working part of the farm. The owners are very environmentally aware: apart from planting 14,000 plus trees since 1994 there are plans to solar heat the pool, and a farm trail to St Winnow (p. 131) on the Fowey (farm museum/café). There's a small local produce shop, and frozen ready meals. One of the highlights is the morning animal feeding – lambs, pygmy goats, pigs – where mown paths through the meadows prevent over-wet feet. The attention to detail here is impressive!

9 s/c cottages, 2–6 people. **Rates** £440–1,960. **Credit** MC, V. **Amenities** babysitting, cot (free), disabled access to some cottages, DIY laundry, parking, indoor pool, games room, animals. **In cottage** cooker/microwave, fridge/freezer, dishwasher (most), Internet, TV/DVD/video/satellite.

Fowey Hall Hotel ★ ★ ★ FIND

Hanson Drive, Fowey, Cornwall PL23 1ET; 01726 833866; www.fowey hallhotel.co.uk. Signed from the top of the town.

A luxury family hotel in a spectacularly situated Georgian mansion – the inspiration for Toad Hall in Kenneth Grahame's *The Wind in the Willows* – at the top of Fowey town, surrounded by beautiful gardens and with glorious views across the river to Polruan. Full attention has been given to the needs of families: each room has complete baby equipment; there's a crèche for children up to eight years old in the old stables (with enclosed yard) and summer sports for older children every evening. The fabulous indoor swimming pool is situated in the terraced gardens, and there's a games room in the stableyard for older children. A children's menu is available at lunch, with separate children's teas and supper, depending on age. The hotel has extremely flexible family accommodation, ranging from doubles plus cot to a two- or three-roomed suite or interconnecting rooms sleeping up to four children plus parents. Fowey town is a short walk away (although via steep steps and alleyways), and

the lovely safe Readymoney Cove only a 10-minute walk.

36 rooms (most suitable for families), including 11 suites and 4 sets of interconnecting rooms. **Rates** £175 (low)–550 (high) half board per room per night (2–6 people: children sharing parents' room free accommodation). **Credit** AmEx, MC, V. **Amenities** babysitting, bar, children's club, cot (free), disabled access, laundry service, parking, indoor pool, restaurant, spa. **In room** fridge, Internet, shower/bath, TV/DVD.

FAMILY-FRIENDLY DINING

INEXPENSIVE

Louis' Tea Rooms & Restaurant ★ ★ ★ FIND

Kit Hill Approach Road, Callington. Cornwall PL17 8AX; 01579 389223. Off the A390 Gunnislake–Callington, 2.4 km east of Callington; local bus Callington–Tavistock.

Tucked away on the slopes of Kit Hill – there are short circular walks in Kit Hill Country Park, just up the road – Louis' Tea Rooms comes as a complete surprise! It's in a great position, with far-reaching views towards Plymouth Sound, and a menagerie of animals to entertain youngsters – chickens, rabbits, guinea pigs, ducks and guinea fowl – plus Shauna the sheep. The owners run a truly child-friendly establishment; the spacious family room comes complete with toys, and the whole place has a homely and functional feel. Food is traditional, homemade and sensibly priced; the 'Early Bird Special' on certain evenings (5pm–6.30pm) is ideal for families with young children. There are all-day breakfasts (£2.70–7.50), ham, egg and chips (£4.50), veggie bangers and mash and macaroni, bangers and fishcakes (£2–3) on the children's menu, and wonderful homemade cakes and puddings. This is not somewhere that simply accepts children – a real effort has been made to ensure they are genuinely welcome and entertained.

Open 9am–5pm summer, 9am–4pm daily winter, every day; also 5pm–9pm Thurs–Sat. *Main course* £4.50–5.50. *Credit* AmEx, MC, V. *Amenities* children's menu, highchair, disabled access, reservations accepted, parking, outside seating, big family room with toys, tours of bird and animal pens, lots of outside space and great views.

The Smugglers' Rest ★★★

Talland Bay, near Looe, Cornwall PL13 2JA; 01503 272259. *Follow signs from the beach at Talland Bay, west of Looe.*

This is a welcome change from the flood of trendy beach cafés hitting the Cornish coast. This attractive little single-storey wooden building with outside decking sits at the top of a large meadow a short walk from the beach at Talland (café, kayaking), with extensive free parking (a huge bonus in summer when beach car parks and lane sides fill up quickly). All food is homemade, fresh and reasonably priced: breakfast (£4.50–5.50), salads (£5.95–6.25), jacket potatoes, sandwiches and baguettes (£2.20–4.40), tempting cakes and cream teas. A real plus is that the café is licensed, and on sunny summer evenings puts on popular BBQs – you can come straight off the beach. A great place to take the children for a relaxed supper.

Open 10am–5.30pm, evening BBQs depending on the weather, Easter–end Sept, Oct half-term. *Main course* £2.95–6.25; BBQ £2–10. *Amenities* childen's menu/half portions available (BBQ), highchair, extensive grassy grounds, reservations (BBQs), parking, takeaway.

Pinky Murphy's Boathouse Café ★★★ FIND

19 North Street, Fowey, Cornwall PL23 1DB; 01726 832512; *www. pinkymurphys.com. On North Street, between town centre and Bodinnick ferry.*

A wonderfully wacky café just off the centre of Fowey – turn the corner and suddenly you've lost the crowds – and there it is, strikingly obvious on account of the startling pink fringed umbrella outside! Bright, colourful, crowded, stuffed with bits and pieces to fascinate small people: sofas, cushions, mobiles, plants, seashells...all crammed together in an old boathouse, and just a fun place to go. Steps lead up and into the ground floor – there are a couple of spaces to sit outside – and there's a bigger sitting area upstairs, ideal for larger families and groups. Breakfast is served until 11.30am – pains au chocolat, croissants. There are fabulous

Try These Too!

- **Whitsand Bay Lodge Park:** Relatively new development on the cliffs above Whitsand Bay incorporating a 19th-century coastal fort. Millbrook, Torpoint, Cornwall PL10 1JZ; ☎ *01752 822597; www. whitsandbayholidays.co.uk.*
- **Courtyard Café & Juice Bar:** Fantastic range of Cornish produce and friendly resident collie, Buster! Purely Cornish Farm Shop and Delicatessen, St Martin by Looe, Cornwall PL13 1NX; ☎ *01503 262680; www.purelycornish.co.uk.*
- **The Devonport Inn:** Historic, weather-beaten, blue-shuttered building with locally inspired menu. The Cleave, Kingsand, Torpoint, Cornwall PL10 1NF; ☎ *01752 822869.*

chocolate melt cakes, chocolate brownies, muffins, cream teas, homemade cakes – plus jugs of squash, organic ginger beer and Cornish apple juice. Unmissable!

Open *9am–5ish Mon–Sat, 9.30ish–4ish Sun all year.* **Main course** *£4.50–6.85.* **Amenities** *half portions available, highchair.*

MODERATE

The Springer Spaniel ★ ★ ★

Treburley, near Launceston, Cornwall PL15 9NS; ☎ 01579 370424; www. thespringerspaniel.org.uk. On A388 Launceston–Callington.

There's a real emphasis on local food at this award-winning pub – much of the meat comes from the owners' organic farm, and other ingredients from top local suppliers: fish from Fowey, salads from Altarnun, fruit from Saltash. It's a friendly, welcoming pub with a deserved reputation for good food, and equal care given to children's and adult menus. The pub dates back 200 years and was originally a cider house; around 17 years ago it was converted to a 'food' pub. The children's menu ('Little Jack Russells' – after Nutmeg, who lives upstairs) is for under 14s: homemade fishcakes, fresh penne bolognaise, Springer burger and chips (£4.50–5.25). Lunch menus include seafood chowder (£5.50) and Mediterranean vegetable tart (£6.25). There's also a tempting range of homemade puddings. Children are not allowed in the restaurant, but there are plenty of other comfortable places in which to enjoy an excellent meal in civilised surroundings.

Open *12pm–3pm, 6pm–11pm daily.* **Main course** *£5.50–9.25 (lunch), £8.75–14.95 (evenings).* **Credit** *MC, V.* **Amenities** *children's menu, highchair, disabled access (not restaurant), reservations, parking, beer garden.*

The Rashleigh Inn ★

'The Inn on the Beach', Polkerris, near Par, Cornwall PL24 2TL; ☎ 01726 813991; www.therashleighinn polkerris.co.uk. Signed from A3082 Par–Fowey.

Keeping it Local – Farmers' Markets & Farm Shops

Callington Farmers' Market, Town Hall, 2nd and 4th Fri
Lostwithiel Farmers' Market, Communiity Centre, fortnightly Fri
Purely Cornish Farm Shop & Delicatessen St Martin by Looe;
☎ 01503 262680
Rilla Mill Farmers' Market, Callington, Rilla Mill Hall, 3rd Sat
Sleepy Hollow Farm Shop and Coffee Shop, Harrow Barrow;
☎ 01579 351010
St Neot Farmers' Market, Market Square, 2nd and 4th Sat
Taste of the Westcountry Farm Shop, St Cleer, Liskeard;
☎ 01579 345985
Tredennick Farm Shop, Widegates, near Looe; ☎ 01503 240992

An atmospheric old inn with a big terrace overlooking the beach at Polkerris – children can play within sight of their parents at the pub. Children are allowed everywhere: the pub has several separate areas, including a slightly more formal restaurant area. The original inn, *The General Elliott*, was destroyed by storms in 1915; the current pub was originally a lifeboat station. Food is served from 12pm–2pm, with snacks (£3.50–5.95) all afternoon, and dinner from 6pm–9pm. Children can have sausages or fish bits and chips (£3.25) or choose something from the main menu: cottage pie (£7.95), homemade fish pie (£8.95), scampi (£7.95). The pub does good steaks (£13.95–17.50) and daily fish specials, depending on the local catch. Be warned: the lane to Polkerris is very narrow, with few passing places; in the height of the summer holidays the car park – a short walk up the lane from the beach – fills up very quickly.

Open 11am–11pm Mon–Sat, 12pm–10.30pm Sun all year. *Main course* £7.95–17.50. *Credit* MC, V. *Amenities* children's menu/half portions some dishes, live music some evenings, highchair, reservations, parking (limited).

INSIDER TIP

The **Lifeboat Café** at Polkerris does cheap and cheerful takeaway food during daylight hours during the high season, plus big plates of pasta and pizza. The chef is Italian, and in the evenings the café turns into a reasonably priced Italian restaurant (£3.25–11.50), right on the beach.

9 North Cornwall

NORTH CORNWALL

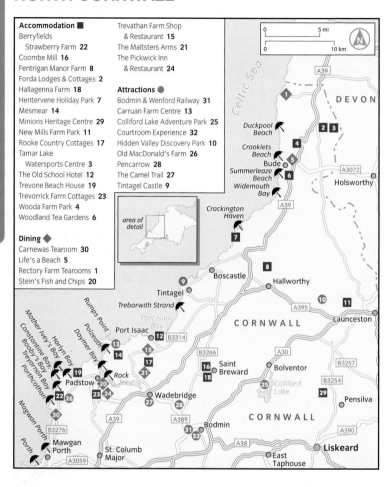

Accommodation ■
Berryfields
  Strawberry Farm **22**
Coombe Mill **16**
Fentrigan Manor Farm **8**
Forda Lodges & Cottages **2**
Hallagenna Farm **18**
Hentervene Holiday Park **7**
Mesmear **14**
Minions Heritage Centre **29**
New Mills Farm Park **11**
Rooke Country Cottages **17**
Tamar Lake
  Watersports Centre **3**
The Old School Hotel **12**
Trevone Beach House **19**
Trevorrick Farm Cottages **23**
Wooda Farm Park **4**
Woodland Tea Gardens **6**

Dining ◆
Carnewas Tearoom **30**
Life's a Beach **5**
Rectory Farm Tearooms **1**
Stein's Fish and Chips **20**

Trevathan Farm Shop
  & Restaurant **15**
The Maltsters Arms **21**
The Pickwick Inn
  & Restaurant **24**

Attractions ●
Bodmin & Wenford Railway **31**
Carruan Farm Centre **13**
Colliford Lake Adventure Park **25**
Courtroom Experience **32**
Hidden Valley Discovery Park **10**
Old MacDonald's Farm **26**
Pencarrow **28**
The Camel Trail **27**
Tintagel Castle **9**

Those families who aren't too bothered about 'artificial' holiday attractions, but who are drawn to fantastic sandy beaches, rugged cliffs, pretty fishing villages and spectacular scenery, would be well advised to consider North Cornwall for their next trip. This part of the county has a totally different feel to the 'safe south' with its tranquil estuaries and sheltered coves. North Cornwall is rugged and windswept, exhilarating, wild and magnificent, with some of the best sections of the South West Coast Path to be explored. Yet the area also boasts dozens of perfect unspoiled family beaches – Harlyn, Trevone, Daymer Bay – with acres of hard sand, ideal for beach games, rock pools, paddling for younger children and surfing opportunities at beaches such as Polzeath and Bude's Widemouth Bay for the more adventurous. Atmospheric old fishing ports such as Boscastle, Port

Isaac and Padstow line the coast, some still home to working fishing fleets. It's a great area for active families too: the Camel Trail cycle route runs from Bodmin Moor via Bodmin and Wadebridge to Padstow.

Travel south from the coast and you'll soon enter a different world: the crags and combes of Bodmin Moor (p. 151), renowned for posterity in Daphne du Maurier's novel *Jamaica Inn*, where small moorland communities shelter in the shadow of the moor's granite crags. Here you can climb to the top of Rough Tor and Brown Willy, marvel at the Cheesewring (Bodmin's most famous granite outcrop), visit 4,000-year-old standing stones and stone circles and Dozmary Pool, linked by legend with Arthur's sword Excalibur.

VISITOR INFORMATION

The best free guide to the area is produced by North Cornwall Tourism (*www.visitnorthcornwall. com*). North Cornwall District Council's **Coast Lines & Countryside News** (free annual paper) is packed with information (*www.ncdc.gov.uk*). Relevant maps are OS Explorers 106 (Newquay & Padstow), 109 (Bodmin Moor) and 111 (Bude, Boscastle & Tintagel).

Information Centres

Bodmin, Shire Hall ☏ 01208 76616; *www.bodminlive.com*

Boscastle, Cobweb Car Park ☏ 01840 250010; *www.visit boscastleandtintagel.com*

Bude, The Crescent ☏ 01288 354240; *www,visitbude.info*

Camelford, North Cornwall Museum ☏ 01840 212954

Launceston, Market House Arcade ☏ 01566 772321; *www. visitlaunceston.co.uk*

Padstow, North Quay ☏ 01841 533449; *www.padstowlive.com*

Tintagel, Bossiney Road ☏ 01840 779084; *www.visitboscastleand tintagel.com*

Wadebridge, Town Hall ☏ 01208 813725; *www.visitwadebridge. com*

Orientation

The area defined as North Cornwall for the purposes of this book extends from the Devon border just north of Morwenstow southwest along the coast to just north of Newquay. The main roads run northwest to southeast: the A39 from Bude via Camelford and Wadebridge, then onto St Columb Major. The Cornwall–Devon border follows the River Tamar, which runs north–south a little west of the A388 Launceston to Holsworthy road. Bodmin Moor straddles the A30, which links Launceston in the east with Bodmin in the west.

Getting Around

Once again car is your most likely option. There are good cycle routes through North Cornwall: the Camel Trail (p. 157) and Bodmin's off-road St Guron's Way. The area is sadly devoid of railways other than in the south: the main railway line passes through Bodmin Parkway east of the town. There's a special Western Greyhound scenic bus route from Wadebridge to Bude (☎ *01637 871871; www.westerngreyhound.com*). For information on all timetables ask in the local TIC or ☎ Traveline *0871 200 2233; www.traveline.org.uk*.

Child-Friendly Events & Entertainment

Padstow 'Obby 'Oss

Padstow comes alive on May Day when the town re-enacts one of

'Obby 'Oss, Padstow

the country's oldest folk traditions, believed to be an ancient fertility rite marking the return of spring. It's quite an unnerving experience, but well worth witnessing: the 'Obby 'Oss swirls and spins in front of dancing revellers, to a throbbing pagan drumbeat and hypnotic singing. *1 May;* ☎ *01841 533449*

Royal Cornwall Show

Cornwall's premier agricultural show, held over three days on a lovely site near Wadebridge has everything you'd expect: top quality livestock, more than 900 trade stands, rare breeds, steam fair, flower show, Cornish food, farming and crafts, and children's events. *Early June;* ☎ *01208 812183; www.royalcornwallshow.org*

WHAT TO SEE & DO

Children's Top 10 Attractions

❶ **Playing** beach cricket on the sands at Harlyn Bay. See p. 156.

❷ **Pressing** the 'guilty' button at Bodmin's Courtroom Experience. See p. 149.

❸ **Steaming along** on Launceston's narrow gauge railway. See p. 153.

❹ **Watching** baby lobsters at the National Lobster Hatchery in Padstow. See p. 151.

❺ **Climbing** the rocky steps up the cliff to Tintagel Castle. See p. 152.

❻ Riding a pony at Old MacDonald's Farm. See p. 154.

❼ Cycling by the Camel estuary on the Camel Trail. See p. 157.

❽ Sitting in Hawker's Hut and Morwenstow and looking for shipwrecks. See p. 164.

❾ Exploring rock pools at Treyarnon Bay. See p. 157.

❿ Running around the giant's stepping stones at Bedruthan. See p. 165.

Towns & Villages

Bodmin

Bodmin tends to be largely ignored by people shooting past on the A30, bound for West Cornwall. But the town has an interesting history, and a lot to offer the family on a 'non-beach' day. There's an excellent **information centre** in the monumental 19th-century Shire Hall on Mount Folly, where you'll also find the **Town Museum** (closed Sundays; 📞 *01208 77607*). **Bodmin Jail**, built in 1778 (the last public hanging took place in 1909) is worth a visit around the three-level museum (free admission), or to stop at the restaurant or gift shop, and hire children's and adult's bikes (📞 *01208 76292; www.bodminjail.org*). For a bit of hands-on activity try the **Paint Your Own Pottery** shop in Turf Street, near the TIC (📞 *01208 76661; www.4u2paint. co.uk*). **Willows Café and Garden** (📞 *01208 78477*), also on Turf Street, welcomes families and serves good homemade food at

sensible prices, and has a children's menu and takeaway. The **Dragon leisure centre** is worth a visit for its 25-metre heated indoor pool (📞 *01208 75715*). And if you want to explore the countryside around the town take the family on a steam train along the **Bodmin & Wenford Railway** (📞 *0845 1259678; www.bodminandwenfordrailway. co.uk*) to Boscarne Junction (links to the **Camel Trail**, p. 157 – cycles are carried for free) or Bodmin Parkway. The railway puts on special events for families in the summer.

> **INSIDER TIP** ›
>
> The Shire Hall in Bodmin also hosts the amazing Courtroom Experience – perfect for a wet afternoon! – where you take part in a 30-minute re-enactment (complete with life-size moving models) of a real murder trial from 1844, held in what was a courtroom for the County Court until 1988. The fun bit comes when you decide whether to vote guilty or not guilty...afterwards you can take a trip to the creepy holding cells, a mere one metre square, and listen to the sad stories of some of the inmates (📞 *01208 76616/79896; www.bodminlive.com*).

Bude

The popular seaside town of Bude sits solidly on a low-lying stretch of coast 6.4 km inside the Cornish border, at the mouth of the River Neet. Bude gets very crowded in summer on account of its beaches – **Summerleaze** (with a large natural saltwater swimming pool) and **Crooklets** – and the

Bude

surfing hotspot of **Widemouth Bay** a few kilometres to the south. The tranquil **Bude Canal** (by the TIC car park), which opened in 1825 (to transport sand inland to improve farmland), reaches the coast at Summerleaze, and a trip by kayak, bike (**Don't Push It Cycle Hire** ℓ *01288 359555*) or on foot along the towpath provides a peaceful break from bustling Bude. An easy 3 km ride will take you to the **Woodland tea garden** at Helebridge. Good for a wet day: **Wonder Years Toy Experience** in Queen Street, where you'll find more than 3,500 toys from the 1950s to the present day (ℓ *01288 359979; www.wonder-years.co.uk*); the **Budehaven** leisure centre (putting, crazy golf, table tennis, tennis – ℓ *01288 353714*); and **The Splash** (ℓ *01288 356191*). In town the **Castle Heritage Centre** in battlemented Victorian Bude Castle details the history of the town and canal

(ℓ *01288 353576*). Finish the day with tea at the **Castle Tearooms** on the Lower Wharf, with lovely views down the canal towards the open sea.

Launceston

Like Bodmin, Launceston is bypassed by the A30 and is often ignored. But this historic town – which was walled by the 12th century (unique in the county – the impressive Southgate is still standing) has much to recommend it. Much of the core of the medieval town is a designated conservation area: visit the **Norman castle** keep, which towers above the town, for great views (ℓ *01566 772365; www. english-heritage.org.uk*). **Lawrence House Museum**, a beautiful Georgian townhouse (ℓ *01566 773277*) on Castle Street will tell you all you need to know about the town's history; **The Bell Inn** (ℓ *01566 775154*) on Tower Street dates from the 14th century. Look out for the carved wooden 14th-century quarterjacks on the **Guildhall's** clock tower, who emerge to strike every quarter hour. Take a ride on Launceston's famous **narrow-gauge steam railway**, which runs for 4 km through the lovely Kensey valley to New Mills (☎ *01566 775665*). You can use the train to reach **New Mills Farm Park**, which has a good range of indoor and out-door activities for children (☎ *01566 777106; www.newmills farmpark.com*).

Padstow

Since the arrival of TV chef Rick Stein this once sleepy little fishing port has changed out of all recognition – on the surface, at least. In holiday times the narrow streets are clogged with visitors, and parking a nightmare: use the Park & Ride, park in Rock and catch the ferry over the Camel, or use the Camel Trail and cycle in from Wadebridge. But despite the crowds Padstow is a delightful place to visit. You can watch baby lobsters hatching at the **National Lobster Hatchery** on the quay (☎ *01841 533877; www.nationallobsterhatchery.co.uk*), take a trip by bike along the **Camel Trail** (p. 157), play crazy golf, take the ferry to Rock, visit 16th-century Elizabethan **Prideaux Place** (closed Friday and Saturday; ☎ *01841 532411;*

Bodmin Moor

Bodmin Moor – part of the same granite sheet that forms Dartmoor, West Penwith and the Isles of Scilly – rises to over 396 m at Brown Willy. Many of Cornwall's beautiful rivers rise on the boggy moorland heights, once known as 'Foweymoor' – the source of the River Fowey is below Brown Willy, from where it flows south to eventually tumble over Golitha Falls, a well-known beauty spot near St Neot. There is evidence of Bronze Age occupation on the moor, mainly in the form of megalithic chambered tombs, dating back 5,000 years. China clay, one of Cornwall's most important sources of wealth, was mined here from 1862 until 2001, and Bodmin granite has been used in many famous structures, including the British Museum and Westminster Bridge. Turn north or south off the main A30 and you enter a world of narrow lanes, solid stone farms and hamlets, archaeological relics and mining sites. The village of Minions sprang up to meet the needs of tin and copper miners in the 19th century; today the **Minions Heritage Centre** provides good background information about the area (☎ *01579 341000; www.caradon.gov.uk*). Note: If you decide to take the family for an exploration on foot across the moor, take care: over recent years there have been several reported sightings of a cat-like creature that has become known as the 'Beast of Bodmin'!

www.prideauxplace.co.uk), or sit on the harbourside eating a real pasty from **Chough's Bakery** (watch out for greedy seagulls). Padstow's wonderful sandy beaches – St George's Cove, Harbour Cove and Hawker's Cove – are found a short way along the Coast Path towards Stepper Point easily accessible with buggies.

Fun Days Out

Tintagel Castle ★★
AGES 5 AND OVER

Tintagel, Cornwall PL34 0HE; ☎ 01840 770328; www.english-heritage.org. uk. On Tintagel Head, 800 m from village on rough track.

Don't expect a 'typical' battlemented castle at Tintagel (the legendary birthplace of King Arthur): the main attraction of what remains of this 13th-century

Tintagel

stronghold lies in its fantastic position on Tintagel island, with long, steep flights of uneven steps linking it to its outer defences on the mainland. There is thought to have been a large monastic community here before the site was abandoned after the 8th century, then refortified in the 13th by the Earl of Cornwall. This English Heritage site is great fun to explore, but there's an 800 m walk from the village to the entrance, and a very long flight of rough steps to access the castle itself. Fun for older and tougher children – not good for the very young or infirm – but there is a café near the entrance where those unable to go further can sit and enjoy the view. A storyteller performs during the summer months, and a children's activity sheet will encourage them to explore the ruins.

Open 10am–6pm Apr–end Sept, 10am–5pm Oct, 10am–4pm Nov–Mar. *Admission £4.50 adult, £2.30 child (5–15), under 5 free, members free.* *Credit MC, V. Amenities café nearby, Land Rover service in summer (charge), picnic area, shop.*

Colliford Lake Adventure Park ★★ AGES 3 AND OVER

Bolventor, Bodmin Moor, Cornwall PL14 6PZ; ☎ 01208 821469; www. collifordlakepark.com. Signed off the A30 on Bodmin Moor between Jamaica Inn and Temple.

Bodmin Moor may not be the most obvious place to find a manmade family attraction, but if you're looking for somewhere that suits a range of ages don't miss this extensive play park,

King Arthur <<

The legend of King Arthur is closely associated with North Cornwall.
According to Tennyson, Merlin plucked the infant Arthur from the sea at Tintagel; King Arthur's Stone at the **Arthurian Centre** (📞 *01840 213947/212450*) at Slaughterbridge near Camelford is said to mark the spot where he fell in battle. The Lady of the Lake is thought to reside in Dozmary Pool on Bodmin Moor, and to have taken King Arthur's sword Excalibur into the pool's murky depths.

about 1 km south of the A30 east of Bodmin. It's something of an Aladdin's Cave, much of it built within a conifer wood and so not immediately visible – and there's much more to do than you might think at first glance. As well as animals and birds to see (in the Animal Kingdom) there's a wealth of indoor and outdoor activities to keep children of all ages occupied for hours: Kids' Kingdom (huge indoor play area, including soft play), Woodland Kingdom (adventure playground, including bumper boats and fun train ride) and Moorland Kingdom (more than 50 acres of moorland with nature trails and bird-watching hides). Every corner turned brings a new surprise! The park runs down to Colliford Lake, with opportunities for walks and cycle rides. The café provides takeaway children's picnic boxes, and there's a campsite next door (separate from the park: **Colliford Tavern Camping** (📞 *01208 821335*).

Open *10am–5.30pm Easter–end Oct.* **Admission** *£6 adult, £5 child 2–11, free under 2, 10% family discount.* **Credit** *AmEx, MC, V.* **Amenities** *café, disabled access, parking, picnic area, shop, nature trails, indoor and outdoor play areas.*

INSIDER TIP >>

Colliford Lake Park has some lovely nature walks – the longest only takes 30 minutes each way to Stuffle Point, jutting out into the lake. Look out for frogs in the marshes, butterflies on the brambles, and see how many different species of bird you can spot on the water. A really good photographic leaflet (available from the shop) will help with identification.

Hidden Valley Discovery Park & Light Railway ★★
AGES 8 AND OVER

Tredidon, St Thomas, Launceston, Cornwall PL15 8SJ; 📞 *01566 86463; www.hiddenvalleydiscoverypark. co.uk. Signed off A395 west of Launceston*

The longer you stay at the Hidden Valley (and the harder you concentrate) the more you'll get out of it! Lovers of the 1990s TV gameshow, the Crystal Maze will be in their element: the main thrust of the attraction is following clues around the site (built to represent an old mining camp) with the aim of completing three challenges which eventually buy time in The Vault, where there are more challenges to tackle, working towards the ultimate prize...it's a

Hidden Valley Railway

real brain-teaser, but good for older children with logical minds. Younger children will need help from parents to complete the challenges, which take around two hours. Your ticket includes a short ride on a narrow-gauge train – hang on tight round the corners! – with a surprise en route. There's also a fabulous model railway garden, with several tracks, stations, villages, bridges, ponds and windmill, and a newly planted beech maze, as well as other challenges scattered round the site. Good for anyone after a bit of mental exercise!

Open 10.30am–5pm Easter holidays, end May–mid Sept, Sun–Fri. **Admission** £4.95 adult, £4.75 child (5–15), under 5 free, £4.50 OAP, £18 any 4 persons. **Credit** MC, V. **Amenities** café, disabled access possible (narrow paths), parking, picnic area, shop.

Animal Attractions

Old MacDonald's Farm ★ ★ ★
AGES UP TO 10

Porthcothan Bay, Padstow, Cornwall PL28 8LW; ☏ *01208 540829. Signed off B3276 Porthcothan to Mawgan Porth.*

When you arrive at Old MacDonald's Farm there are few obvious clues as to what goes on there – but as you walk through the entrance and into the three-level grassy acres beyond you quickly realise this is everything a small child dreams of having in the back garden: calves, piglets, rabbits, geese, pygmy goats, owls, pony rides on chestnut Teddy or grey Murphy, a lovely sandy playground with swings, slides, trampolines and ride-on toys, and a toddlers' play area. Older children can play crazy golf, table tennis or table football; adults can sample local scrumpy cider in the shop. It's all nicely low-key and relaxed, with none of the pretensions and 'flashiness' of some bigger family attractions. There's a good café with inside and covered outside seating (and Wendy house and toy box inside), and half-price return tickets available.

Open 10am–5pm Easter–end Sept. **Admission** £4.50 adult/child, under 2 free, £16 family. **Credit** MC, V. **Amenities** café, disabled access, parking, picnic area, shop.

INSIDER TIP

Camping is available at Old MacDonald's Farm: a three-acre family site with around 45 pitches (same contact details), just 800 m from lovely Porthcothan Bay. Children staying at the campsite have free access to the farm park, and can help feed the animals in the mornings.

Carruan Farm Centre ★ ★
AGES UP TO 10

Polzeath, Cornwall PL27 6QU; 01208 869584; www.carruan. co.uk. On the St Endellion–Polzeath road.

This is a working farm – with a small farm shop – where visitors are invited to wander at leisure through the animal paddocks to see goats, sheep, cows, chickens and ducks. The owners are keen to teach visitors about the whys and wherefores of farming in an informal manner. The spacious (and licensed) café serves a good range of reasonably priced food, with excellent Sunday lunches (£6.50 adult, £4 child). There's a lovely outside seating area with a safe play area for under 10s adjacent, and ride-on diggers. During peak holiday times the farm comes alive: tractor and trailer tours, birds of prey, nature walks, sheepdog demonstrations, sheep racing, storytelling and animal feeding. In the summer holidays there are weekly farmhouse suppers, BBQs and hog roasts for all the family.

Open 8am–8.30pm Mon–Fri, 9am–8.30pm Sat/Sun peak season; 9am–6pm spring/autumn; 10am–4pm winter. Admission free; charge for some activities. Credit MC, V. Amenities café, disabled access, parking, shop.

Gardens

Pencarrow ★ ALL AGES

Washaway Bodmin, Cornwall PL30 3AG; 01208 841369; www. pencarrow.co.uk. 6.5 km northwest of Bodmin off A389 and B3266.

This lovely Georgian house set in 50 acres of landscaped gardens is still very much a family home, and a trip to Pencarrow feels as if you're visiting friends. The gardens were originally planted in the mid-19th century, fell derelict and were restored in the 20th century. Whereas children are often uninterested in looking round houses this one has a real family feel – you may well be joined by the resident pet dogs! Outside there's a beautiful sunken Italian garden, an American garden, Victorian rockery made with granite from Bodmin Moor, lake and fabulous rhododendrons and camellias. The children's play area is the near the Peacock Café, with rabbit, guinea pigs, peacock and peafowl, and a Cornish slate Wendy House to keep little ones occupied.

Open 11am–5pm Apr–end Oct, Sun–Thurs. Admission £4 adult, £1 child (5–16) garden only, free under 5; £8 adult, £4 child guided house tour. Credit MC, V. Amenities café, disabled access possible, parking, picnic area, shop.

Best Beaches

Boobys Bay, St Merryn Wide sandy beach, rock pools. Surfing. Park at Constantine and walk.

Constantine Bay Long sandy beach, rock pools. Surfing. Small car park.

Crackington Haven Large sandy beach, rock pools. High cliffs. Surfing. Café, car park.

Crooklets Beach, Bude Sandy beach, popular. Café, car park.

Daymer Bay, Rock Sheltered sandy beach, rock pools. Popular with families, busy in summer. Car park.

Duckpool Beach, nr Bude Sheltered pebble beach, sand at low tide. Surfing. Limited parking.

Harlyn Bay, near Padstow Fantastic wide, sandy and popular family beach. Surfing. Café, car park.

Mawgan Porth Wide sandy beach. Surfing. Café, car park.

Mother Ivey's Bay Lovely sandy beach; 20-minute walk from Harlyn Bay.

Padstow (St George's Cove, Harbour Cove, Hawker's Cove) Three lovely flat sandy beaches (joined at low tide) within walking distance of Padstow on the Camel estuary.

Polzeath Big sandy family beach, rock pools. Very busy in summer but huge. Surfing. Café, car park.

Porthcothan Pleasant family beach. Shop, car park.

Rock Long sandy beach on Camel estuary, sand dunes, popular. Café, car park.

Summerleaze Beach, Bude Excellent sandy beach, tidal swimming pool. Surfing. Café, car park.

Trebarwith Strand Long sandy beach, covered at high tide. Access over rocks. Surfing. Café, car park.

Trevone Bay, near Padstow Wonderful sandy family beach,

Trebarwith Strand

Surfing

Many of North Cornwall's beaches are perfect for surfing, from beginner level up. Lessons cost around £20 for a half day (two hours) to £35 for a full day (four hours). Check the lower age limit in advance.

Adventure International, Bude; ☎ *0870 7775111; www.budesurfing experience.co.uk*

Animal Surf Academy, Polzeath; ☎ *0870 242 2856; www.animalsurf academy.com*

Atlantic Pursuits Kilkhampton, Bude; ☎ *01288 321765; www.atlantic pursuits.co.uk*

Big Blue Surf School, Bude; ☎ *01288 331764; www.bigbluesurfschool. co.uk*

Harlyn Surf School, Harlyn Bay, near Padstow; ☎ *01841 533076; www. harlynsurfschool.co.uk*

Outdoor Adventure, Widemouth Bay, Bude; ☎ *01288 362900; www. outdooradventure.co.uk*

Padstow Surf School, Trevone Bay; ☎ *01841 520275*

Shoreline Outdoor Pursuits, Crooklets Beach, Bude; ☎ *01288 354039; www.shorelineactivities.co.uk*

Raven Surf School, Bude; ☎ *01288 353693; www ravensurf.co.uk*

Surf's Up Surf School, Polzeath; ☎ *01208 862003; www.surfsupsurf school.com*

Waves Surf School, Padstow; ☎ *01841 521230; www.wavessurf school.co.uk*

---

tidal pool. Blowhole in cliffs to east. Surfing. Café, car park.

Treyarnon Bay Excellent sandy family beach, rock pools. Surfing. Café, car park.

Widemouth Bay, Bude Large sandy beach. Surfing. Café, car park.

For Active Families

The Camel Trail AGES 5 AND UP
One of Cornwall's most popular off-ride cycle routes – and with good reason. The whole route runs for 29 km from Poley's Bridge on Bodmin Moor to Padstow, but there are lots of shorter options: Bodmin or Wadebridge to Padstow, or start from Padstow and cycle as far inland as you like. The run from Wadebridge to Padstow is particularly lovely, following the route of the old railway line (1889–1967) along the Camel estuary. It's level, easy, with lovely views and good picnic spots. It's about 10 km down to Padstow, but the ride is easy and the return journey not arduous; but if you only want to go one way Bridge Bike Hire will arrange to pick up you, your bike and

your family and transport you back to your start point.

Wadebridge to Padstow 10 km.
Cycle hire *Bridge Bike Hire (Wadebridge);* ☏ *01208 813050* **www.bridgebikehire.co.uk**, *Bridge Cycle Hire (Wadebridge);* ☏ *01208 814545, Camel Trail Cycle Hire (Wadebridge);* ☏ *01208 814104, Trail Bike Hire (Padstow);* ☏ *01841 532594;* **www.trailbikehire.co.uk**.

INSIDER TIP ▶

The **Tamar Lakes Watersports and Angling Centre** (☏ *01288 321712; www.swlakestrust. org.uk*) near Kilkhampton offers sailing, windsurfing, canoeing, kayaking and multi-activity days and courses. There's a campsite, tea room, children's play area, bird hide and walks leading onto the Bude Aqueduct walk.

FAMILY-FRIENDLY ACCOMMODATION

INEXPENSIVE

Berryfields Strawberry Farm ★

Berryfields, Porthcothan Bay, Near Padstow, Cornwall PL28 8PW; ☏ *01841 520178. Just above Porthcothan on the lane to Treyarnon Bay.*

A quiet families-only campsite just a few metres from the beach at Porthcothan. Originally a strawberry farm, Berryfields is now run as a small family campsite, with an excellent café and gift shop on site. The café has an outside seating area and a flower-filled conservatory (cheerful even on the dullest day), open from

10am–6pm every day (breakfast is served to 11.30am) throughout the summer. Food is traditional and reasonably priced (unlike some of the more trendy beach cafés that have been springing up all over Cornwall recently). The owners make their own scones and jam – strawberry, raspberry, gooseberry – a Berryfields' cream tea is highly recommended, and the milkshakes are to die for! The campsite is level, grassy, safe and very peaceful: a larger campsite (Carnevas ☏ *01841 520230*) just up the road takes larger groups.

40 camping pitches, 25 caravan/ campervan pitches, 4 static caravans. **Rates** *£3 (low)–4 (high) per pitch per night, plus £2 pppn; tourers £14–18 per night; caravans (4–6 people) £200–450 per week* **Credit** *MC, V.* **Amenities** *café, games room, crazy golf, mini pitch and putt, croquet lawn.*

Wooda Farm Park ★★★

Poughill, Bude, Cornwall EX23 9HJ; ☏ *01288 352069; www.wooda.co.uk. Just off A39 2.5 km north of Bude.*

A really lovely spacious campsite with every facility any family could possibly want. The hedged camping fields stand on high ground a few kilometres inland, with wonderful views out to sea; the extensive facilities – Courtyard Bar, games room, TV room, sports barn, fitness suite and restaurant – are housed in converted farm buildings at some distance from the camping area, linked by a concrete lane – you can get as involved as you want. There's a huge grassy play area, pitch and putt, pond, woodland walk and nature trail; a vast dog-walking field and kite-flying area; and goats, chickens and lambs near the farmhouse. Despite the high number of pitches the site is so extensive, and the facilities so good, that it doesn't feel cramped – lovely beaches are at Sandymouth and Bude 4 km and 2.5 km away respectively. Two cottages sit in enclosed gardens backing onto the kite-flying field, separate from the campsite but within easy reach of facilities.

40-acre site: touring caravans and tents, 54 luxury holiday caravans, 2 s/c cottages. **Rates** *£11 (low)–24 (high) per 2 people pitch; £2 child (3–15); £190–690 holiday caravan (5–6 people); £330–950 cottages (6 people).* **Credit** *MC, V.* **Amenities** *bar, restaurant/takeaway, games room, farm walks, tractor and trailer rides, 9-hole golf course, clay pigeon shooting, coarse fishing, indoor archery, badminton, tennis, fitness suite.*

MODERATE

Coombe Mill ★ ★ ★ FIND

St Breward, Cornwall PL30 4LZ; 01208 850344; www.coombemill.com. St Breward lies on the west side of Bodmin Moor off the B3266 10 km south of Camelford.

A pre-school paradise! Sixteenth-century Coombe Mill, situated in 30 acres of fields and woodland in the beautiful upper Camel Valley, offers a really good choice of family accommodation: converted mill buildings, riverside lodges, and three large, modern Scandinavian lodges (heated by solar panels, new for 2008). The needs of young children are

clearly to the fore: children meet every morning for a tractor ride to feed (and cuddle!) the animals – Sally the pig, donkeys, sheep, rabbits, ducks, chickens and rheas (giving one parent the chance to pack a picnic while the children are occupied). Children will find fun wherever they wander, with two excellent outdoor play areas (one specifically for under fives); two properties have their own play dens for toddlers. You can buy home-cooked meals from the freezer, get basic supplies from reception, borrow children's overalls and baby monitors, books and videos – even wellies if you've forgotten to pack them. This tranquil spot is only 15 minutes from lovely beaches such as Polzeath and Trebarwith Strand, and from Wadebridge (on the Camel Trail, p. 157).

20 s/c properties: 2–14 people. **Rates** *£195 (low)–£1,300 (high).* **Credit** *MC, V.* **Amenities** *babysitting, cot (free), disabled access some properties, extra bed available in 1-bed properties, parking, fishing, outdoor play areas, badminton and volleyball area, purpose-built BBQs, animal feeding.* **In properties** *cooker/microwave, shower/bath, washing machine/dishwasher in most, TV/DVD.*

INSIDER TIP ≫

One of the best ways to explore Bodmin moor is on horseback. Hallagenna Farm at St Breward (01208 851500; www.hallagenna.co.uk) runs pub rides to Blisland and also has a Saturday morning children's club – booking highly recommended.

Coombe Mill, St. Breward

Forda Lodges & Cottages ★★

Kilkhampton, Bude, Cornwall EX23 9RZ; ☎ *01288 321413; www. forda.co.uk. From the B3254 at Kilkhampton take the road to Tamar Lakes; Forda is on the right after 1.2 km.*

This is a pretty special place – the Scandinavian-style lodges stand out in an area where so much holiday accommodation is in converted farm buildings – and it's extremely well set up for older children and teenagers. Just a stone's throw from the Tamar Lakes (p. 158) and within easy reach of Bude (p. 149) and the north Cornish coast beaches, Forda – 'a small and tranquil holiday haven' – offers a range of interesting and very well-equipped accommodation:

A-frame Scandinavian lodges along the lakeside, single-storey timber lodges, and two lovely conversions from old farm buildings, one with its own enclosed garden, all surrounded by rolling green lawns and three fishing lakes. There's a real feeling of space here – the properties are well spread out. The on-site facilities are of a quality usually associated with a far larger site.

*10 lodges and 2 cottages, 4–8 people. **Rates** £295 (low)–990 (high). **Amenities** cot (free), extra bed some properties, disabled access: one property fully adapted, parking, DIY laundry, fishing, indoor swimming pool, sauna, tennis court, games room, BBQs available. **In properties** cooker, microwave, shower/bath, TV/video/DVD.*

Trevorrick Farm Cottages ★ ★ GREEN

St Issey, Near Padstow, Cornwall PL27 7QH; ☎ 01841 540574; www. trevorrick.co.uk. Off the A389 at St Issey, between Wadebridge and Little Petherick.

There's a very friendly, laid-back feel when you arrive at Trevorrick Farm, welcomed by a bustling flock of bantams and Aylesbury ducks. It's in a peaceful position, situated on a peaceful dead-end lane just above Little Petherick Creek, a lovely 3-km walk into Padstow along the Camel Trail. It's a wildlife paradise: a big safe field above the cottages is ideal for ball games, with good play equipment and a trampoline; there's a separate lawned play area for younger children nearer the farm – including a Wendy house and play combine harvester. The

indoor swimming pool and games room (pool table, table football, table tennis, snooker, plus toys for younger children) are inside an old barn, and trundle toys are ready and waiting for a trip round the yard. The six cottages are all converted farm buildings (the farm was working up to 1980); the present owners have an 11-acre smallholding. DIY laundry is available in a farm outbuilding, with visitor information.

*6 s/c cottages, 2–5 people. **Rates** £240 (low)–995 (high). **Credit** MC, V. **Amenities** babysitting, cot (free), disabled access possible 1 cottage, DIY laundry, parking, indoor pool, games room, outdoor play areas, in cottage cooker/microwave, fridge/freezer, shower/bath, TV/DVD or video, toys/ books.*

Trevone Beach House ★ ★ ★
GREEN

Trevone Bay, Padstow, Cornwall PL28 8QX; ☎ 01841 520469; www. trevonebeach.co.uk. On the beach road in Trevone (off B3276 west of Padstow).

Trevone Bay is one of the best of many family beaches in north Cornwall: acres of golden sand, rock pools, and a natural swimming pool in the rocks. Trevone Beach House, dating from the 1930s, is a delightfully solid family house that has had a complete facelift over the last few years – it's hard to believe that it was once a plumber's shop! It's fresh, bright, relaxed, simply decorated, with local artists' work adorning the walls. There's a spacious breakfast room and guest lounge (with children's games, DVDs, books), an outside decking area and storage for wetsuits and surfboards (discounts given at the Rocky Point Surf Shop on the beach). Every guest (including adults) is greeted by a teddy bear on the bed. The owners have three young children and are right on the ball when it comes to family holidays. They live next door and are extremely environmentally aware; the B&B is run on green principles wherever possible. A great family-friendly B&B.

Rooms 9 double/twin (5 with sea views). *Rates* £34 (low)–39 (high) pppn; £220 (low)–265 (high) pppw. £10 children (2–12) sharing with 2 adults. *Credit* AmEx, MC, V. *Amenities* honesty bar, cot (free), disabled access, extra bed, laundry service, Internet access available in office, parking. *In room* shower, TV.

The Old School Hotel ★ ★

Fore Street, Port Isaac, Cornwall PL29 3RD; ☎ 01208 880721; www.the oldschoolhotel.co.uk. On Port Isaac's main street, above the harbour.

One of the best things about Port Isaac is that it still has a small working fishing fleet. Another plus is that there is no car park in the old village – cars do park on the beach at low tide, but there's always that risk of misjudging just when you should get back to your car… – so the village doesn't get quite as packed as others along this coast. The Old School Hotel does have parking – in the former playground – and is a really fun place to stay, in a magical position overlooking the harbour. The school dates from 1875, and was in use until 1977 – there are still rows of pegs in the hall! The interior has been renovated to provide stylish, comfortable accommodation with loads of character – the 'old school' atmosphere hasn't quite gone (the dining room is in the old school hall, now decorated in blue and white). Local fish features strongly on the menu, and the children's options are good and healthy. Young children love Port Isaac: there are few cars, rock pools on the beach at low tide and fishing trips from the harbour. The old village is a labyrinth of passages and alleyways – look out for Squeezy Belly Alley – and there are excellent beaches a short drive away.

Rooms 12 double/en suite, inc 3 family rooms (4–6 people). *Rates* £127 (low)–137 (high) family suite per night. *Credit* AmEx, MC, V. *Amenities* babysitting/baby monitors, bar, cot (free), extra bed (charge), laundry service, parking, restaurant, Internet access in bar area. *In room* shower/ bath, TV/DVD,

Fentrigan Manor Farm ★ ★

Warbstow, Launceston, Cornwall PL15 8UX; ☎ 01566 781264; www. fentriganmanor.co.uk. 3.2 km north of Hallworthy A395/B3262 junction.

Something of a find in the part of inland north Cornwall few would consider for a holiday unless they already knew the area, but which has the advantage of space, peace and quiet, fantastic rural views – as far as the coast and, on a good day, to Lundy Island (p. 48) – yet with Boscastle, Crackington Haven and wonderful remote beaches such as The Strangles within easy distance. Before 1540 Fentrigan Manor was part of Tywardreath Priory, a resting place for monks travelling between Barnstaple and Truro; the owners' family has lived here since the 17th century. A 220-acre working farm, the former wagonhouse and stables have been beautifully converted into holiday accommodation, each with its own enclosed garden with sitting-out area. There are animals to feed, eggs to collect, pony rides and lambs to feed in spring and early summer; older families can play tennis, fish for carp on the lake and enjoy the games room. There's a spacious games field, and swings, tree house and a sandpit for little ones.

*7 s/c cottages, 5–8 people. **Rates** £288 (low)–1,345 (high). **Amenities** babysitting, cot (free), disabled access some cottages, extra bed (charge), parking. **In cottage** cooker/microwave, fridge/freezer, washing machine (tumble dryer available), shower/bath, TV/DVD.*

EXPENSIVE

Rooke Country Cottages ★★★

Chapel Amble, Wadebridge, Cornwall PL27 6ES; ☎ 01208 880368; www.rookecottages.net. 1.2 km north of Chapel Amble.

A wonderfully peaceful rural retreat, tucked away down narrow country lanes yet within easy striking distance of North Cornwall's beaches. Rooke is a

Duchy of Cornwall farm, and a range of grand stone early 19th-century farm buildings have been beautifully converted into self-catering accommodation, some detached and standing in their own grounds – one has its own drive, another has the old open-sided linhay (holiday cottage) in its garden, now housing a sandpit – all with lovely enclosed gardens. One huge barn has been left unconverted, effectively dividing the properties from the working farm. A great deal of care has been given to the exterior finish and interior fixtures and fittings: flowering baskets and shrubs abound, and the overwhelming impression is one of peace and tranquillity. A big meadow is kept mown for ball games, kite flying and walking the dog, and there's a children's adventure garden with a huge sandpit.

*Rooms 7 s/c cottages (plus 1 riverside apartment in Wadebridge), 2–8 people. **Rates** £427–2,596. **Credit** MC, V. **Amenities** babysitting, cot (free), disabled access possible 1 property, parking, children's adventure garden. **In cottage** Internet access, cooker/microwave, fridge/freezer, dishwasher, washing machine/tumble dryer, shower/bath, TV/DVD.*

FAMILY-FRIENDLY DINING

INEXPENSIVE

Rectory Farm Tearooms ★★★

Morwenstow, Cornwall EX23 9SR; ☎ 01288 331251; www.rectorytearooms.co.uk. Signed off the A39 between Clovelly and Kilkhampton.

You'd probably never find Morwenstow if you didn't already know about it. Just 800 m in from the rugged north Cornish coast, only a few kilometres from the Devon border, it's an idyllic spot blessed with a wonderful tearoom – and a fascinating history. Morwenstow is best known for its connection with the eccentric 19th-century vicar, Reverend Robert Stephen Hawker, and the graveyard of the church is filled with shipwreck victims: Hawker insisted on giving every one a Christian burial. The 13th-century farmhouse tearooms by the church have a wonderful atmosphere – dark wooden furniture, beams, flagstone floors – and delicious freshly prepared lunches, teas and snacks. The children's menu (£4.95) includes mini pizzas, beans on toast, honey and banana sandwiches; half portions of scrumptious cakes are available, and wonderful cream or cheese teas (£6.50), with scones baked from an old family recipe. The tearoom is cosy inside – the tables are quite close together – but there's a very pretty garden too. Lunch specials include goat's cheese, red onion and avocado tartlets (£9.50) and salmon and asparagus quiche (£8.95) plus baguettes, jackets and sandwiches.

Open *11am–5pm week before Easter–end Oct; in winter will open for large groups.* **Main course** *£3.80–9.50.* **Credit** *MC, V.* **Amenities** *children's menu, highchair, garden seating, disabled access, reservations accepted, parking, Sunday lunches.*

> **INSIDER TIP**
>
> If you need to stretch your legs after a visit to the tearooms take a short walk along the grassy path leading to the cliffs. There you'll find **Hawker's Hut**, a little wooden, turf-roofed building – originally built of driftwood – from where the Reverend Hawker kept an eye out for shipwrecks (meditated, wrote poetry and took drugs!). This is a particularly spectacular part of the Cornish coast, and if your companions aren't up to tackling the switchback Coast Path you'll get a taste of it from here. The second-highest sheer cliff in England – after Beachy Head – lies just over the valley to the north. And if a pub is more your style than a tearoom, Morwenstow has the answer: the 13th-century Bush Inn – originally a monks' resthouse – is open all day and has a children's play area.

Carnewas Tearoom ★★

Bedruthan Steps, St Eval, Wadebridge, Cornwall PL27 7UW; ☎ 01637 860701. In the NT car park for Bedruthan Steps, off B3276 Padstow–Newquay.

Two small, single-storey granite buildings – one (now the NT shop) originally the Count House for Carnewas mine – sit solidly on the clifftop above Bedruthan Steps. These great granite stacks and wonderful sandy beach became popular with tourists 150 years ago, and there's been a tearoom here for as long as anyone can remember. It's bright, cheerful, simple and relaxed, with a breezy little walled garden. The menu is small, but everything is homemade and locally sourced;

Bedruthan Steps

one nice touch is the children's lunchbox (£3.75: ham or cheese sandwich, apple or yoghurt, chocolate biscuit, fruit juice, crisps and a toy). There are toasted sandwiches, filled rolls, jacket potatoes and daily specials: fish pie (£6.50), pasty with cider chutney (£3.75). Cream teas are renowned, and a box of books and magazines adds to the homely atmosphere – and after the trek down to Bedruthan Steps you'll be in need of a treat!

Open *10.30am–5pm Mar–end Oct; some winter weekends (depending on weather).* **Main course** *£3.30–6.75.* **Amenities** *highchair, disabled access, reservations accepted, parking, walled garden.*

INSIDER TIP ›
It's a long walk down to the beach at Bedruthan Steps – lots of flights of steps – but it's worth it to get a closer look at the rock stacks, caves and rock pools (no swimming allowed). It is said that the giant Bedruthan used the rock stacks as stepping stones, but that's thought to be an invented late 19th-century legend!

Trevathan Farm Shop & Restaurant ★★

St Endellion, Port Isaac, Cornwall PL29 3TT; ☎ *01208 880164; www. trevathanfarm.com. On B3314 at St Endellion.*

All manner of good things rolled into one! For a start there's the farm shop, selling a huge range of local produce. Secondly there's the café, serving breakfast until 11am, good children's meals (£2.25–3.95), salads, sandwiches, cod and chips (£6.95), ham, egg and chips (£5.95), and a great choice of cakes, biscuits and cream teas.

Thirdly – probably most impor-tant – is the excellent range of unobtrusive children's play equipment. The farm shop/café is situated at the top of a huge field, with inside seating and lots of outside chairs and tables. Ranged along the field edge are pens with rabbits and sheep, swings, adventure play area, sandpit and zipwire; ride-on tractors, mini diggers, and giant jenga. There are acres of space for children to run around, and fantastic views inland. You can pick your own strawberries in June – and there's excellent self-catering accommodation available at the farm just down the road (with the same feeling of space and views; ℓ *01208 880248*).

Open *9.30am–5.30pm early Mar–end Oct. Main course £5.95–8.50. Credit AmEx, MC, V. Amenities chil-dren's menu, highchair, play area, disabled access, reservations accepted, parking.*

Stein's Fish and Chips ★

South Quay, Padstow, Cornwall PL28 8BL; ℓ 01841 532700; www.rick stein.com. On the South Quay in Padstow (quayside car parks).

Wander along the quayside in Padstow any night of the week and you may come across queues of people stretching across the car park, waiting for the chance to sample Rick Stein's fish and chips. Eat in or takeaway is available (if you eat in you'll pay a bit more but you get to sit down at a scrubbed wooden table – and perhaps have a glass of wine or beer with your meal – but you'll eat out of the same cardboard container in which you would otherwise carry away your supper!). The vast majority of the fish served comes from Cornwall, and there's a huge choice: sea bass, John Dory, gurnard, monkfish, as well as the more usual cod and plaice.

Try These Too!

- **Hentervene Holiday Park:** A small, very quiet, family site on a peaceful lane near a fantastic beach. The Strangles, Crackington Haven, Bude, Cornwall EX23 0LF; ℓ *01840 230365; www.hentervene. co.uk*.

- **Mesmear:** Beautifully 18th-century converted barns on a 'bou-tique' hotel basis run on sound environmental principles. St Minver, Cornwall PL27 6RA; Telephone ℓ *01208 869731; www.mesmear. co.uk*.

- **The Pickwick Inn & Restaurant:** The original part of this building dates back 200 years – lovely views over the Camel estuary. Burgois, St Issey, Near Padstow, Cornwall PL27 7QQ; ℓ *01841 540361*.

Choose between grilled or battered (the restaurant uses traditional beef dripping for most of its dishes, but also offers squid and goujons fried in vegetable oil); children can have cod chunks or goujons (£4.65). It's relaxed, friendly, informal – and fun.

Open *12pm–9pm Mon–Sun (take-away), 12pm–2.30pm, 5pm–9pm Mon–Sat, 12pm–7pm Sun (restaurant).* **Main course** *£6.20–11.80 (eat in; takeaway £2 less).* **Credit** *MC, V.* **Amenities** *children's menu, high-chair, disabled access, parking.*

EXPENSIVE

The Maltsters Arms ★★

Chapel Amble, near Wadebridge, Cornwall PL27 6EU; ☎ 01208 812 473. In the centre of Chapel Amble, off A39 Wadebridge–Bude.

Chapel Amble is one of Cornwall's prettiest inland villages, with a broad main street and wide grassy verges flanked by terraces of pretty cottages. It's the sort of place you'd expect to find a really good pub, and The Maltsters Arms is just that: an excellent place to take the family for an end of holiday treat. The pub has several rooms – upstairs – and can accommodate a high number of diners (children are allowed everywhere); there's a good 'buzz' about the place, but since each room is fairly small it manages to maintain an intimate atmosphere. Food is locally sourced, freshly prepared and reliably good: there

are daily specials – tuna steak with sweet chilli sauce (£13.95), moules mariniere (£10.95), steak and ale pie (£11.50), plus spring lamb (£15.50), with beautifully cooked and presented vegetables. The children's menu is quite small (£7) but half portions of adult dishes are available.

Open *11.30am–3pm, 6.30–midnight Mon–Sat, 12pm–3pm, 7–11pm Sun.* **Main course** *£12.95–18.95 (evenings).* **Credit** *MC, V.* **Amenities** *children's menu/half portions available, highchair, disabled access possible, reservations advisable evenings, parking.*

Life's a Beach ★★

Summerleaze Beach, Bude, Cornwall EX23 8HN; ☎ 01288 355222; www. lifesabeach.info. On Summerleaze Beach, beyond the beach car park.

Beach café by day, award-winning seafood bistro by night! The bistro has a stunning position above popular Summerleaze Beach in the centre of Bude, and in the daytime serves nachos, bruschettas, baguettes, shell-on prawns and good salads. There's loads of seating both inside and out on the veranda, and a lovely long blue bar where you can sit and drink in the view. In the evenings start with goat's cheese salad or Fowey scallops (£5–7), and move on to roasted monk-fish and prawn with chorizo and saffron broth, ravioli filled with butternut squash, wok-fried tiger prawns and John Dory. Those children who are a little 'iffy'

Keeping it Local – Farmers' Markets & Farm Shops

Bodmin Farmers' Market, Public Rooms, 4th Sat
Bre-Pen Farm Shop, Mawgan Porth, Newquay; ☎ *01637 860420*
Bude Farmers' Market, Parkhouse Centre, alternate Fri
Camel Valley Farm Shop, St Kew Highway, Wadebridge; ☎ *01208 841343*
Carruan Farm Centre, Polzeath; ☎ *01208 869584*
Launceston Farmers' Market, Town Square, 1st Sat Apr–Oct
Padstow Farm Shop, Trethillick Farm, Padstow; ☎ *01841 533060*
St Kew Harvest Farm Shop, St Kew Highway, Wadebridge; ☎ *01208 841818*
Trevathan Farm Shop, St Endellion, Port Isaac; ☎ *01208 880164*

about fish can choose chicken, steak, pasta or lamb. A lovely relaxed spot for a special supper on a sunny summer's evening – and from where you can watch the sun go down.

Open 10.30am–4pm daily, 7pm–late Tue–Sat high season; closed Jan/Feb. **Main course** £15–17 (evenings). **Credit** AmEx, MC, V. **Amenities** children's menu/half portions available, highchair, disabled access, reservations advisable eves, parking.

MID CORNWALL

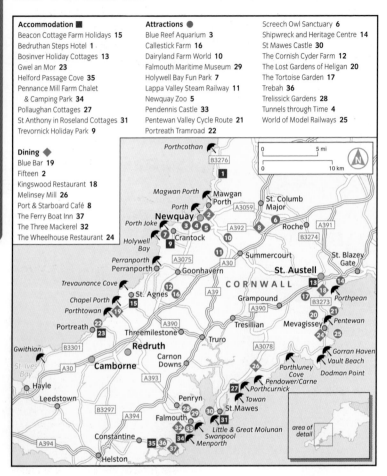

Accommodation ■
Beacon Cottage Farm Holidays **15**
Bedruthan Steps Hotel **1**
Bosinver Holiday Cottages **13**
Gwel an Mor **23**
Helford Passage Cove **35**
Pennance Mill Farm Chalet
   & Camping Park **34**
Pollaughan Cottages **27**
St Anthony in Roseland Cottages **31**
Trevornick Holiday Park **9**

Dining ◆
Blue Bar **19**
Fifteen **2**
Kingswood Restaurant **18**
Melinsey Mill **26**
Port & Starboard Café **8**
The Ferry Boat Inn **37**
The Three Mackerel **32**
The Wheelhouse Restaurant **24**

Attractions ●
Blue Reef Aquarium **3**
Callestick Farm **16**
Dairyland Farm World **10**
Falmouth Maritime Museum **29**
Holywell Bay Fun Park **7**
Lappa Valley Steam Railway **11**
Newquay Zoo **5**
Pendennis Castle **33**
Pentewan Valley Cycle Route **21**
Portreath Tramroad **22**

Screech Owl Sanctuary **6**
Shipwreck and Heritage Centre **14**
St Mawes Castle **30**
The Cornish Cyder Farm **12**
The Lost Gardens of Heligan **20**
The Tortoise Garden **17**
Trebah **36**
Trelissick Gardens **28**
Tunnels through Time **4**
World of Model Railways **25**

Tʜe area denoted as 'Mid Cornwall' in this book stretches right across the county. From the tough north coast, famed for its surfing beaches, especially around Newquay, to the sheltered, indented coastline of the south. From these wooded river estuaries – beloved of the sailing and boating fraternity – around Falmouth, and the beautiful rugged coastline from St Anthony Head northeast we head towards historic Charlestown (p. 175) and St Austell. North and south are completely different; your choice of destination will depend on your family's requirements. To the north is the magnificent coastline around St Agnes Beacon and the famous tourist hotspot of Newquay, known for years for cheap holiday accommodation and uncomplicated beach fun, today famous for world-class surfing, trendy beach cafés and Jamie Oliver's Fifteen restaurant. The south coast is uniquely beautiful, sheltered and luxuriant. It has glorious gardens at Trebah and Glendurgan, historic Falmouth, old fishing villages such as Portloe and Mevagissey and the wonderfully tranquil and unspoilt Roseland Peninsula where a short walk or boat ride will lead you to deserted sandy coves, perfect for sandcastles and rock pool exploration.

VISITOR INFORMATION

The southern part of Mid Cornwall is particularly well covered. 'Your passport to Cornwall's best-kept secret', **King Harry's Cornwall Guidebook**, is published annually – a mine of useful information on the Falmouth area and Roseland Peninsula. Two smaller annual publications – **The Roseland Visitor Guide** and the **Cornish River guide** (covering Falmouth, Truro and the Roseland Peninsula – *www.acornishriver.co.uk*) – are packed with tips. All can be picked up free of charge at TICs, campsites, in pubs and so on. The best maps to use are OS Explorers 104 Redruth & St Agnes, and 105 Falmouth & Mevagissey.

Information Centres

Falmouth, Market Strand, Prince of Wales Pier; 01326 312300; www.acornishriver.co.uk

Mevagissey, 14 Church Street; 01726 842266; www.mevagissey-cornwall.co.uk

Newquay, Municipal Buildings, Marcus Hill; 01637 854020; www.restormel.gov.uk

Perranporth; 01872 573368

St Agnes, 20 Churchtown; 01872 554150; www.st-agnes.com

St Austell, Southbourne Road; 01726 223300; www.restormel.gov.uk

Truro, Municipal Buildings, Boscawen Street; 01872 274555; www.truro.gov.uk/tic

Orientation

Two major A roads pass through this area from east to west. For the north coast the A30 is best; the notorious bottleneck at Goss Moor was removed in 2007, and dual carriageway now runs virtually all the way from Bodmin (and points east), west past Indian Queens, and on to Redruth and Cambourne. The A38 leads from St Austell towards Truro, Cornwall's county town – the A3078 branches off south for the Roseland Peninsula – then the A39 takes you all the way to Falmouth.

Getting Around

Once again – sadly – a car is your best bet for getting around, especially in the centre or north of the area. But along the south coast there's a great ferry network, often linking with bus routes: visit *www.kingharrys cornwall.co.uk*.

The main railway line runs through the area from Par, south of St Austell, then west via Truro. The Atlantic Coast line leads from Par to Newquay; the Maritime Line runs from Truro to Falmouth.

There's a special Western Greyhound scenic bus route from Newquay to Padstow (☎ *01637 871871; www.westerngreyhound. com*). For information on bus and train timetables ask in the local TIC or ☎ Traveline *0871 200 2233; www.traveline.org.uk*.

Child-Friendly Events & Entertainment

Falmouth Week

Week of activity both on and off the water, from Falmouth Classics yacht races (great to watch) to all manner of land-based family activities: live music, continental market, children's workshops, crabbing sessions, events at Pendennis Castle (p. 179). Mid Aug, *www.falmouth week.co.uk*. Also **Falmouth Oyster Festival** mid Oct, *www. falmouthoysterfestival.co.uk*.

Mevagissey Feast Week

This festival celebrates the feast of St Peter, the patron saint of fishermen: carnival, music, procession, raft races, children's entertainment, flora dance, crab-catching competition and fireworks.

Late June, www.mevagissey.net

Stithians Show

Cornwall's biggest one-day agricultural show is not to be missed! Typical quaint country fair: farm animals, show ring, horse events, craft tents, beer tent, children's 'garden on a tea tray' competitions, local food, wonderful.

Mid-July, www.stithiansshow.org.uk

WHAT TO SEE & DO

Children's Top 10 Attractions

❶ **Paddling** a kayak from lovely Swanpool Beach. See p. 182.

❷ **Feeding** chickens and ducks every morning at Bosinver. See p. 186.

❸ **Bumping along** behind a tractor on a trailer ride at the Cornish Cyder Farm. See p. 176.

❹ **Getting close** to a bird of prey at the Screech Owl Centre. See p. 177.

❺ **Hiding** under giant gunnera at Trebah garden. See p. 179.

❻ **Digging** in the sand at Great Molunan beach on the Roseland Peninsula. See p. 181.

❼ **Cycling** along the old Portreath tramroad. See p. 183.

❽ **Climbing** huge trees – safely! See p. 183.

❾ **Sailing** a model dinghy at Falmouth's Maritime Museum. See p. 174.

❿ **Messing about** in a boat on the Helford river. See p. 175.

Maritime Museum, Falmouth

Towns & Villages

Falmouth

Situated on the third largest natural deepwater port in the world, Falmouth has its roots planted firmly in maritime tradition. Henry VIII built **Pendennis** and **St Mawes castles** (p. 179) to defend the Carrick Roads; for over 150 years from the late 17th century the Falmouth Packet Service established the town as a vital link in global communications. Falmouth Docks were founded in 1860, a huge boost to the local economy; the railway arrived three years later. Today Falmouth is a comfortable mix of holiday resort, fishing port and ship-repair centre. There's a real buzz, a good mix of high street and individual shops, and lots of family activities: **Pendennis Castle** (p. 179) and ferry trips to St Mawes, **Trelissick Gardens** and the Roseland Peninsula; the **Ships & Castles Leisure Centre** (📞 01326 212129); the fabulous **Maritime Museum** (p. 174); afternoons on Gyllyngvase Beach, with an ice cream at the excellent **Gylly Beach Café**; award-winning fish and chips at **Harbour Lights** on Arwenack Street; or explore **Falmouth Lifeboat Station** by the marina.

Newquay

Newquay is undergoing a transformation. The coming of Jamie Oliver's **Fifteen** to lovely Watergate Bay (north of the town, p. 188), and increasingly good air connections to Newquay airport have put the town firmly on the map. For families Newquay has great beaches, plenty of places to eat and lots to get involved in. But there's nothing particularly Cornish here, despite its fishing-port origins. Its population swells enormously in summer as huge numbers of teenagers descend to the UK's premier surfing destination, drawn by sun, sand, and cheap campsites. Best to leave it to them, stay elsewhere and enjoy using the facilities associated with a big seaside town. **Trenance Leisure Park** is home to the award-winning **Newquay Zoo** (📞 01637 873342; www.newquayzoo.org. uk) and Waterworld (📞 01637 853828; www.newquaywaterworld.co.uk) which has two superb pools, one a Tropical Fun Pool with flumes, slides, spitting snake and crocodile! More watery fun may be had at the **Oasis Fun Pool** at Hendra Holiday Park (📞 01637 875778;

www.hendra-holidays.com), and at Holywell Bay a few kilometres to the south of the town **Holywell Bay Fun Park** (℡ *01637 830095; www.holywell bay.co.uk*) will provide a good day's entertainment. **Tunnels through Time** on St Michaels Road (℡ *01637 873379; www. tunnelsthroughtime.co.uk*) is great for a wet day: stories and legends of Cornish life are brought to life by more than 70 life-size characters. **The Windswept Café** on South Fistral Beach is highly recommended for families.

Fun Days Out

National Maritime Museum
★ ★ ★ VALUE   AGES 3 AND OVER

Discovery Quay, Falmouth, Cornwall TR11 3QY; ℡ 01326 313388; www. nmmc.co.uk. Signed throughout Falmouth.

There are so many factors that make Falmouth's maritime museum great for a visit whether or not you're interested in boats. For a start there's the incredibly impressive building, a massive construction by the docks: from the top of the tower (there is a lift) binoculars and telescopes help you make the most of the incredible views. Then there's the innovative way in which craft of all shapes and sizes are displayed, suspended on wires in a huge central space, around which run easily accessible wide walkways. Fascinating information about boats, weather, sail-making, and boat-building is presented in a really simple manner, with hands-on displays to entertain

and inform adults and children alike. You can grab hold of a tiller and steer a computerised course, slide a depression over Cornwall and watch what happens to the weather, even steer a little sailing boat into wind on the fantastic indoor sailing lake. Actual boats on display include an Inuit kayak and the canoe used to break the world altitude canoeing record: 17,500ft in a lake on Everest in 1977!

Open 10am–5pm daily except Christmas Day/Boxing Day. Admission £7.50 adult, £5 child (6–15), under 6 free, £6 OAP, £20 family. Credit MV, V. Amenities café, disabled access, parking, shop, special children's events and workshops.

> **INSIDER TIP**
>
> If you're going to the Maritime Museum why not get in the mood and arrive by boat! **Falmouth Park & Float** runs classic wooden ferries every 20 minutes from Ponsharden, a lovely stress-free trip down the Penryn river to Falmouth's Customs House Quay.

Shipwreck and Heritage Centre ★   AGES 5 AND OVER

Quay Road, Charlestown, St Austell, Cornwall PL25 3NJ; ℡ 01726 69897; www.shipwreckcharlestown.com. 3.2 km south of At Austell on A3061; signed off the A30. Bus from Fowey, Mevagissey, St Austell.

The historic port of Charlestown comes as a real surprise after driving along the busy A30 through the outskirts of St Austell. This remarkably unspoiled Georgian working port – with tall ships in the harbour – has often been used as a film location; you almost expect to see people emerging from the terraced 18th-century cottages dressed in period costume! It's fitting that Charlestown is also home to the largest private collection of shipwreck and maritime artefacts in Europe. Visitors start off in dark tunnels, along which wagons used to deliver china clay to the dockside, then move into the body of the museum: a mass of historic tableaux, exhibitions, stories of shipwrecks, even a recreation of divers working on the actual remains of the *Grand Turk*, which went down off Barnstaple in 1808. It's a real maze, and although there isn't much interactive material here for young children they can download the museum's I-Spy Trail or colouring sheet before you go and fill these in as they go round.

Open 10am–5pm 1 Mar–end Oct. **Admission** £5.95 adult, £2.95 child 10–16 (under 10 free), £3.95 OAP/student/disabled. **Credit** MC, V. **Amenities** café, disabled access, shop.

INSIDER TIP ≫

On Tuesday and Friday evenings and Saturday afternoons throughout the summer there's racing in the Carrick Roads off Falmouth. Good vantage points for watching the magnificent **Falmouth Working Boats** in all their glory – some are over 100 years old, and are traditional oyster-dredging boats – are Pendennis Castle, anywhere on the Coast Path between Flushing and Mylor, and St Mawes Castle.

Messing About in Boats

The creeks and estuaries of the Fal and Helford rivers are ideal for all sorts of activity on the water, whatever your level of expertise – and there are plenty of companies out there willing to help, whether you're into hiring a motorboat for an afternoon or want to learn how to sail a traditional wooden boat. You can hire easy-to-handle, stable six-person motorboats (or sailing boats) from £20 per hour from **Mylor Boat Hire** (📞 01326 377745; www.mylorboathire.co.uk) and go exploring anywhere from Truro and beyond all the way down to Falmouth. Safety is a priority, and full instruction is given before you're allowed to set off. Wooden sailing day boats can be hired from **Fal Wooden Boat Hire** in Penryn (📞 07967 381299; www.falwoodenboathire.com). **Roseland Paddle and Sail** (📞 01872 580964; www.paddleandsail.com) offer a variety of RYA courses for children and adults from Portscatho. **Sailaway St Anthony** (📞 01326 231357; www.StAnthony.co.uk) operates from beautiful Gillan Creek south of the Helford, and **Helford River Boats** (📞 01326 250770; www.helford-river-boats.co.uk) from Helford Passage. And if you feel like a little luxury why not charter *Wando Lady*, a fantastic fully crewed 20 m wooden classic motor yacht, for a day cruise or overnight trip (www.wandolady.com)

Jump on a Ferry

Getting around by ferry is far more satisfying, more restful, more environmentally friendly – and much more fun – than going everywhere by car. Fal River Links (*www.falriverlinks.co.uk*) has a mass of information on getting round this part of south Cornwall without the car.

King Harry Ferry (☎ *01872 862312; www.kingharryscornwall.co.uk*) Access to the Roseland Peninsula from the west is via this long-established route from Feock. There's been a ferry crossing the Fal here for over 500 years; the new ultra-efficient ferry runs every 20 minutes, daily. It's on the Pilgrim's Way to St Michael's Mount, and is named after the Lancastrian King Henry VI.

St Mawes Ferry (☎ *01872 861910* (office); ferry mobile ☎ *07855 438674; www.stmawesferry.co.uk*) Operating three times an hour in summer, the ferry connects St Mawes with the bustling port of Falmouth.

Place Ferry (☎ *01872 861910* (office); ferry mobile ☎ *07791 283884; www.placeferry.co.uk*) Operating seven days a week, the Place Ferry runs every 30 minutes between St Mawes and Place Creek on the Roseland Peninsula.

Helford River Boats (☎ *01326 250770; www.helford-river-boats.co.uk*) Ferries across the Helford River between Helford Passage and Helford village (the Old Ferry); and also the Garden Ferry to Glendurgan and Trebah Gardens (p. 179) on request in the summer months.

The Cornish Cyder Farm ★★
ALL AGES

Penhallow, Truro, Cornwall TR4 9LW; ☎ 01872 573356; www.thecornishcyderfarm.co.uk. Off the A3075, 13 km southwest of Newquay.

Anywhere with the slogan 'Legless but happy' has to be worth checking out! This working cider farm has cleverly adapted itself to accommodate visitors while still producing around 590,000 litres of cider a year. A guided tour explores the cider-making process (free sampling in the shop, fruit juices for children) via the press house bottlery and brandy distillery, then into the jam kitchen where delicious preserves are produced. The first batch of Cornish whisky is also being distilled at present. A fun (but bumpy) tractor and trailer ride takes you round the orchards. There's no outdoor play equipment here; this is very much a working farm, though it has a good, relaxed feel (assisted by the heady scent of fermenting apples!). Younger children will be more interested in the farm animals, and in sampling locally made Callestick ice cream (p. 177).

Pay with Cider ◁◁

Around 150 years ago cider was made at the farm to pay the labourers' wages – on average they downed four or five pints a day (and up to 10 pints a day at harvest time)!

Open *9am–6pm Mon–Fri, 10am–6pm Sun all year round; to 8pm July/Aug.* **Admission** *free to site; guided tour £6 adult, £4 child 6–16, under 6 free. £5 OAP; tractor ride £3.50 adult/OAP, £2.50 child.* **Credit** *MC, V.* **Amenities** *café, disabled access, parking, picnic area, ice cream/cream tea kiosk, shop, farm animals.*

> **INSIDER TIP >>**
>
> If you're in need of more ice cream **Callestick Farm** can be found just down the lane from the Cornish Cyder Farm (☎ *01872 573126; www.callestickfarm. co.uk*). There are farm animals to see and a very attractive café and ice cream parlour where you can try different flavours – mango sorbet strongly recommended!

Lappa Valley Steam Railway ★★★ FIND ALL AGES

St Newlyn East, near Newquay, Cornwall TR8 5LX; ☎ 01872 510317; www.lappavalley.co.uk. Follow brown tourist signs from A3075.

A magical discovery on a lovely 1.6 km-long trip through the pretty Lappa valley behind a shiny narrow gauge steam engine (Zebedee or Muffin) to emerge at East Wheel Rose, an old tin-mining site complete with renovated chimney and engine house in a beautiful natural setting. Go canoeing on the lake, take a ride on two miniature railways (one of which goes to the picnic area and family games field), have a go on the pedal cars and see if you can find your way around the brick maze. Those interested in the history of the site can explore the engine house (access was denied when I visited due to nesting bees – there's a strong emphasis on wildlife conservation) or watch the video which details the site's industrial heritage. This is a very well thought out and presented attraction: there are some lovely play trains at Benny Halt, where you start your journey, to keep youngsters occupied while waiting for the train. Trains runs every 40 minutes there and back.

Open *first train 10.30am early Apr–late Oct (closed some days Oct); last train late afternoon.* **Admission** *£8 adult, £7.20 child (3–15), under 3 free, £7.20 OAP, £28 family, 50p dog.* **Credit** *MC, V.* **Amenities** *café, disabled access, parking, picnic area, shop.*

Animal Attractions

Screech Owl Sanctuary ★
AGES 5 AND OVER

Trewin Farm, Goss Moor, Cornwall TR9 6HP; ☎ 01726 860182; www. screechowlsanctuary.co.uk. Follow the signs from the A30 on the Indian Queens bypass, or from the A39 between Wadebridge and Truro.

Did you know that owls love to sunbathe? Or that Harris hawks drop sticks and catch them again when bored? An hour or two at Cornwall's owl rehabilitation and education centre will provide the answers to these and many other questions! There are regular flying displays, and 'Close Encounters' when you can handle some of these fascinating birds. Younger children may be more interested in the playground by the café or in feeding fish and ducks on the lakes (food available from the tearoom). The centre is well laid out and maintained, and offers adoption or sponsoring schemes. Conservation and breeding programmes are promoted, as is work with schools and disabled groups. This is a place worth supporting, good for a non-beach morning or afternoon.

Open *10am–6pm 1 Mar–31 Oct; 10am–4pm 1 Nov–28 Feb, daily.* **Admission** *£6.95 adult, £5.50 child (3–14), under 3 free, £6.50 OAP, £22 family.* **Credit** *MC, V.* **Amenities** *café, disabled access, parking, picnic area, shop, outdoor play area with trampoline (6–12 years), no dogs.*

Screech Owl Sanctuary, Trewin Farm

INSIDER TIP »

If you're interested in what goes on under the sea take a trip to the **Blue Reef Aquarium** on Newquay's Towan Beach (☎ *01637 878134; www.bluereefaquarium. co.uk*). There are family fun days and an amazing underwater walk-through tunnel from where you get a really good sight of all sorts of exotic species. Some family days are specifically baby-friendly.

Dairyland Farm World ★★
ALL AGES

Near Newquay, Cornwall TR8 5AA; ☎ 01872 510246; www.dairyland farmworld.co.uk. Signed from the A30; 6.5 km from Newquay. Bus from Truro, Newquay.

One of those big and initially confusing places where there is far more to get stuck into (and learn) than you think at first glance. Sit down and study the map before venturing too far! There's a strange mix of attractions here, but there is something of interest for every age group. Built onto a working dairy farm, there's a strong educational element that's not immediately apparent. You can get a bird's-eye view of the cows being milked every afternoon in a fantastic space-age orbiter (the first in Europe), and learn about how milk is produced from excellent wall panels. There's a recycling exhibition, an old Newquay exhibition, a very good Cornish heritage area with Victorian agricultural and household equipment, and solar-powered pumps and waterwheels in the Alternative Energy Centre.

All this plus endless outdoor play areas for all ages, huge indoor play barn (socks required, separate area for under fives), nature trails, assault course, animal petting, vintage tractors, pony rides and rheas, llamas and deer to visit by tractor and trailer, and a daily programme of activities.

Open 10am–5pm end Mar–end Oct. **Admission** £7.95 adult, £6.95 child (3–15), under 3 free, £5.50 OAP, £28 family. **Credit** MC, V. **Amenities** café, disabled access, parking, picnic area, shop, no dogs.

INSIDER TIP ›

And now for something completely different... **The Tortoise Garden** (📞 01726 65670; www.thetortoisegarden.co.uk) at Lower Sticker, a few kilometres southwest of St Austell, is an absolute must! Many children will never have seen a tortoise yet there are over 400 of them at this rescue and conservation centre, ranging in size from a 50p piece to a massive 38 kg (and still growing!). This is the largest collection of tortoises in the country – at the time of writing 107 inmates (including boarders). Entry is by donation – be sure to look out for the tortoise finger puppets!

Gardens

Trebah ★ ★ ★ FIND ALL AGES

Mawnan Smith, Falmouth, Cornwall TR11 5JZ; 📞 *01326 252200;* www.trebah-garden.co.uk. *From the A39 Falmouth follow brown tourist signs. Bus from Falmouth, Helston. Ferry from Helford village.*

The balmy climate of the Helford River creates the ideal environment for several wonderful gardens (some by ferry, p. 176). Trebah, a uniquely beautiful 26-acre Cornish ravine garden descending 60 m to a private beach, is particularly special – and particularly family friendly. Find the Koi pool at the top of the ravine and follow the stream as it cascades downhill via ponds and falls. There's something new

Castles on the Fal Estuary

Two magnificent castles watch over the Carrick Roads, both in the care of English Heritage and both well worth a family visit. **Pendennis** and **St Mawes** castles were built as part of Henry VIII's south coast defence system, which also incorporated St Catherine's Castle at Fowey (p. 131), an artillery fort built in 1510. Pendennis Castle (📞 *01326 316594*) was strengthened again prior to the Civil War and holds a commanding position at the mouth of the Fal estuary. Apart from the magnificent views there's a new interactive exhibition in the restored Royal Artillery Barracks, children's activity sheets, special children's workshops and events throughout the summer holidays: pirate week, jousting, 'medieval mayhem'! St Mawes (📞 *01326 270526*), a smaller, clover-leaf-shaped fort, is the most beautiful of Henry's fortresses. Here a free audio tour brings the history of the castle to life. www.english-heritage.org.uk/events

round every corner: tiny paths twist and turn through stands of exotic plants – children especially enjoy the Gunnera Passage, where 'giant rhubarb' towers above the path – and 'Bamboozle' (the bamboo maze). Have an ice cream or picnic on the beach before wandering back up to find Tarzan's Camp (adventure playground) and Fort Stuart (safe play area for the under fives). There are several special trails for children – Mr Frog's Hop-a-Long trail, for example – aimed at different age groups, which change regularly during holiday times. Special children's workshops are also held: mask making, outdoor theatre, a fairy day with storyteller. Delicious local food is served in Planter's Café, which appears to rise almost organically out of the exotic flowering trees and shrubs.

Open *10.30am–5pm (last entry, closes at 6.30pm) 1 Apr–end Oct (phone for out of season opening times).* *Admission* *£5.80 adult, £2 child 5–15, under 5 free, £5.30 OAP (reduced in winter).* *Credit* *AmEx, MC, V.* *Amenities* *café, disabled access possible – motorised buggies available, parking, picnic area, shop.*

The Lost Gardens of Heligan ★ ALL AGES

Pentewan, St Austell, Cornwall PL26 6EN; ☎ *01726 845100; www.heligan. com. Signed off the B3273 St Austell–Mevagissey. Bus from Eden Project, St Austell, Newquay. Bike via loop off Pentewan Valley cycle route.*

Heligan is big. There are 200 acres of garden, pasture and woodland to explore! Take it

Dovecote at Heligan Gardens

gently: allow several hours, and don't rush: it's a longish walk (with steep descents and ascents) to the furthest parts, the luxuriant Jungle (accessed via boardwalks – not suitable for buggies) and the Lost Valley. Don't miss the Giant's Head and the Mud Maid, natural sculptures by the Woodland Walk en route for the Jungle. There is no play equipment or children's trails – this is a working garden – but it's a wonderful place, and the story behind its discovery in 1990 after 75 years of neglect is fascinating. Those feeling less energetic can stick to the level Northern Gardens with the Melon Yard and pineapple pit, walled vegetable garden and Ravine, a giant rockery. There are guided Wild Walks in the Lost Wood, where you can sample edible plants and identify butterflies. And don't miss Lobbs wonderful farm shop.

Open *10am–6pm Mar–Oct, 10am–5pm Nov–Feb daily.* *Admission*

The Giant's Head is based on a huge tree root. Monbretia growing on top of his head provides his hair, and his eyes and nose are made out of chips of china and glass found on the old bottle dump at Heligan.

£8.50 adult, £5 child 5–16, under 5 free, £7.50 OAP, £23.50 family. **Credit** *MC, V.* **Amenities** *café, tea-room, disabled access (35 acres), parking, picnic area, shop.*

Best Beaches

Castle Beach, Falmouth Rocky, sandy beach, great rock pools.

Chapel Porth Small sandy cove, wide beach at low tide; surfing. Kiosk, car park.

Crantock Beach Pleasant sandy beach, extensive dunes. Nearby car park. No swimming near Gannel river.

Crinnis, Caerleon Bay Large beach, car park, good for flying kites. Naturist beach at far end.

Fistral Beach, Newquay Huge sandy beach, one of best surfing beaches in UK. Café, car park.

Gorran Haven Popular small sandy beach in village, car park, shop.

Gyllyngvase, Falmouth Main town beach; soft sand, very busy in summer. Café, car park.

Holywell Bay Huge sandy beach, extensive sand dunes. Surfing. Café, car park.

Little & Great Molunan, St Anthony Head Very sheltered sandy beaches; worth the walk from the car park.

Surfing

Put very simply, the south coast of Mid Cornwall is for messing about in boats, the north coast is for surfing: Newquay's beaches are acknowledged as some of the best in the world. Contact the following for details of lessons; remember to check the lower age limit.

Blue Wings Surf School, Newquay; ☎ *01637 874445; www.blue wingssurfschool.co.uk*

Extreme Academy, Watergate Bay, ☎ *01637 860543*

Lusty Glaze Adventure Centre, Newquay; ☎ *01637 872444/878718; www.adventure-centre.org*

Piran Surf, Perranporth; ☎ *01872 573242*

Reef Surf School, Newquay; ☎ *01637 879058; www.reefsurfschool.com*

The Winter Brothers Surf School, Newquay; ☎ *01637 879696; www. winterbrothers.com*

Perranporth

Maenporth, Falmouth
Sheltered beach, flat, sandy, low cliffs, rock pools. Great for families. Café, car park.

Par Sands
Wide sandy beach popular with families. Café, car park.

Pendower/Carne
1.6 km long sandy beach; dunes; safe for children. Café, car park.

Pentewan
Large sandy beach; busy (holiday park). Café, car park.

Perranporth
3.2 km long sandy beach and dunes. Surfing. Café, car park.

Porthbeor, Bohortha
Very secluded, steep descent, long sandy beach and rock pools.

Porthcurnick, Portscatho
Wide sandy beach, rock pools. Kiosk in summer. Nearby parking.

Porth, Newquay
Wide sandy beach. Café, car park.

Porth Joke
Narrow sandy cove, caves, rock pools. Surfing. Car park.

Porthluney Cove, Caerhayes
Quiet family beach, rock pools, car park, kiosk.

Porthpean, St Austell
Small sheltered family beach, rock pools, dinghies. Parking, shop, toilets.

Porthtowan
Spacious sandy beach, good for families. Rock pools and seawater pool at low tide. Surfing. Café, car park.

Swanpool, Falmouth
Small safe sandy beach, perfect for families. Café, car park.

Towan, Portscatho
Long sandy beach, rock pools at low tide. Car park.

Trevaunance Cove, St Agnes
Sandy cove. Surfing. Café, car park.

Vault Beach, nr Gorran
Long climb down from NT car park, quiet, worth it!

Watergate Bay, Newquay
3.2 km long sandy beach, good for families. Surfing. Very busy in summer. Café, car park.

For Active Families

Portreath Tramroad
AGES 5 AND OVER

A fascinating cycle ride just bursting with industrial and natural history, along the route of Cornwall's first tramway (constructed to link Portreath to Poldice Mine in 1809). It's flexible too: younger children may only get a little way along the early off-road section before turning round – older and more competent ones can continue on to cross above the A30 and cycle the Wheal Busy Loop, in the heart of the mid-19th-century tin and copper mining area. The whole route runs for 22.5 km across the county to Devoran, but a there-and-back option is more adaptable for the needs of different family members. Most of the route to the A30 is off road and reasonably gentle, with a short section on pavement in the middle. The start and finish of the Wheal Busy Loop (an optional extension) involves cycling along the pavements of some fairly busy roads near the A30, and is harder than the main tramroad – more like a novice mountain bike route.

But it's packed with interest, passing Killifreth Mine's Hawke's Shaft pumping house (the tallest chimney in Cornwall) and descending through Unity Wood, where opencast mining was carried out in medieval times.

Pentewan to A30 8 km each way; optional 5.6 km extension. **Cycle hire** *Elm Farm;* ☎ *01209 891498; www. elm-farm.co.uk; Bissoe Tramways Cycle Hire;* ☎ *01872 870341; www. cornwallcyclehire.com*

Pentewan Valley Cycle Route
AGES 5 AND OVER

This gentle route starts by the cycle hire shop in Pentewan and is a good starter route for families with young children: all off road and very easy. It's not desperately exciting but is straightforward, following the line of the old Pentewan railway (closed in 1918) along the banks of the St Austell river. Once you reach Tregorrick at the edge of St Austell you can cycle a small loop (on road) then

---

FUN FACT » **Tree Climbing** «

Something most children really enjoy is climbing trees, yet in these health-and-safety conscious days it's an activity that many children never get the chance to experience. **The Mighty Oak Tree Company** at Nanswhyden near Newquay provides the complete (and safe) tree-climbing experience for all members of the family, with the aid of harnesses and ropes ☎ *07890 698651; www.mighty-oak.co.uk*

return to Pentewan. There is a loop off the valley route to **Heligan** (p. 130), but it involves a steep climb through woodland, then a short section on a busy road and a long, steep lane on the return (not recommended for youngsters). Those with older children who are capable of going further (and are safe on roads) have the choice of a number of longer routes: to **Mevagissey**, historic **Charlestown** (p. 175) or all the way to the **Eden Project** (p. 131), where those arriving by bike enjoy cheaper entry.

Pentewan to St Austell 5.6 km each way. **Cycle hire** *Pentewan Valley Cycle Hire;* ☎ *01726 844242; www. pentewanvalleycyclehire.co.uk.*

INSIDER TIP ⟫

The creeks and estuaries of Mid Cornwall's south coast are very much the preserve of the sailor. Learn to sail there perfectly safely if you have an approved instructor, but you may prefer to give the family a bit of practice on an inland water before committing them to the 'high seas'. The **SW Lakes Trust Watersports Centre** at Stithians Lake, near Redruth (☎ *01209 860301; www.swlakes trust.org.uk*) runs courses in sailing, windsurfing, canoeing, kayaking and rowing.

FAMILY-FRIENDLY ACCOMMODATION

INEXPENSIVE

Beacon Cottage Farm Holidays ★★

Beacon Drive, St Agnes, Cornwall TR5 0NU; ☎ *01872 552347/553381;* *www.beaconcottagefarmholidays. co.uk. Take the B3277 from the A30 Chiverton roundabout to St Agnes, then signs for Chapel Porth, then for the farm.*

Legend has it that the Cornish Giant Bolster could stand with one foot on Carn Brea, a highpoint above Redruth, and with the other on St Agnes Beacon! He chose well: Beacon Cottage Farm has an enviable position on the slopes of The Beacon (worth climbing for views), a few minutes' walk from a magnificent stretch of coastline. The lovely sandy beach at Chapel Porth is only a 20-minute walk across open moorland. All in all this quiet, out-of-the-way spot (a 400 acre working farm which has been welcoming guests since 1927) has everything required for a good family camping holiday: three grassy camping fields, two with superb views over the coast, the other (more sheltered) tucked behind the farm; outdoor playground; small shop supplying essential items; family shower room; and St Agnes (part of the Cornwall Mining World Heritage Site) within easy reach. The two self-catering cottages (one an old carriage house) both have private gardens.

60 pitches (some with electric hookups). **Rates** *£14 (low)–£20 (high) 2 adults; £3 child 2–11; under 2 free. 2 s/c cottages 2–4 people (one with disabled access).* **Rates** *£275–730.* **Credit** *MC, V.* **Amenities** *DIY laundry, family shower room, shop, parking, children's playing field, dog exercise field.*

Pennance Mill Farm Chalet & Camping Park ★★

Maenporth, Falmouth, Cornwall TR11 5HJ; ☏ 01326 317431; www.pennance mill.co.uk. From the A39 outside Falmouth turn right at Hillhead roundabout; follow brown camping signs, then the Maenporth beach road. Bus from Falmouth.

Situated in a quiet valley between lovely safe sandy beaches at Swanpool and Maenporth, Pennance Mill Farm is ideally placed for those families wanting to benefit from the nearby facilities afforded by a big town – Falmouth – while staying in a wonderfully quiet location. It's a very attractive spot: the first thing you notice is the huge waterwheel near the farmhouse, and the children's play meadow. Three south-facing meadows are available for campers, and the on-site farm shop is open twice daily. In high season weekly skittles and games nights are held in the barn, and a bus service runs into Falmouth. You can watch the cows being milked – the farm has a herd of 60 dairy cows. Maenporth beach is about 1 km away, with opportunities for scuba diving and windsurfing. The four wooden chalets on site have enclosed gardens and parking space.

*70 pitches, some with electric hook-ups. **Rates** £4.50 (low)–£5.50 (high) per adult; £1.50–2 child 4–16, under 3 free. 4 s/c chalets, 2–7 people. **Rates** £195 (low)–480 (high). **Amenities** DIY laundry, farm shop, parking, children's play meadow, dogs accepted, woodland walk.*

MODERATE

St Anthony in Roseland Cottages ★★★ FIND

Portscatho, Truro, Cornwall TR2 5EZ; ☏ 01295 680265; www.roseland cottages.co.uk. South of Portscatho on the Roseland Peninsula; reached via the A3078 from the A390 St Austell–Truro, or via the King Harry ferry off the A39 north of Falmouth.

The Roseland Peninsula is my favourite part of mid-south Cornwall. It's out of the way, tranquil, with beautiful sandy beaches – and no beach cafés! If you're looking for a traditional bucket-and-spade holiday in one of southern Cornwall's most beautiful spots – and don't mind driving a few kilometres to Portscatho for supplies (or taking the ferry to Falmouth or St Mawes to go shopping) – a cottage on the Place Estate would be perfect. Place House – the estate has been in the same family for 400 years – was built in 1840 on the site of an Elizabethan house: estate buildings now provide excellent holiday accommodation, some with enclosed private gardens. One was the former potting shed; Place Lodge was home to the coachman in the 19th century; the oldest is 300-year-old Cellars, which has an indoor children's play area and direct access to the beach. Moorings can be arranged, dinghies parked by the slipway (great for crabbing), and boats hired locally. A number of quiet sandy beaches lie within ½ km, ideal for safe swimming, rock pooling and messing about in boats.

5 s/c cottages, 2–9 people. **Rates** *£155–1605.* **Amenities** *cot (free), extra bed (charge), showers/ baths, TV/DVD, dogs welcome.*

Bosinver Holiday Cottages ★ ★ ★ FIND

Trelowth, St Austell, Cornwall PL26 7DT; ☎ 01726 72128; www.bosinver. co.uk. 1.6 km west of St Austell on the A390 to Truro; off the slip road to Trelowth/Sticker/Polgooth.

Perfect for families who don't want to drive miles down narrow country lanes to reach their accommodation. Close to the A390 – yet seemingly deep in the countryside – Bosinver has that special 'something'. Nineteen individual cottages surround the 16th-century farmhouse; there's a safe, cosy 'village' atmosphere. All have gardens and sitting-out areas, flowering trees and shrubs. There's excellent outdoor play equipment, a games room for teenagers, solar-heated swimming pool and (new for 2007) a huge play barn, the walls decorated with children's drawings from the visitor's book. A huge amount of attention has been paid to detail here in all areas (a welcome cake in your cottage on arrival). For children the highlight is making friends with others at the daily pets' corner, where ducks, chickens and Chalky the goat are fed, and eggs taken home for breakfast. Then there's the trip to bring Secret the pony in from the field (and pony rides on some days). Add to all that meadows and woodland to play in, a lake for fishing, and

Bosinver Cottage

great beaches just down the road, and it's not surprising that families come back year after year.

19 s/c cottages, 3–12 people. **Rates** *£275 (low)–£2200 (high).* **Credit** *MC, V.* **Amenities** *babysitting (contacts), cot, booster seat, bed guard (free), disabled access, extra bed (some properties), DIY laundry, parking, outdoor pool, sauna, meals available, games room and play barn, outdoor play area, fishing, lake, woodland walks, farm animals.*

Pollaughan Cottages ★ ★ ★ GREEN

Portscatho, Truro, Cornwall TR2 5EH; ☎ 01872 580150; www.pollaughan. co.uk. Follow the A3078 from Tregony–St Mawes, then signs for Portscatho.

You just have to look in the visitors' books to understand why Pollaughan Cottages (recipient of the first Gold GTBS award in Cornwall) has received so many accolades – 'a recipe for a perfect family holiday'!

Pollaughan is a peaceful, tranquil place where the owners' aim is simple: to provide everything families need to make their holiday as stress-free and enjoyable as possible, right down to the provision of Aga-cooked meals, ordered from the farm and delivered to your door – even breakfast! Five beautifully appointed cottages are available, each with an enclosed garden (small trampoline, trike and paddling pool if required); the family-size cottages have level, grassy, family-size gardens. All baby equipment is on hand: cots, highchairs, ride-on toys, three-wheeler pushchairs. There are lambs, chickens, pigmy goats and ducks to feed every morning, eggs to collect, a full-size trampoline and all-weather tennis court to enjoy. There are two wildlife lakes, a vegetable patch where visitors can help themselves... and wonderful safe sandy beaches a stone's throw away.

5 s/c cottages, 2–6 people. **Rates** *£300 (low)–£1320 (high).* **Credit** *MC, V.* **Amenities** *babysitting contacts, cot (free), extra bed possible, disabled access possible 3 cottages, parking, Internet access, cooker/microwave, dishwasher, washing machine/tumble dryer, shower/bath, TV/DVD/video/ digital, Aga-cooked meals available to order, no dogs.*

Helford Passage Cove ★

Helford River Holidays, The Boathouse, Helford Passage, Falmouth, Cornwall TR11 5LB; ☎ *01326 250278; www.holiday cornwall.co.uk. Helford Passge is on the north side of the Helford river, south of Falmouth; signed from Mawnan Smith. Bus from Falmouth and Helston at top of hill. Ferry from Helford village.*

This has a lovely spot on the Helford River with a great variety of individual properties and apartments around the Ferry Boat Inn (p. 189) for families to rent. These range from budget-conscious apartments round the Courtyard next to the inn to a detached house with its own private terrace. Some have private gardens, some shared, and all have access to the lovely outdoor swimming pool. Small motor boats and sailing dinghies can be hired to explore the Helford River; Daphne du Maurier's Frenchman's Creek joins the river just above of Helford village. Helford River Holidays also has more luxurious self-catering properties at Maenporth Cove (Maenporth Estate) as well as individual properties around the Helford area.

13 s/c properties, 2–8 people. **Rates** *£125 (low)–1160 (high).* **Credit** *MC, V.* **Amenities** *vary according to property; see website for details, safe sandy beach, parking, outdoor swimming pool.*

EXPENSIVE

Bedruthan Steps Hotel ★★★

Mawgan Porth, Cornwall TR8 4BU; ☎ *01637 860555; www.bedruthan. com. On B3276 just north of Mawgan Porth. Bus from Newquay, Padstow.*

A genuinely family-friendly luxury hotel where the needs of children of every age are of the utmost importance – and where parents can really relax and be as involved as they want, while knowing that offspring will be well looked after at certain times of the day. It's in a fantastic cliff-top position with a big terraced garden (lots of slopes and steps) plus wonderful sheltered swimming pools, tennis court, a range of outdoor play equipment, and room to kick a ball around. Family accommodation is flexible – rooms, apartments, villas. Breakfast and lunch are family times; later in the day there are children's teas, and a supper club, depending on age; older children can eat in the very plush dining room with parents. Entertainment is laid on for younger children during the early evenings; there's a great indoor play area, a teenagers' room, and a quiet adults' only lounge. Everything is in place for the perfect hotel family holiday.

Rooms 100 (most family suites; apartment suites up to 6 depending on age). *Rates* £80 (low)–124 (high) pppn dinner/B&B; children's rates dependent on age; villas/apartments plus £40/44 per room per day. *Credit* MC, V. *Amenities* babysitting, bar, children's club, cot (free), extra bed (charge), gym, laundry service, parking, pool (indoor & 3 outdoor), restaurant, spa, in room Internet access, shower/bath, TV.

FAMILY-FRIENDLY DINING

INSIDER TIP >>

Treat the family to breakfast at Jamie Oliver's **Fifteen Cornwall** restaurant (📞 *01637 861000; www.fifteencornwall.co.uk*)

overlooking the wonderful 3.2 km of sandy beach at Watergate Bay. Children are welcome for lunch (12.00-5.00pm) and breakfast (8.30–10.30am, last orders 10am) and it's not too pricey. Choose from pancakes, granola, smoked salmon or the Fifteen Fry-up, and do your bit in helping disadvantaged young people from Cornwall to get a foot on the career ladder.

INEXPENSIVE

Melinsey Mill ★★

Veryan, nr Truro, Cornwall TR2 5QQ; 📞 *01872 501049. Signed off A3078 Tregony–St Mawes.*

There's an almost magical atmosphere at this little 16th-century watermill – one of the smallest in Cornwall – nestling in a wooded valley near Veryan, accessed by steep narrow lanes. You can sit by the tranquil millpond listening to the prolific birdsong, or inside the crooked mill building, and enjoy delicious 'doorstep' sandwiches, homemade soup, ploughman's, homemade cakes and fruit pies. Daily specials (around £6.50) might be smoked trout and salad, or homemade pie. A little walkway leads along the millstream and across boardwalks, with fun things to look out for: teapots hanging in the branches, a big willow-work spider dangling from the trees, a couple of lovely wood and willow shelters to sit inside. A footpath leads from the mill along the Secret Valley to Pendower beach.

FUN FACT » Fish & Chips «

It may sound a little strange, but it's possible to have award-winning fish and chips slap bang in the middle of Cornwall! The **Port and Starboard Café/ Fish & Chip Shop** at Indian Queens (☏ *01726 860270*) has been supplying the needs of locals and visitors alike for over 50 years and has a deserved reputation for serving up locally sourced and delicious meals. Fun for the whole family.

Open *10am–5.30pm Apr–end Oct daily; closed Mon Apr, May, Oct.* *Main course* *£4–6.80.* *Credit* *MC, V.* *Amenities* *highchair, disabled access (downstairs only), parking, millpond and 'magic' walk.*

INSIDER TIP »

For those with an interest in ancient buildings the mill has been restored to working order, and you can go into the working part of the building to see the 1882 iron over-shot wheel, which replaced the previous wooden one. At one time there were around 700 mills in Cornwall – sadly there are only half a dozen left.

MODERATE

Blue Bar ★★

Beach Road, Porthtowan, Cornwall TR4 8AD; ☏ 01209 890329; www. blue-bar.co.uk. Right on the beach in Porthtowan, between St Agnes and Portreath. Bus from Newquay, Truro, Redruth, Camborne, St Ives.

Porthtowan isn't one of Cornwall's prettiest coastal settlements, but it has a great beach and is fast becoming a surfing hotspot. By the beach (rock pools and saltwater pool at low tide) you'll find all the usual clothes shops, surf hire, snack and beach shops alongside the excellent Blue Bar. A spacious one-storey building in a great position – with outside seating overlooking the beach (and a cash machine) – it's a good place for teenagers: the main room has a pool table, there's live music at weekends, and summer BBQs. The quieter Board Room (think surfing) has more of a relaxed restaurant feel; children are allowed everywhere. The children's menu (£3.75–5) offers homemade fishcakes, pasta and bean burgers; there are pizzas, baps, mezze platter (£9), tortillas (£5.75), chargrilled sardines (£8) and daily fish specials. At weekends brunch is served from 10am–12pm.

Open *11am–11pm Mon–Fri, 10am– 12pm weekends, all year; shut for 5 weeks from 1st Jan.* *Main course* *£7.50–12.50.* *Credit* *MC, V.* *Amenities* *children's menu/half portions, highchair, disabled access, reservations accepted in Board Room, beach car park, on beach.*

The Ferry Boat Inn ★★

Helford Passage, Falmouth, Cornwall TR11 5LB; ☏ 01326 250625. Helford Passage is on the north side of the Helford river, south of Falmouth; signed from Mawnan Smith. Bus from Falmouth and Helston at top of hill.

There's been a ferry crossing the Helford river from Helford Passage since medieval times, and on a sunny afternoon it's wonderfully relaxing to sit outside the

0 Mid Cornwall

In 1855 a Miss Fox (possibly from Glendurgan) paid for a wooden ferry shelter on the south side of the river where passengers could sit and wait for the boatman to finish drinking in the Shipwright's Arms in Helford!

Ferry Boat Inn and watch all the comings and goings. The little beach provides a safe playing place for children; a little kiosk provides ice creams and boat hire; you can take a ride across the water to pretty Helford village. The pub provides a good range of freshly prepared food (it gets very busy at holiday times – with summer BBQs for big parties), with daily fish specials (fish comes off the beach). Children can enjoy fresh local cod, lasagne, sausages and mash (£5.25–6.95); the adult menu includes ham, egg and chips (£6.95) and bean, chickpea and vegetable pot (£8.95). Note: children must be accompanied at all times inside the inn, and shoes must be worn.

Open 11am–11pm Mon–Sat, 12pm–10.30pm Sun all year round. **Main course** *£6.95–14.50.* **Credit** *MC, V.* **Amenities** *children's menu/half portions available, highchair, disabled access possible, reservations accepted for large groups, short steep walk downhill from village car park, on riverside beach.*

The Wheelhouse Restaurant ★★

West Quay, Mevagissey, Cornwall PL26 6UJ; ☎ 01726 843404; www.wheelhouse.me.uk. On the harbourside in Mevagissey; parking on the edge of the village.

This is a fun family restaurant with a well-deserved reputation

for fish dishes on the quayside in Mevagissey, still a working fishing port with a bustling harbour. The first pier here dated from the 15th century. Today fishing boats can still be seen in the harbour, though the village has lost some of its intrinsically Cornish charm under the weight of the tourist trade. The Wheelhouse has been run by the same family for 40 years, and has a decidedly nautical feel: life-size models of Captain Cook and pirates Lawrence and Jeremy adorn the interior! A good range of food is served all day, from all-day breakfasts from 9am to dinner in the restaurant which specialises in local fish (no under fives in the evening). There's a dedicated family room, the Gun Deck, accessible to both buggies and wheelchairs. Children can have half portions of many dishes. The Wheelhouse's sister restaurant next door, **Quay West**, caters more for the fish 'n' chip brigade.

Open 9am–4.30pm, 6pm–late. **Main course** *£9.95–16.95 (dinner).* **Credit** *MC, V.* **Amenities** *children's portions available (min £4.50), highchair, disabled access (toilets available next door), reservations accepted.*

If you're in Mevagissey on a wet afternoon wondering what to do, take a look round the **World of Model Railways** in an old mackerel-processing factory on

Try These Too!

- **Trevornick Holiday Park** One of the loveliest beaches on this stretch of the coast, with huge sand dunes, offshore stacks and surfing. Holywell Bay, nr Newquay, Cornwall TR8 5PW; ☎ *01637 830531; www.trevornick.co.uk*
- **Gwel an Mor** Scandinavian style lodges with feel of an exclusive club where children can feed animals on nearby farm. Tregea Hill, Portreath, Cornwall TR16 4PE; ☎ *01209 842354; www.gwelanmor.com*.
- **Kingswood Restaurant** The kind of place you can go to straight off the beach with an old-fashioned feel and Early Bird Special. London Apprentice, St Austell, Cornwall PL25 7AP; ☎ *01726 63780; www.eatoutincornwall.co.uk*.

Meadow Street (signed from the car parks – ☎ *01726 842457; www.model-railway.co.uk*). It's a treasure trove for both the model railway enthusiast and the unconverted! Small children can press a button and start Thomas the Tank Engine on his way; there's a wonderful model fairground (also with buttons to push) and a huge layout in 00 scale, complete with a drive-in cinema featuring *The Railway Children*.

Trevornick Camping

EXPENSIVE

The Three Mackerel ★★★

Restaurant Bar, Swanpool Beach, Falmouth, Cornwall TR11 5BG; ☎ 01326 311886; www.thethree mackerel.com. Follow brown tourist signs from Falmouth. Bus from Falmouth.

This single-storey white-painted restaurant enjoys a fabulous position above Swanpool beach on the edge of Falmouth. It has a really contemporary feel, and an extensive area of wooden decking where you can sit and drink in the views towards Pendennis Castle and St Anthony Head. Being a little out of town Swanpool beach tends to be less busy than Gyllyngvase, but is still a safe, gritty sandy beach, with beach café, watersports, crazy golf and nature reserve. Although The Three Mackerel has an excellent dinner menu it's a fun place to go for lunch or a 'smart' snack during the day: the all-day tapas menu is very popular (£2.95–5.95) and nibbling olives while sipping a cool white wine in a

Gwel an Mor Lodges

spot like this is hard to beat! Children are well catered for too: battered catch of the day, grilled mackerel fillets, fettuccini, sausage and mash (£4.95). Tubs of Roskilly's ice cream (p. 213) and free colouring books help to ensure that children (and parents) will have a good time.

Open *10am–11pm daily end May–Sept; phone for out of season opening.* **Main course** *£6.95–11.95 lunch, £11.95–17.95 dinner.* **Credit** *AmEx, MC, V.* **Amenities** *children's menu, highchair, disabled access,* *reservations accepted, few parking spaces + beach car park.*

INSIDER TIP

Swanpool Beach Watersports (☎ *01637 877701; www.element aluk.com*) provide all kinds of fun things to do in or on the water: sailing, kayaking, windsurfing, canoeing and raft building. The Eels (5–9 years), Dolphins (9–13 years) and Sharks (13+) are out and about at weekends in term time and every day in school holidays; there are special sessions for mums and dads too.

Keeping It Local – Farmers' Markets & Farm Shops

Falmouth Farmers' Market, On the Moor, every Tues
Lobbs Farm Shop, Heligan, St Ewe, St Austell; ☎ 01726 844411
Longclose Barn Farm Shop, Tregew Farm, Flushing; ☎ 01326 373706
On the Table Farm Shop, Goonhavern Garden Centre, Truro; ☎ 01872 571400
Redruth Farmers' Market, Market Way, 2nd and 4th Fri
St Austell Local Produce Market, Cornerstone Cafe, Trinity Street, every other Fri
Trevilley Farm Shop, Newquay; ☎ 01637 872310
Truro Farmers' Market, Lemon Quay, every Sat and Wed

11 Southwest Cornwall

SOUTHWEST CORNWALL

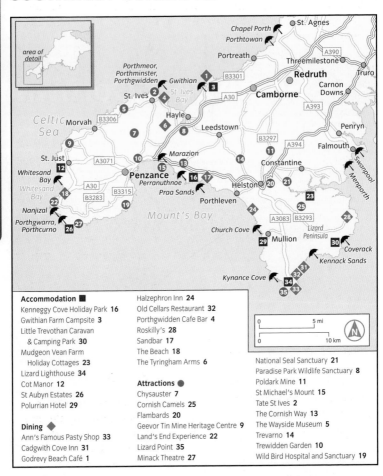

By the time you reach Cornwall's furthest-flung extremities – Land's End and the Lizard Peninsula – you've entered a different, less comfortable world. West Penwith district is where a real feeling of Cornish independence, borne of physical remoteness from London, becomes very striking. If you want a taste of how tough life has been here follow the narrow, twisting road along the west coast, from St Ives south through St Just and onto Land's End. This tortuous road wends its way through a strip of hedge-banked fields and small farms that sit between the rugged coast and granite moorland, where mega-lithic burial sites and Bronze Age stone circles abound. The solid for-mer mining settlements of West Penwith – Pendeen and St Just – are flanked by the atmospheric remains of old mines, some, such as Geevor (p. 203), now visitor attractions. Much of the area is an AONB, and has long attracted artists and craftspeople, inspired by the extraordinary quality of the light. The huge and intrusive visitor attraction on Land's End gives no clue as to what lies beneath the surface of this uniquely beautiful part of the county.

The **Lizard Peninsula** (AONB) – culminating in the British mainland's most southerly point – is a strangely flat, open place. Driving south from Helston to The Lizard you'd be forgiven for thinking you were passing through a wasteland – especially when you see the space-age structures at Goonhilly Satellite Earth Station. But nothing could be further from the truth: much of this area is the Lizard National Nature Reserve (SSSI), renowned for its flora and fauna. The ancient serpentine rocks date back around 400 million years, and the serpentine soils and maritime climate have combined to support the beautiful and rare Cornish heath, which flowers in late summer and is unknown elsewhere in the UK. And all around the coast can be found delightful fishing villages, wonderful rocky coves, and magical beaches such as at Kynance, one of the most beautiful in the country.

VISITOR INFORMATION

For more information on the area visit *www.visit-westcornwall.com* and *www.go-cornwall.com*. Two specific websites – *www.landsendarea.co.uk* and *www.thelizard.co.uk* – examine southwest Cornwall in greater depth. In the summer the free paper **Lizard & Meneague** (available almost everywhere) is packed with information on the Lizard, Helford River, Helston and Porthleven areas. The most detailed maps are OS Explorers 102 Land's End and 103 The Lizard.

Information Centres

Hayle Library, Commercial Road; ☎ *01736 754399*

St Just Library, Market Square; ☎ *01736 788165*

St Ives, The Guildhall; ☎ *01736 796297*

Penzance, Station Road; ☎ *01736 362207*

Orientation

The part of Cornwall covered by this chapter is roughly the area covered by the Penwith district (excluding the Isles of Scilly). The A30 goes all the way to Penzance; from there the A30 leads to Land's End, and the A3071 to St Just. Roads off these tend to be narrow and in places single track (especially west of Penzance: Mousehole, Lamorna, Porthcurno and so on). If you want to explore the Penwith Moors consult the OS map (many of the junctions are unsigned and it is easy to get lost). The Lizard Peninsula lies south of the A394 Falmouth–Helston road; the A3083 leads from Helston to the UK's most southerly point.

Getting Around

Bus timetables are available from Penzance bus station (next to the railway station). From Easter to late October there's a circular bus service – the Penwith Explorer – around the Land's End peninsula, usually a double-decker and open-topped: a great way to see the coast of West Penwith, and to visit Penzance, Land's End and St Ives. There are also special scenic bus routes round the Lizard – the Lizard Rambler –and from Falmouth to Helston (*01872 273453; www.truronian.com*). The main railway line runs through the middle of the area from Truro through Redruth and Camborne to terminate at Penzance; the St Ives Bay branch line runs from Penzance to St Ives, neatly removing the problem of trying to park in St Ives. For more information go to local TICs or *Traveline 0871 200 2233; www. traveline.org.uk*.

Child-Friendly Events & Entertainment

Golowan Festival & Mazey Day

A wonderful revival of an ancient festival, to celebrate the arrival of midsummer. Penzance buzzes during a 10-day period through this huge and colourful celebration of music and the performing arts. Fantastic

costumes, wonderful processions – and a real pagan feel.

*End June, all over Penzance; * 01736 362207; www.golowan.org.*

Helston Flora Day

The little town of Helston (p. 197) comes alive in May when townspeople don their finery and dance through the streets from 7am until 5pm in celebration of the arrival of spring. The town is decked out with flags and flowers, and there's the famous mummers' play, Hal-an-Tow.

8th May (unless Sun/Mon, when held preceding Sat); www.helstonflora day.org.uk.

Newlyn Fish Festival

Newlyn lands more fish than any other port in England and Wales; this festival celebrates the town's fishing and seagoing heritage which has been a vital part of Cornish life since time immemorial. The harbour is filled with all kinds of boats, many open to visitors; all manner of fish are on display; and there are stalls and street entertainment.

*Aug Bank Hol Mon; * 01736 362207; www.newlynfishfestival.org.uk.*

WHAT TO SEE & DO

Children's Top 10 Attractions

❶ **Eating** delicious Cornish ice cream at Roskilly's. See p. 213.

❷ **Staying in** a real lighthouse at Cornwall's most southerly point! See p. 211.

❸ Being photographed on the back of a camel at Cornish Camels. See p. 204.

❹ Laughing at mum and dad as they try to stay upright on a surfboard. See p. 215.

❺ Panning for real diamonds at Poldark Mine. See p. 201.

❻ Feeding a rainbow parakeet while it sits on your head! See p. 205.

❼ Building sandcastles on Porthgwidden's sandy beach. See p. 208.

❽ Exploring the maze of paths at Trevarno gardens. See p. 206.

❾ Camping near Prussia Cove, where notorious smugglers used to land their booty. See p. 210.

❿ Bobbing over the waves in a fishing boat to St Michael's Mount. See p. 200.

Towns & Villages

Helston ★

This ancient stannary (tin mine) town has a gentle feel. Best known today for its annual Flora Day festival (see previous page) on 8th May – and its proximity to RNAS (Royal Naval Air Station) Culdrose – it has some fine buildings and an interesting Town Trail. The TIC has gone, but the **Folk Museum** in the Market Place (☏ *01326 564027; www. kerrier.gov.uk*) is the place to go for information. You can take in the 25-metre pool at the sports centre (☏ *01326 563320*) or see a film at the **Flora** (☏ *01326 569977;*

www.merlincinemas.co.uk). Buy a pasty from the bakery and eat it in the beer garden of **The Bell Inn** in Meneague Street – 'We've got the pub, you bring the grub' – or go to the thatched 15th-century **Blue Anchor Inn** (☏ *01326 562821; www.spingoales.com*) in Coinagehall Street, home to Spingo ales, the oldest brewery in the county. At the bottom of town is **Coronation Park,** where the old cattle market is being extensively redeveloped: boating lake, a new café, all-weather events space, skate park and excellent playground. A good place for picnics and feeding the ducks.

Marazion ★

Cornwall's oldest charter town, dating from 1257, was the main trading port in Mount's Bay until Penzance took over in the 16th century. It's well worth a visit, with stunning views to St Michael's Mount (p. 200), a fantastic beach, a good playground by the beach car park, and **Marazion Marsh** RSPB nature reserve (☏ *01736 711682; www. rspb.org.uk*), the largest reedbed in Cornwall. Good eats may be found at **The Godolphin Arms** (☏ *01736 710202; www.godolphin arms.co.uk*) which has a large terrace overlooking the causeway. And if you want to picnic on the huge sandy beach, **Philps** wonderful bakery (☏ *01736 710332*) in Market Place sells excellent pasties and takeaway cream teas. Philps bakeries can also be found in Hayle and Praze an Beeble.

Marazion

Penzance

Penzance, an important pilchard fishing centre in medieval times, is the main centre for Penwith. The town (along with Newlyn and Mousehole) was destroyed by Spanish raiders in 1595, but by the early 17th century fortunes had revived on account of the export of tin, and it became a fashionable place. Follow the Town Trail (from the information centre), and visit **Penlee House Gallery and Museum** in Morrab Road, which runs children's workshops in school holidays, and the Orangery café and shop (✆ *01736 363625; www. penleehouse.org.uk*); take in a movie at the Savoy cinema (✆ *01736 363330; www.merlin cinemas.co.uk*), go swimming at the leisure centre (✆ *01736 874744*) or in the open-air **Jubilee Bathing Pool** on the Promenade (✆ *01736 369224*). The coming of the Great

Western Railway in Victorian times gave the town another boost; today a trip on the **St Ives Bay Line** makes a good day out. You can explore the coastline on a sea safari with **Marine Discovery** (✆ *01736 874907; www.marinediscovery.co.uk*), jump on a bike and cycle to **Marazion** (p. 197), wander around lovely **Trewidden Garden** just outside the town (✆ *01736 366800; www.trewiddengarden. co.uk*), and visit the little fishing village of Mousehole (pronounced 'Mowzei'), famed for 'stargazey pie' and the **Wild Bird Hospital and Sanctuary** (✆ *01736 731386; www.mouseholebird hospital.org.uk*). The harbour is full of interest: check out the **Trinity House National Lighthouse Centre** (✆ *01736 360077*) and watch the *RMV Scillonian* set off for the **Isles of Scilly** (p. 219).

Sennen Cove

This favourably positioned village, on the western end of Cornwall, is a place of two halves. If arriving by car, the first thing you see is the beach car park, the **Beach Café** (p. 214), surf hire and shops; but keep going past **The Old Success Inn** – with fabulous Whitesand Bay stretching away before you – and you'll find the real village. Old cottages and boatsheds cluster round the working harbour; there are bucket-and-spade shops, takeaway pasties and cream teas at **Myrtle's Cottage**. **Sennen Lifeboat Station** is open to visitors, and the work of local artists is on display and for sale at the **Round House and Capstan Gallery** (📞 *01736 871859; www.round-house.co. uk*). If you're feeling energetic follow the Coast Path to **Land's End**: it's only a kilometre or so, and heavily used, but the coastal scenery is fantastic. This gives you free access to the natural Land's End, and also sight of the artificial **Land's End Experience,** which is accessed via the A30 (📞 *0870 458 0044; www.lands end-landmark.co.uk*).

St Ives

This picturesque old fishing town was, from medieval times, an important pilchard-fishing port. Wander through the maze of narrow lanes and courtyards of 'Downlong' round the harbour and you'll get an inkling of life in the 18th and 19th centuries before the coming of the railway saw the start of the tourist invasion. St Ives gets very crowded, but with good reason: there are three excellent beaches; numerous places to eat, ranging from takeaways and traditional pubs to smart harbourside restaurants; a leisure centre (📞 *01726 797006*) and the **Royal cinema** (📞 *01726 796843; www.merlincinemas.co.uk*); trips to see the seals, self-drive motor

St Ives

Penzance and St Ives TICs both run a series of hour-long ghost walks on some summer evenings. Go exploring as light falls in the company of a real ghost hunter!

boats...as well as wonderful walks along the coast towards Clodgy Point. St Ives has long been famous for attracting artists. Ben Nicholson and his wife, the sculptor Barbara Hepworth, came here in 1939 and turned St Ives into one of the leading centres of British art. Those interested must not miss the magnificent **Tate St Ives** gallery, built in 1993 above Porthmeor Beach (good for a rainy day, with lots of activities for children – free entry), and the **Barbara Hepworth Museum and Sculpture Garden** on Barnoon Hill (📞 *01726 796226; www.tate.org.uk*).

Fun Days Out

St Michael's Mount ★★

AGES 5 AND UP

Marazion, nr Penzance, Cornwall TR17 0EF; 📞 *01736 710507, 01736 710265 (tide and ferry); www.st michaelsmount.co.uk. Accessed from Marazion on foot (low tide) or boat (high tide).*

Craggy St Michael's Mount, rising out of the waves of Mount's Bay, is an awe-inspiring sight. Although crossing over on the causeway is fun (a bit like walking through a giant rock pool) there's something really exciting about going by boat to this extraordinary rocky outcrop, crowned by a medieval church and a 'real' castle. It's not great

St Michael's Mount, Marazion

Poldark Mine, Trenear

for small children unless parents are prepared to carry them up the very steep, uneven, rocky steps to the castle. Wear decent shoes, and don't take the dog; dogs are not allowed in the castle or garden and there are no facilities for them in the village. There's a children's quiz in the castle, and an excellent one in the terraced gardens – lots of steep and narrow steps – on the east side; look out for Tommy the tortoise, Henry the hedgehog and Boris the bat. The St Aubyn family, who acquired the castle after the Civil War, still live here (now in the hands of the National Trust).

Open *10.30am–5.30pm Apr–end Oct (closed Sat). Gardens Mon–Fri May/June; Thurs/Fri Jul–Oct.* **Admission** *£6.40 adult, £3.20 child (under 16), under 5 free, £16 family, members free. Garden £3 adult, £1 child.* **Credit** *MC, V.* **Amenities** *café, picnic area, restaurant, shop.*

Poldark Mine ★ ALL AGES

Trenear, Wendron, Helston, Cornwall TR13 0ES; 📞 *01326 573173;* **www. poldark-mine.co.uk.** *Signed off the A3297 Helston–Redruth, 3.2 km from Helston.*

The Poldark Mine will keep all members of the family occupied – whether or not they're interested in the history of the Cornish tin-mining industry. Children can pan for gold or search for real diamonds (22 found in 2006!), make candles, throw a pot or paint ceramics. There's a toddlers' playroom and outside play area, and all sorts of craft shops. But the best part, to my mind, is the hour-long tour of the mine, which was worked from 1710–90. Don't go if you're claustrophobic or unstable: the tour involves going 45 m underground, through narrow, rough-hewn tunnels and up and down ladders. Water drips constantly down the walls; it's wonderfully atmospheric. Children cannot be carried, and under fives are only allowed at the guide's discretion. There's an excellent museum detailing the history of the tin-mining industry, and a Cornish beam pumping engine (the last one to have worked in the county, up to 1959).

*Open 10am–5.30pm Apr, mid Jul–end Aug daily; end Apr–mid Jul, Sept/Oct closed Sat. **Admission** £7.90 adult, £4.90 child, £7.60 OAP, £20 family. **Credit** MC, V. **Amenities** café, disabled access (not to mine), parking, picnic area, shop.*

INSIDER TIP »
Take your holiday postcards with you when you go into Poldark mine and post them in the deepest postbox in the country – it's around 20 m below the ground. And if you really want to you can get married there too!

Flambards ★★★ ALL AGES

Clodgey Lane, Helston, Cornwall TR13 0QA; ☏ 01326 573404; www.flambards.co.uk. Follow brown tourist signs from Helston; south of the town just off A394 to The Lizard. Bus from Truro, Penzance, Redruth.

Flambards is legendary throughout the West country for providing good all-round family entertainment. For older children there's the theme park, with all manner of thrilling and scary rides, such as the Hornet Crater and Thunderbolt. Younger children can have fun on the Wobbly Bridges and Sealegs Safari (during holiday times there

Flambard's Log Flume

are special days for younger children, such as circus workshops). There's educational value here: grandparents can take a trip down memory lane and experience a reconstructed dimly lit bombed street (Britain in the Blitz), or wander through the 50 plus shops in the Victorian village (both indoor attractions). There are go-karts to ride, chariot racing, the Flambards Aircraft Park (where it all began 30 years ago) and gardens to enjoy. A great family day and something to keep up your sleeve for a rainy day.

*Open 10.30am–5pm Apr–Jul, 10am–5.30pm half term and summer holidays, 10.30am–4.30pm Sept/Oct. **Admission** £12.95 adult, £8.95 child (3–10), under 3/over 80 free, £6.95 OAP, £41 family. **Credit** MC, V. **Amenities** cafés, refreshment kiosks, disabled access, parking, picnic area, shop, garden centre.*

Geevor Tin Mine Heritage Centre ★ `AGES 8 AND UP`

Pendeen, Cornwall TR19 7EW;
📞 01736 788662; www.geevor.com.
Signed off B3306 at Pendeen
between St Just and St Ives. Bus
from Land's End, Penzance, St Ives.

There's a touch of the *Marie Celeste* about Geevor: apart from the fact that it's eerily quiet, it's almost as if the miners have simply disappeared in the middle of the working day. And that's not surprising: Geevor only closed in 1990, and 400 men once worked here. One of the earliest structures dates from the 16th/17th centuries. This sadly uneconomic enterprise is now a popular World Heritage attraction, made all the better by the fact that ex-miners lead the underground tour. Geevor once extended to a depth of 640 m, and (from Levant) went nearly 1.6 km out under the sea; you can see the cages in which miners were lowered down the shafts. A short walk towards the sea gives a better idea of the extent of the workings. There's a good café (accessible without going to the museum), and a shop with an excellent selection of books on Cornwall.

Open 9am–5pm Sun–Fri (4pm Nov)
daily (closed Christmas/New Year).
***Admission** £7.50 adult, £4.50 child 5*
and over/student, under 5 free, £7 OAP,
£22 family. **Credit** *MC, V.* ***Amenities***
café, parking, picnic area, shop.

INSIDER TIP ≫

If you visit Geevor on a less-than-clement day make sure you're properly wrapped up – the mine

sits on the clifftop in a pretty exposed position. Also make sure that you are wearing stout footwear for the 30-minute underground tour (children cannot be carried or picked up).

The Wayside Museum ★★★
`FIND` `VALUE` `AGES 5 AND UP`

Zennor, nr St Ives, Cornwall TR26
3DA; 📞 01736 796945. On B3306 St
Ives–St Just.

Although I've been to Zennor many times (on foot) I'd never made it into this extraordinary treasure trove of a museum. It's a charming place which has, deservedly, been widely featured on TV, and is known the world over for its magical collection of artefacts which reflect the lives of those who have lived in this unique area from 3000BC to the 1950s. It all started when a retired Indian army colonel moved to Zennor in 1924 and began collecting archaeological bits and pieces from the moors: today the museum houses over 5,000 artefacts, beautifully displayed in a number of small linked rooms (including a disused watermill, due to be restored 2007/8, and a 16th-century miller's cottage). There's a schoolroom, blacksmith's forge, village cobblers and wheelwrights...mining memorabilia, childhood memories and old photographs, all beautifully displayed and annotated. Keep an eye on small children as you go round – there's a lot to tempt small fingers (and a range of fascinating items to keep them interested); grandparents will be transported back to their childhoods.

Open *11am–5pm Apr–Oct, 10.30am–5.30pm May–Sept daily.* **Admission** *£3.25 adult, £2 child (5–16), under 5 free.* **Credit** *MC, V.* **Amenities** *refreshments, parking nearby, shop.*

Animal Attractions

Cornish Camels ★★ ALL AGES

Rosuick Organic Farm, St Martin, Helston, Cornwall TR12 6DZ; ☎ *01326 231119/231302; www.cornish camels.co.uk. Signed off B3293 Helston–St Keverne.*

During the summer you may catch sight of a camel or two as you drive over Goonhilly Downs – it's not a mirage! Rosuick Organic Farm, home to the Oates family since the 1750s, is also home to nine Bactrian camels (plus rheas, pigs, goats, cattle, sheep, wallabies, chickens and ducks). In the summer you can have a 15-minute camel ride round the farm, or a one-hour trek over the Downs (14 years and over) – a first for Cornwall! Smaller children can be photographed sitting on a camel, and have fun in the outside play area, giant sand pit, tractor trailer rides and on the farm trail. Camels are bred at the centre – in the spring of 2007 Myrtle gave birth to Archibald – and the older camels are being trained up for the summer treks. The organic shop sells home-produced meat and wool, organic vegetables, ready meals and local crafts. Spend a day here – there's an organic café

Lizard Point

If you really want to get to the 'end' of something in Cornwall, try Lizard Point rather than Land's End (unless you plan to access Land's End via the Coast Path). In terms of coastal scenery there is much better to be had away from both these points, but The Lizard is far less commercial – and still receives an incredible 2,500 visitors a day in the summer months. You can park for free in the village and walk down to the point, or park in the NT car park by the lighthouse. The **Lizard Lighthouse** (☎ *01326 290202; www.trinityhouse.co.uk*) is open to visitors from March to September (not Thurs/Fri) – so long as you're over one metre tall and don't suffer from vertigo! Have a cup of tea overlooking the old lifeboat station from the **Polpear Café,** the most southerly in the country. There are a couple of serpentine workshops on the point, and the **Wavecrest Café** up on the Coast Path. Along the Coast Path to the east can be found **The Lizard Wireless Station,** set up by Guglielmo Marconi in 1900 (with eight other coastal stations) to enable ships at sea to communicate with each other. But perhaps the biggest plus for Lizard Point is the presence of the lovely red-beaked red-legged **Cornish chough,** breeding here again after an absence of almost 30 years.

selling delicious food or drink –
or stay longer in one of the farm's
three lovely self-catering properties, each in its own grounds and
with access to the farm's tennis
court and farm trail.

Open 10.30am–5pm May half-term
to early Sept, Fri/Sat rest of year.
Admission free. *Credit* AmEx, MC,
V. *Amenities* café, disabled access,
parking, picnic area, shop, 1 self-
catering cottage, 2 farmhouses, 6–10
people. *Rates* £200 (low)–£950 (high).

National Seal Sanctuary ★★
ALL AGES

*Gweek, Nr Helston, Cornwall TR12
6UG; ☎ 01326 221361; www.seal
sanctuary.co.uk. Gweek is about 6
km east of Helston, signed off A394
(Falmouth) and A3083 (Lizard). Bus
from Falmouth and Helston.*

Everyone loves seals don't they? A
visit to Cornwall wouldn't be
complete without a trip to this
beautiful 43-acre site on the
Helford creek. The centre rescues
and rehabilitates sick and injured
grey seal pups from all over the
UK, and there's loads of information about seal welfare the world
over. Visitors can see pups at various stages of recovery (around
40–45 are brought in each winter). Watch the underwater
action in the sea lion lagoon and
otter creek, and let the children
learn about what they might find
in rock pools through the
Cornish Coast experience.
There's also a fun children's quiz
dotted around the site. Feeding
time takes place at regular intervals throughout the day. There's a
café, picnic area and children's
play area (toddlers–12 years),

with lovely views over the creek.
The seal pools are about a 10-
minute walk from the entrance,
but for the less able (and tired
toddlers) the Safari Bus makes
regular trips to and from the
entrance.

Open 10am–5pm daily (check for
winter opening times). *Admission*
£10.95 adult, £7.95 child (3–14),
under 3 free, £9.95 OAP, £33.80 family. *Credit* AmEx, MC, V. *Amenities*
café and refreshment kiosk, disabled
access (but some steep slopes),
parking, picnic area, shop, dogs
on leads.

Paradise Park Wildlilfe
Sanctuary ★★★ VALUE
ALL AGES

*16 Trelissick Road, Hayle, Cornwall
TR27 4HB; ☎ 01736 751020; www.
paradisepark.org.uk. Signed off A30
Hayle/St Ives roundabout. Bus from
Newquay, Truro, Helston, Penzance.*

Paradise Park on a hot sunny day
is indeed paradise! Set in the
grounds of a Victorian house
and walled garden, originally

Paradise Park, Hayle

home to tropical birds, award-winning Paradise Park is now a centre for the conservation of many animal and bird species, including the rare Cornish Chough, their pens and aviaries surrounded by mature trees and exotic flowering plants – a wonderful place to amble around. The air is filled with the constant cries of lorikeets, eagles, parrots and toucans. There are regular feeding (otters, penguins) and free-flying events – the flight of the rainbow parakeets gives children and adults the chance to feed these brilliant birds. The huge indoor play barn – all reds, blues and oranges – is great for rainy days (remember to bring socks), and you can explore the park on the Jungle Express train. And beyond the penguins and otters and parrots there's the fun farm and pets' corner. You need a whole day here to really make the most of it (the return ticket only costs £2.50). The World Explorer quiz ensures children pick up some useful information about birds and animals (and Cornwall) too.

Open 10am–5pm every day except Christmas. **Admission** £9.95 adult, £8.95 child 3–15, under 3 free, £7.95 OAP, £36 family. **Credit** MC, V. **Amenities** cafés, disabled access, parking, picnic area, shop, adventure playgrounds, animal feeding.

INSIDER TIP

Check out what's showing at the amazing open-air **Minack Theatre** (01736 810181; www.minack. com), carved out of the cliffs above Porthcurno. The Minack began as a makeshift theatre in

1929 for a village play, staged in Miss Rowena Cade's cliff-side garden. She then proceeded to build the 750-seat theatre virtually single-handed. Plays are put on throughout the summer, some suitable for children. Take cushions and a picnic! If you don't want to see a performance it's worth visiting the exhibition centre to learn more about the story behind this unique theatre.

Gardens

Trevarno ★★★ ALL AGES

Crowntown, nr Helston, Cornwall TR13 0RU; 01326 574274; *www.trevarno.co.uk. Signed off A394 Helston–Penzance and B3302 Hayle–Helston.*

The historic Trevarno estate lies tucked away in the Cornish countryside just north of Helston. At the heart of the estate lie 70 acres of beautiful gardens (dating back to 1246), with level formal areas set above a wonderfully luxuriant valley, a lake and cascade. Garden experts will appreciate Cornwall's largest and most diverse collection of plants; children will have fun leading grandparents round the gardens, following the lettered trail on the map, exploring the grotto, finding out who's buried in the pet cemetery, and answering the quiz (sticker and prize). There's a really good, solid, fenced adventure playground – accessed via a creepy yew tunnel – tucked away amongst the trees, and a 2-km walk, which leads through the countryside around the estate. You can enjoy tea in the Fountain Garden Conservatory, sit on the lawns and enjoy the peacocks, go round the National Museum of Gardening, or have fun reminiscing in the Toy Museum.

Open 10.30am–5pm daily except 25th/26th Dec. *Admission* £5.75 adult, £2.10 child (5–14), under 5 free, £4.90 OAP, £3 disabled, £13 family. *Credit* MC, V. *Amenities* café, wheelchair route, parking, children's trail, shop and workshops, dogs on leads.

Best Beaches

Church Cove, Helston
Picturesque sandy cove with lots of rock pools, car park.

Coverack Shingle beach close to harbour. Good for swimming. Café, car park.

Gwithian, Hayle Long sandy beach, surfing. Café, car park.

Kennack Sands Sandy, rock pools, popular with families.

Surfers on east beach. Kiosk, car park.

Kynance Cove (NT) one of most beautiful in Cornwall; sandy, rock pools; watch out for tides. Café, car park.

Marazion Huge sandy beach, gently shelving. Note that at low tide it's a long walk to reach the sea. Car park.

Mount's Bay, Penzance Mix of sand and pebbles; facilities near by. Car park.

Nanjizal Beautiful, remote, no access by car – some years sandy.

Perranuthnoe Sandy and rocky – favourite with small children. Café, car park.

Porthcurno (NT) Big sandy cove, steep shelf; white sand, turquoise sea, cliffs; popular. Café, car park.

Sennen Cove Boats

Porthgwarra Small sandy cove. Café, car park.

Porthgwidden, St Ives Small, sandy, suntrap, ideal for small children, popular. Café, car park.

Porthmeor, St Ives Sandy, gently shelving; popular with surfers. Café, car park.

Porthminster, St Ives Sandy, gently shelving. Café, car park.

Praa Sands 2.4 km long, gently sloping, sandy beach. Surfing. Café, car park.

St Gothian Sands/Gwithian Towans Eastern end of 4.8 km of sandy beach on St Ives Bay. Surfing. Car park, cafés. Rock pools towards Godrevy Point.

Whitesand Bay, Sennen Cove Huge, sandy beach, gently shelving. Surfing. Car park.

For Active Families

The Cornish Way AGES 5 AND UP

The Cornish Way cycle route runs from Land's End to Holsworthy in Devon, where it joins the West Country Way onto Bristol. You can take the family on a short, safe, level section of it along the edge of Mount's Bay, starting from Marazion and finishing at Penzance. There's a short stretch of roadwork as you leave Marazion, but you soon join a level track that runs along the back of the huge beach fringing Mount's Bay. The route passes the heliport, from which helicopters fly regularly to the Isles of Scilly, and becomes busier as you approach Penzance (look out for pedestrians). The Cornish Way continues ahead

Iron Age Life at Chysauster

West Penwith is dotted with sites of archaeological interest: Chun Quoit Neolithic tomb, the **Nine Maidens Bronze Age stone circle,** the inscribed stone of **Men Scryfa.** In terms of entertaining children there's not a huge amount to see at most sites, with one exception. The most impressive – and where you get a real sense of community life 2,000 years ago – is **Chysauster Iron Age village.** There's so much here that it's not hard to imagine living in one of the eight solid once-thatched courtyard houses (a style unique to West Penwith and the Isles of Scilly), lining a 'village street'. The remaining walls are up to 1.8 m high in places, and a hearth and water channel can be identified in one of them. Chysauster was a farming community, and was occupied for a while between the first and third century AD; garden plots can be identified, and there are terraced fields along the hillside. It's a fascinating and atmospheric place to look around, and fun for children. English Heritage has a shop and information, and there are toilets.

4 km northwest of Gulva, off B3311. (*07831 757934; www.english-heritage.org.uk.*

along the road towards Newlyn, but is not recommended for families with young children. Those with older children could extend the route from Marazion by following minor roads north to the Hayle estuary.

Marazion to Penzance station 8 km (there and back). **Cycle hire** *Mount's Bay Cycle Hire, Marazion;* ℂ *01736 363044; The Cycle Centre, Penzance;* ℂ *01736 351671; Pedals Bike Hire, Penzance;* ℂ *01736 360600; www. penzance.co.uk.*

INSIDER TIP ≫

If older children are after more action – surfing, climbing, horse riding and the like – contact the West Cornwall Activity Centre (ℂ *01736 871227; www.west cornwallactivitycentre.com*), which is linked to a number of activity providers in the southwest and will answer your requirements, make necessary bookings, and so on, in advance of your holiday. Mount's Bay Sailing Club (ℂ *01736 710620; www.mbsc. org.uk*) offers taster dinghy-sailing sessions; visit Mobius Kite School – based at Perranporth and Marazion (ℂ *08456 430 630; www.mobiusonline.co.uk*) – to find out how you can have a go at the relatively new and exciting sport of kitesurfing.

FAMILY-FRIENDLY ACCOMMODATION

INEXPENSIVE

Kenneggy Cove Holiday Park ★★

Higher Kenneggy, Rosudgeon, Penzance, Cornwall TR20 9AU;
ℂ *01736 763453; www.kenneggy cove.co.uk. Signed off the A394 between Crowlas and Helston.*

If you're after peace and quiet and simple family fun look no further than this idyllic campsite situated on a dead-end lane a few minutes' walk from sandy Kenneggy Cove (the cove is inaccessible by car, so never busy). It's one of the best locations I've seen for a family camping holiday: you can set up camp and forget about the car (other than the odd trip into nearby Penzance). Pitches are generously large, and views over Mount's Bay are glorious. Prussia Cove, renowned for the exploits of the infamous smuggler John Carter, lies just around the corner. The Victoria Inn at Perranuthnoe – where there is also a beach café and refreshments at Perranuthnoe Village Crafts – can be reached via a lovely walk along the Coast Path.

50 spacious camping pitches. **Rates** *£12–21 per night 2 people, £4 extra child 4–14, under 3 free. 9 static caravans, 2–6 people.* **Rates** *£185–525.* **Credit** *MC, V.* **Amenities** *cot/highchair/garden furniture, takeaway meals some evenings, outside play area, parking, electricity on some pitches, shop (breakfast items a speciality!), BBQs, laundry, sandy beach within walking distance.*

Gwithian Farm Campsite ★★★

Gwithian, Hayle, Cornwall TR27 5BX; ℂ *01736 753127; www.gwithian farm.co.uk. On the B3301 Hayle–Portreath.*

Gwithian Farmhouse

The little village of Gwithian sits at the eastern end of 4.8 km of golden sands, backed by high dunes, stretching from Hayle Towans (Cornish for 'sand dunes') to Godrevy Point. A perfect spot for a traditional family campsite, Gwithian Farm really fits the bill. There's no play equipment or games room, but seven acres of beautifully maintained sloping grassland backing onto the dunes and beach. The centre of the site is kept clear for children to play, and the very high standard showers and toilets (built 2005) include a family shower room, family bathroom and disabled facilities. There are no statics, which will please some campers. A local surf school and Godrevy lighthouse are a short walk away. The site has a well-stocked shop (with wet suit hire), a good pub (Red River Inn) over the road, no fewer than four beach cafés and bars within walking distance, and cream teas served in the 16th-century farmhouse.

130 camping pitches (some with electric hook-ups). **Rates** *£9 (low)–£18 (high) 2 adults; £2 child over 5, £1 under 5.* **Amenities** *disabled facilities, DIY laundry, shop, parking, recreational area, 10 min walk to beach, cream teas in farmhouse.*

MODERATE

Mudgeon Vean Farm Holiday Cottages ★

St Martin, Nr Helston, Cornwall TR12 6DB; ☎ 01326 231341; www. mudgeonvean.co.uk. Take the B3293 (St Keverne); follow signs to St Martin then get a map!

The area around the Helford river – and Daphne du Maurier's 'Frenchman's Creek' – is full of elegant second homes, and has become an enclave of the rich and famous: it is undeniably beautiful. Eighteenth-century Mudgeon Vean farm lies at the

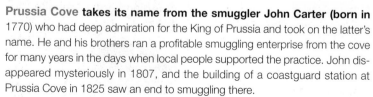

FUN FACT ▶ **Smuggler John Carter**

Prussia Cove takes its name from the smuggler **John Carter** (born in 1770) who had deep admiration for the King of Prussia and took on the latter's name. He and his brothers ran a profitable smuggling enterprise from the cove for many years in the days when local people supported the practice. John disappeared mysteriously in 1807, and the building of a coastguard station at Prussia Cove in 1825 saw an end to smuggling there.

Note that the Lizard lighthouse is not the place for light sleepers – in misty conditions the electronic foghorn will operate automatically – ear plugs are provided!

end of a labyrinth of narrow lanes, and the cottage accommodation – within walking distance of the river (through National Trust woods) – would suit families looking for a simple holiday in this somewhat 'refined' area! It's a comfortable, cosy, relaxed place; two of the cottages are open plan downstairs, and have enclosed sitting-out areas; the third adjoins the farmhouse and has a small enclosed garden. There's a woodland walk, outside play area and space for football or cricket; children will enjoy the chickens, ducks, pigmy goats and pigs. The farm also has a games room for teenagers, and video and DVD library. An added bonus: the farm is the home of delicious Helford Creek apple juice (*www.helfordcreek.co.uk*).

3 s/c cottages, 2–6 people. Rates £150 (low)–£425 (high). Amenities babysitting, cot (free), extra bed (charge), DIY tumble dryer, parking, games room, outdoor play area, in cottage fridge, cooker/micowave/ washing machine, shower or bath, TV/DVD/video.

Lizard Lighthouse ★★

Lizard, Helston, Cornwall TR12 7NT; 01736 240333; www.mullion cottages.com. Signed from Lizard village on the A3083 from Helston.

What could be more exciting than staying in a lighthouse – especially one marking the most southerly point of the mainland?

The Lizard lighthouse was originally established (unsuccessfully) in 1619, and commissioned under Trinity House in the mid-18th century. It was automated in 1998. Six newly refurbished and modernised ex-lighthouse keepers' cottages are available for rent, each romantically named after a lighthouse off the southwest coast, such as Godrevy, Longships and Seven Stones. Wolf Rock, which sleeps six, incorporates the unused West Tower as part of the accommodation, with steps leading up to the observatory. There's outside seating in a small courtyard, and acres of open grassy space on the clifftop around the lighthouse. Lovely Housel Beach is nearby along the Coast Path, and beautiful Kynance Cove, with its glistening turquoise waters and excellent cafe, just 3.2 km away.

Lizard lighthouse

*6 s/c cottages, 4–8 people. **Rates** £298 (low)–£1072 (high). **Amenities** cot (free), disabled access (1 property), fridge, cooker/microwave/ washing machine/dishwasher, shower/bath, TV/DVD.*

> **INSIDER TIP** ›
>
> For brilliant pasties don't miss **Ann's Famous Pasty Shop** (📞 01326 290889), a bright yellow building found just off the green in Lizard village. Well worth a visit!

EXPENSIVE

Cot Manor ★★★

*Cot Valley, St Just, Cornwall TR19 7NT; 📞 01647 433593; **www.helpful holidays.com**. Signed off B3306 just south of St Just.*

St Just, England's most westerly town, sits solidly a kilometre or so inland from the coast. In medieval times it was known as Lafrowda, and developed as a religious and market centre for the surrounding fishing and farming communities. The town feels ancient and tough: a medieval amphitheatre and uncompromising granite buildings flank the Market Square. But between St Just and the coast can be found some of the most sheltered and luxuriant valleys in the whole of Cornwall. Lovely Cot Manor is down a narrow dead-end lane ('unsuitable for vehicles') in the depths of the beautiful Cot Valley, which leads to little Porth Nanven cove (sandy at low tide): an idyllic place for families with small children who want to get away from it all. Set in five acres (fields and garden, with stream)

Cot Manor originated in Tudor times and almost seems to grow out of its unspoilt surroundings. Accommodation is spacious and 'gracious'; there's a big family room with flagstone floor and woodburner – and a priest's hole! The owners live next door and will pick up from Penzance station and the end of walks. Ready-cooked meals also available.

*Sleeps 9. **Rates** £385 (low)–1926 (high). **Credit** MC, V. **Amenities** cot (free), cooker/microwave, dishwasher/tumble dryer, fridge/freezer, shower/bath, TV/DVD/satellite, private garden, garden furniture, BBQ, no dogs.*

St Aubyn Estates ★★★

*Manor Office, Marazion, Cornwall TR17 0EF; 📞 01736 710507; **www.staubynestates.co.uk**.*

If you want to stay in a truly beautiful, remote coastal location, have a look at what the St Aubyn family (of St Michael's Mount, p. 200) have to offer in terms of self-catering accommodation. Their seven cottages and houses, all beautifully renovated and in fantastic positions, will appeal to those families who like staying in places where the views and surrounding landscape just take the breath away. No swimming pools here, no play equipment, no handy shop just around the corner – but solid stone Cornish houses, glorious views, peace and quiet, and that lovely feeling that comes with having found somewhere really special. Choose from a converted fisherman's cottage in tiny Porthgwarra (that once housed two families with 11 children!), Faraway Cottage at the end of a bumpy farm track at Nanjizal – one of southwest Cornwall's most beautiful and least-known coves – or Venton Farmhouse above Marazion, from where you can scramble down to the rocky beach below or just sit and gaze across Mount's Bay at sunset.

7 s/c properties, 2–10 people. **Rates** *£315 (low)–1,995 (high).* **Credit** *MC, V.* **Amenities** *cot (free), no dogs, family room in larger properties, cooker/microwave, dishwasher, TV/DVD.*

Polurrian Hotel ★★

Mullion, Cornwall TR12 7EN; 📞 *01326 240421; www.polurrianhotel.com. Mullion is 9.6 km from Helston on the A3083, then B3296; follow signs for the hotel.*

If you want to give the family a bit of a treat take them to the Polurrian Hotel, a rather grand yet friendly and beautifully situated hotel above sandy Polurrian Cove (easy access to the beach). All ages are well catered for: a crèche for younger children, children's game room, climbing frames and huge outdoor pool; older teenagers can enjoy the gym, squash court and fitness suite. Younger children have high tea, and are looked after by staff until 9pm, giving parents (and grandparents) the chance for a relaxed dinner in the very smart dining room, with wonderful views over Mount's Bay. For less formal dining there's the High Point bistro, open all day (and to non-residents) with a spacious terrace overlooking the

beach. And if you find the hotel a little too pricey you can rent one of the nearby bungalows, with access to the hotel facilities.

39 rooms, inc 1 family suite and 3 family rooms. **Rates** *£53 (low)–£134 (high) adult pppn; £15 (low)–£42 (high) child pppn. 8 s/c bungalows, 4–6 people.* **Rates** *£300 (low)–£1,020 (high).* **Credit** *MC, V.* **Amenities** *babysitting, crèche, bars, cot (free), disabled access, extra bed (some rooms; also in properties – charge), fitness suite, laundry service, parking, indoor/outdoor pool, tennis court, restaurants, dogs accepted.* **In bungalow** *fridge, cooker/microwave, washing machine/dryer, TV/video.*

FAMILY-FRIENDLY DINING

INEXPENSIVE

Roskilly's ★★★ FIND

Tregellast Barton, St Keverne, Helston, Cornwall TR12 6NX; 📞 *01326 280479; www.roskillys.co.uk. B3293 (St Keverne), fork to Coverack and follow signs.*

It's very hard knowing quite where to place Roskilly's. It's a great, relaxed place to eat, with a lovely courtyard, inside seating, BBQs and music on some summer evenings (children allowed to 8.30pm). There's loads to see and do (craft shops, Jersey calves, milking, woodlands, meadows and ponds to explore), plus three self-catering cottages, and another in Coverack: and then there's the ice cream. You'll see Roskilly's ice cream on sale all over Cornwall, and it is wonderful! The farm has come a long

Roskilly's Jersey calf

way since the early days when all the ice cream was made on site, but it still retains the feel of a working farm. The Croust House restaurant is the perfect place for an easy family lunch; the court-yard (former farmyard) has a wonderfully continental feel on a hot day. Daily specials – salmon and dill fishcakes (£6.25) – com-plement baguettes, sandwiches and salads, all freshly made and delicious, as are the homemade cakes and puddings. The chil-dren's menu is cheap and cheerful (£1.20–3.50). And if you can't quite decide which ice cream to go for, buy some to take away!

Open *10am–6pm/9pm summer, and winter weekends.* **Main course** *£3.85–6.80.* **Credit** *MC, V.* **Amenities** *children's menu, summer evening BBQs, pond and woodland walks, disabled access, parking, farm ani-mals. 4 s/c cottages, 4–6 people.* **Rates** *£195 (low)–640 (high).*

INSIDER TIP

There are 24 fabulous flavours to choose from at **Roskilly's** (p. 213) – malty mystery, mint choc chip, trifle, strawberry, chocolate – and a whopper cone will give you three different flavours. You can watch the farm's Jersey cows being milked at certain times of day, and from 2008 can see the ice cream being made just down the lane from the farm.

Godrevy Beach Café ★

Godrevy Towans, Gwithian, Hayle, Cornwall TR27 5ED; ☎ *01736 757999. Off the B3301 just north of Gwithian, on the road to Godrevy lighthouse.*

The eastern end of St Ives Bay culminates in Godrevy Point with its famous lighthouse (upon which Virginia Woolf based her novel of the same name). This lovely area is owned by the National Trust: sandy beaches, high rocky cliffs, superb Coast Path walking, wildflowers and wildlife – if you're lucky you may spot a seal. The Godrevy Beach café is in the first NT car park (free for members). It's a small wooden building with seating on the balcony, and gets busy at weekends and during the holiday season. But you can get good quality food at reasonable prices a stone's throw from a wonderful beach. Grab breakfast from 10am–12pm – the children's breakfast sandwiches at £2.95 are good value. Children also have their own 'wrapsicles': cheese, tuna, bacon, sausage...

Open 10am–5pm daily, 6pm–last orders Fri/Sat high season; phone for winter opening times. *Main course* £3.95–6.95 (lunch). *Credit* MC, V. *Amenities* children's menu, half portions available evenings, highchair, close to beach, disabled access, reservations accepted (evenings only), NT car park.

MODERATE

Sandbar ★ ★ ★ FIND

Praa Sands, Penzance, Cornwall TR20 9TQ; ✆ 01736 763516; www.sandbarpraasands.co.uk. Praa Sands is signed off the A394 between Helston and Penzance. Bus from Helston and Penzance.

On a sunny day this place really does have the 'Wow!' factor – it has got an unbelievable position, situated on this fantastic long, sandy beach – a little bit of California in southwest Cornwall. Airy, spacious, with huge windows and a big outside seating area overlooking the beach (and steps down to the sands) this is a brilliant place for families with children of all ages. There are big sofas, bright colours and trendy fixtures and fittings (pool tables and table football are separate

Surfing

In recent years there has been an explosion in the number of surf schools around the Cornish coast, and the seas are regularly full of wet-suited hopefuls kneeling on boards in the shallows. Lessons cost around £20 for a half day (2 hours) to £35 for a full day (4 hours). Check the lower age limit in advance; some schools only teach, say, eight years and above.

Freetime Holidays, St Levan, Penzance; ✆ 01736 871302
Global Boarders Surf Shop and Surf School, Marazion; ✆ 0845 330 9303
Gwithian Academy of Surfing, St Ives Bay; ✆ 01736 755493; www. surfacademy.co.uk
Lizard Surf School, Lizard Peninsula; ✆ 07980 010090/01209 831422
Reeflex Surfing, Stones Reef, Praa Sands; ✆ 01736 672991
St Ives Surfing Centre, Porthmeor Beach; ✆ 01736 793366
Sennen Surfing Centre, Sennen Cove; ✆ 01736 871458; www. sennensurfingcentre.com
Shore Surf School, Hayle; ✆ 01736 755556; www.shoresurf.com

from the bar and eating areas). Food is, as expected, contemporary: char-grilled tuna steak (£12.50), mussels (£9.50), fajitas stuffed with roasted vegetables and chickpeas (£8.95). There are Beach Bites – burgers, baguettes and light meals – and Junior Bites at £4.75 (sausage and mash, scampi, hummus). There's a popular Sunday carvery (with organic meat sourced from local farms).

Open 11am–11pm Mon–Fri (from 10am in summer), 10am–2am weekends all year. Main course £8.95–13.75. Credit MC, V. Amenities children's menu, half portions of some dishes, highchair, disabled access, reservations accepted, on the beach, pool table, table football.

INSIDER TIP »

While you sip a cocktail at the Sandbar you can let the children have a go at learning how to surf. The seas of the south Cornish coast are 'flatter' than those of the north in the summer months, and **Stones Reef Diving and Watersports** (under the Sandbar) will happily take them off your hands for an hour or so and teach them the basics of keeping upright on a surfboard (☎ *01736 762991*). Adults also welcome!

Halzephron Inn ★★

Gunwalloe, Helston, Cornwall TR12 7QB; ☎ 01326 240406; www.halzephron-inn.co.uk. Gunwalloe is signed off the A3083 Helston–The Lizard at RNAS Culdrose.

'Halzephron' comes from the Cornish *Als Yfferin*, 'cliffs of hell'. The 'hellish cliffs' referred to are those along the Lizard

coast: the inn dates back around 500 years and is steeped in tales of smugglers and shipwrecks. Today this pretty blue-and-white building, with seating at the front and in an enclosed courtyard overlooking fields behind, sits on a quiet dead-end lane leading to the NT's lovely Church Cove. It has a reputation for excellent food, and has won several awards. There's a dedicated family room (separate from the bar area) and an extensive menu, locally sourced wherever possible. Children have their own interesting menu – tuna and mozzarella fishcake (£3.95), scampi and chips (£4.95), tagliatelle bolognaise (£3.95); adults have a huge choice, ranging from sandwiches and salad platters to pan-fried skate wing (£13.95) and beef and Halzephron gold ale ragout (£11.95). Also lots of delicious homemade puddings, and local ice creams.

Open 11am–2.30pm, 6.30pm–11pm Mon–Sat, 12pm–2.30pm, 6.30pm–10.30pm Sun. Main course £8.95–14.50. Credit AmEx, MC, V. Amenities children's menu, half portions of some dishes, highchair, disabled access, reservations accepted, outside seating areas, B&B accommodation.

INSIDER TIP »

Babies and toddlers might be better off at **The Old Cellars Restaurant** (☎ *01326 290727*), just downhill from the pub in Cadgwith. Housed in what was once a pilchard cellar (1782) – for over 100 years Cadgwith was

Try These Too!

- **Little Trevothan Caravan & Camping Park** For a slightly alternative stay try these traditional Mongolian yurts complete with horsehair interior! Coverack, Nr Helston, Cornwall TR12 6SD; ☎ *01326 280260; www.littletrevothan.co.uk.*
- **The Beach** Contemporary wooden and glass building at trendy end of Sennen Cove hanging over one of the area's best beaches. Sennen Cove, Cornwall TR19 7BT; ☎ *01736 798798; www.beach restaurant.co.uk*
- **Cadgwith Cove Inn**: Proper local pub dating back 300 years in idyllic fishing village serving locally sourced seafood. Cadgwith Cove, Helston, Cornwall TR12 7JX; ☎ *01326 290513; www.cadgwith coveinn.com.*

dependent on pilchard fishing – it's an atmospheric spot and good for lunch, tea or a snack. There's room for buggies, indoor and outdoor seating, and the restaurant is sometimes open in the evenings (licensed). And if you feel like going out to explore the coves round Cadgwith contact Nigel Legge (☎ *01326 290716; www.lobsterpots.co.uk*) who makes lobster pots and runs **boat trips** from the cove.

The Tyringham Arms ★★

Family Carvery & Restaurant, Old Coach Road, Lelant Downs, nr St Ives, Cornwall TR26 3EZ; ☎ 01736 740434; www.tyringhamarms. co.uk. South of St Ives off B3311 to Penzance; follow signs for Hayle. Bus from St Ives and Penzance.

A good place to take the family for a straightforward, reasonable, down-to-earth meal in interesting surroundings. In a former life The Tyringham Arms was Trevarrack Council School – school group photos dating from the 1930s hang on the walls – the old school hall now houses the main dining room. But there's nothing drab and 'educational' about the place: clever use of brightly coloured banners effectively 'lower' the ceiling, and the atmosphere is light, airy and cheerful. You could have a relaxed meal here with children of all ages (there's a pool table off the bar and an outside play area for 4–10 year olds). The Sunday and summer evening carvery is extremely popular. Booking is recommended (£8.95 adults, £4.75 children under 10).

*Open 12pm–2pm lunch, 2pm–5.30pm cream teas, 5.30pm–9pm dinner summer holidays; winter shut Mon/Tues and afternoons. **Main course** £8.95–11.95. **Credit** MC, V. **Amenities** children's menu and carvery, highchair, outside play area, disabled access, reservations accepted, parking.*

Porthgwidden Café Bar ★★★

FIND

Porthgwidden Beach, St Ives, Cornwall TR26 2NW; 📞 *01736 796791; www.porthgwidden cafe.co.uk. On the Island in St Ives.*

A real find: tucked away on the edge of the Island in the middle of St Ives is a wonderful small, compact, enclosed sandy beach – ideal for small children. The lovely blue-and-white Porthgwidden café sits right on the beach – only accessed by stairs – and has a wonderful breezy terrace, with blue cushions and tiled tables – sit there on a hot day and you could well be in Greece. Children are welcome from breakfast onwards, though under 14s must leave by 8pm. Food is original and freshly prepared: herby pancake with seafood filling, chicken breast stuffed and sun-dried tomatoes and mozzarella (£10.95); lunchtime baguettes (crayfish tails, brie and cranberry) come with salad and chips; the children's menu (£5.50) lists fish and chips and pasta. There are daily specials and delicious homemade cake and pastries, all served with a smile in an almost picture-perfect setting.

*Open 9am–10pm high season; out of season phone for details. **Main course** £7.95–12.95. **Credit** MC, V. **Amenities** children's menu, half portions available to 8pm, on beach, highchair, reservations recommended in high season, paying car park nearby.*

Keeping It Local – Farmers' Markets & Farm Shops

Bill and Flo's Farm Shop, Nance Lakes, Lelant, St Ives; 📞 *01736 798885*

Carnon Downs Farmers' Market, Village Hall, last Sat.

Gear Farm, St Martin, Helston; 📞 *01326 221150*

Godolphin House, Helston; 📞 *01726 763194*

Grange Fruit Farm, Gweek, Helston; 📞 *01326 221718*

Helston Farmer's Market, Guild Hall, Mons

Higher Trenowin Farm Shop, Nancledra, Penzance; 📞 *01736 362439*

Penzance Market, Wharfside Shopping Centre, Sats

Richards of Cornwall, Carwin Farm, Hayle; 📞 *01736 757888*

Trevaskis Organic Farm Shop, Connor Downs, Hayle; 📞 *01209 713931*

Vicarage Farm Shop, Wendron, Helston; 📞 *01326 340484*

12 Isles of Scilly

ISLES OF **SCILLY**

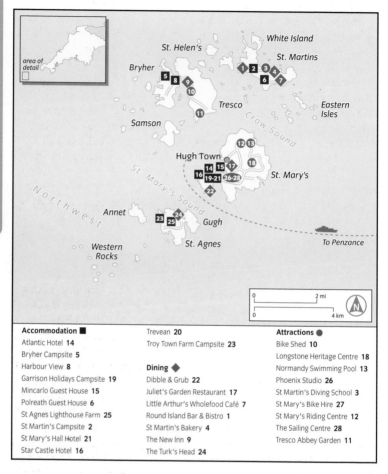

Accommodation ■
Atlantic Hotel **14**
Bryher Campsite **5**
Harbour View **8**
Garrison Holidays Campsite **19**
Mincarlo Guest House **15**
Polreath Guest House **6**
St Agnes Lighthouse Farm **25**
St Martin's Campsite **2**
St Mary's Hall Hotel **21**
Star Castle Hotel **16**

Trevean **20**
Troy Town Farm Campsite **23**

Dining ◆
Dibble & Grub **22**
Juliet's Garden Restaurant **17**
Little Arthur's Wholefood Café **7**
Round Island Bar & Bistro **1**
St Martin's Bakery **4**
The New Inn **9**
The Turk's Head **24**

Attractions ●
Bike Shed **10**
Longstone Heritage Centre **18**
Normandy Swimming Pool **13**
Phoenix Studio **26**
St Martin's Diving School **3**
St Mary's Bike Hire **27**
St Mary's Riding Centre **12**
The Sailing Centre **28**
Tresco Abbey Garden **11**

┃magine taking the family to a remote rocky island with no cars, deserted silver-white beaches, turquoise sea, sub-tropical vegetation, unpolluted air, fantastic wildlife, and where the children can run free...yet with a good local shop, café and pub within walking distance, and similar islands to explore just a boat ride away. Sounds like paradise, doesn't it? And yet you don't have to travel too far to find it: just as far as the magical Isles of Scilly, only 50 km off Land's End.

The Isles of Scilly are, quite simply, unique. England's smallest AONB (Area of Outstanding Natural Beauty) (just 41 square km) is blessed with a stunning natural environment. There are five inhabited (six, if you count the one house on Gugh off St Agnes) and 50 uninhabited low-lying granite islands, divided by shallow seas, with long sandy beaches and sub-tropical vegetation. The islands enjoy a wealth of wildflowers and migrant butterflies and moths, and attract hundreds of birdwatchers every year, keen to spot rare migrants.

For generations the flower industry and fishing were the main sources of income; today tourism has largely taken over, with more than 80% of Scilly businesses linked to tourism. The islands' population stands at around 2,000, of which 1,700 are on the main island St Mary's.

Holiday accommodation fills up quickly, especially on the out islands where opportunities are limited – many families book up year on year. Accommodation varies in quality and price, from camping at the country's most southwesterly farm on St Agnes to a family house in Hugh Town on St Mary's to luxurious living at the Island Hotel on Tresco. No holiday on Scilly is cheap. For a start there's the cost of travel to the islands, and possible car storage at Penzance. Accommodation is limited, and demand is high. But the minute you reach St Mary's you can feel Scilly starting to work her magic on you – and if you're staying on an out island you'll be sorely tempted to miss the boat home.

VISITOR INFORMATION

The TIC on Hugh Street, St Mary's is the place to go. The very helpful staff will answer all your queries (see also *www.scilly online.co.uk*). If staying on one of the out islands information about boat trips and the like will be displayed outside the shop or pub – or ask an islander. The **Isles of Scilly AONB** (☎ *01720 423486; www.ios-aonb.info*) produces a good information pack, detailing every aspect of the islands' history, archaeology, flora and fauna, arts and crafts, and ideas for what to do with children. A real bonus for visiting children is the excellent DVD written and presented by pupils at The Five Islands School: **Children's Guide to Scilly** (available from the TIC, Hugh Town, St Mary's ☎ *01720 422536; www.simplyscilly.co.uk*).

Orientation

There are five inhabited islands: St Mary's (the largest at about 6½ km square, and the hub of the transport system), St Martin's, Tresco and Bryher (across Crow Sound to the north of St Mary's) and St Agnes. At times of exceptionally low tide it is possible to walk from Tresco to Bryher (and, occasionally, to another island Samson). St Agnes (with Gugh, to which it is linked at low tide) lies to the southwest of St Mary's and is the smallest and most self-contained island in the group, separated from the rest by the deep waters of St Mary's Sound.

The most economic way for a family to travel to Scilly is by the **Scillonian III**, which sails from Penzance to St Mary's from late March to early November, and takes about 2½ hours. Travelling by boat to a remote island group brings with it a real sense of adventure. The 'fully flexible' adult return fare £92. (📞 0845 710 5555; www.ios-travel.co.uk).

Skybus flies to St Mary's from Southampton, Bristol, Exeter, Newquay and Land's End (you can leave your car at Penzance heliport – £6 per day – and take a shuttle bus to St Just). The plane only takes eight passengers, and is unsuitable for anyone who is claustrophobic or nervous – the 'airfield' is just that! The flight (from St Just) takes around 20 minutes at a cost of £125 adult fully flexible return (contact details as above).

The third option – to my mind the most pleasurable – is to take a comfortable 20-minute ride on a British International helicopter from Penzance heliport. There are regular flights throughout the day Mon–Sat to St Mary's and Tresco, at a cost of £152 for a normal adult return (📞 01736 363871; www.islesofscilly helicopters.com). During the summer, flights are booked up often well in advance. They are also subject to good weather conditions.

Getting Around

The inter-island boat service works like clockwork. Boats leave Hugh Town around 10am and 2pm every day, and return boats leave the out islands at lunchtime and late afternoon. Tickets can be purchased at the **Boatmen's Association** kiosk on the quay (📞 01720 423999; www. scillyboating.co.uk) – no need to book in advance. The harbour buzzes with activity as the inter-island boats (with wonderfully evocative names – *Seahorse, Surprise, Sapphire, Guiding Star*) arrive to pick up their passengers. You'll find masses of boat trips advertised along the quay: evening supper trips to the Turk's Head on St Agnes (p. 234), trips to uninhabited islands such as Samson or Annet, seal watching on the Eastern Isles, or to the Bishop Rock lighthouse.

If you're staying on the out islands each one has its own boat service (p. 222).

The best way to get around St Mary's (and Tresco) is by bike (available to hire on both islands). There are 14½ km of road and lane on St Mary's, but few cars, and cycling is safe and fun, and there are deserted beaches and the odd café where you can take a break. The recommended 8-km circuit takes about one hour. A good way to learn more about St Mary's is to hop on an **Island Rover** (📞 01720 422131; www. islandrover.co.uk) open-top bus tour, which run at least twice a day at 10:15am and 1:30pm Mon–Sat, with a full commentary. The trip lasts just over an hour. If you're just popping over to the island for the day, tickets can be bought aboard the Scillonian III (p. 221) from Penzance.

INSIDER TIP »

While waiting on Hugh Town quay for your boat to come in take a look at the Isles of Scilly Wildlife Trust Visitor Centre – excellent for occupying impatient children. There are activity sheets, a colouring desk, pebbles and seaweed to identify. There are two nature trails on St Mary's, and excellent leaflets telling you what to look for. Call into the Centre on your way home and report what flora and fauna you've seen (☎ 01720 422153/422156; www.ios-wildlife trust.org.uk).

Child-Friendly Events & Entertainment

Walk Scilly

The Isles of Scilly Walking Festival first took place in 2007 and attracted walkers from far and wide. As well as all sorts of themed walks, exploring miles of protected footpaths, the festival includes beachcombing, treasure hunts and a family charity walk.

Late Mar; ☎ 01720 422536; www. walkscilly.co.uk

WHAT TO SEE & DO

Children's Top 10 Attractions

❶ **Building** sandcastles on an uninhabited island: Tean, St Helens, Great or Little Arthur.

❷ **Hunting** for beads in the sand at Beady Pool, St Agnes. See p. 224.

❸ **Sipping** a delicious hot chocolate at St Martin's on the Isle. See p. 234.

❹ **Swimming** with fishes on a guided snorkelling trip. See p. 236.

❺ **Cheering** on your island's gig at the weekly gig races off St Mary's. See p. 226.

❻ **Munching** homemade pizza and watching the sun go down on St Martin's. See p. 232.

❼ **Making** your own stained glass yacht or dolphin to take home. See p. 225.

❽ **Cycling** around Tresco, and visiting the exotic Abbey Gardens. See p. 236.

❾ **Eating** fish and chips on Porthcressa beach on St Mary's. See p. 231.

❿ **Watching** the Atlantic waves crash onto the rocks at Hell Bay on Bryher. See p. 224.

The Out Islands

Any holiday on Scilly is a treat, and the main island of St Mary's a wonderful place to stay, but to get a taste of real island life stay on St Martin's, Bryher or St Agnes. Tresco (like the other islands owned by the Duchy of Cornwall but – unlike the others – leased to a private family) has a smarter, more contemporary ambience. It's interesting to note that the Isles of Scilly are sinking very, very slowly; it's estimated that in 3,500 years time the Garrison will be all that is left of St Mary's, and that St Agnes will have shrunk to one-tenth of its present size.

St Martin's The most easterly of the inhabited islands, St Martin's is a 3.2-km-long narrow ridge of land, with a wild, rugged northern side – Great Bay is one of the most beautiful beaches on Scilly – and a gently sloping southern side facing Tresco, where small walled fields (and the campsite) back the sandy shoreline. One narrow concrete lane links Lowertown Quay to Highertown Quay, via Highertown and the famous bakery (p. 232). White Island, on St Martin's northeast tip, is only accessible at low tide.

Tresco Tresco sits between St Martin's and Bryher, and is the most 'civilised' of the out islands – even the Reading Room has been converted to holiday accommodation – and it's almost as if someone sweeps the lanes each night! The island is renowned for the beautiful Abbey Gardens (p. 225) and the Island Hotel at Old Grimsby on the northeast coast. The north of the island is wild and rugged; the south is low lying and gentle, with some fabulous beaches. The Great Pool at the heart of the island attracts exotic migrant birds.

Bryher Bryher is the most westerly of the 'group of three', and its west coast gets a real hammering from Atlantic storms over the winter months. By contrast the southern and eastern shores are sheltered and peaceful; the campsite is in the shadow of Shipman Head Down, where there is an exceptional concentration of Bronze Age cairns. Rushy Bay on the island's southernmost point is particularly beautiful.

St Agnes The most remote of the inhabited islands – and most southwesterly community in the British Isles – St Agnes (and Gugh) is separated from the rest of the group by deep St Mary's Sound, and looks west towards the Bishop Rock lighthouse beyond the Western Rocks. Step off the boat and you really do feel as if you've reached the end of the world. Walk all round the island – look out for the Nag's Head, St Warna's Well, and the Maze on Castella Down. Don't miss Periglis and Cove Vean, perfect beaches, or the freshwater Big Pool, renowned for attracting migrant birds – and spend time at Beady Pool, site of a 17th-century shipwreck, where even today samples from its cargo of beads may be found. The only inhabited island without a hotel, St Agnes has a unique appeal.

Fun Days Out

Longstone Heritage Centre ★ ★ ★ ALL AGES

St Mary's TR21 0NW; ☎ *01720 423770; www.longstonecentre. co.uk. Off Telegraph Road, overlooking Holy Vale.*

A long bumpy track leads to this single-storey blue-painted wooden building – don't give up (especially if you're on bikes) – it's well worth the effort. The Longstone Heritage Centre is a must for any visitor, and has been carefully thought out so that all ages will be kept interested. Everything you ever wanted to know about Scilly is here: visitor numbers and provenance, shipwrecks, flower farming, coastguards, World Wars I and II, the building of the Bishop Rock lighthouse and so on. There are children's activities all round the centre, cleverly positioned below 'adult' interest so

Get Crafty! «

The Isles of Scilly are a magnet for artists and craftspeople, drawn to this magical spot by the amazing quality of the light. Galleries and workshops are dotted all over the islands – and some offer the chance to have a go yourself (an excellent way of occupying the children on a rainy afternoon). The **Phoenix Studio** at Porthmellon (St Mary's) runs workshops for adults and children in stained glass, ceramic painting, fabric painting and kite making. Children under eight have to be accompanied by an adult. Workshops take place on weekday afternoons all year – call in for details. ☎ *01720 422900; www.phoenixstained glass.co.uk*

that no one is inconvenienced. Apart from activity sheets there's a blackboard area to scribble on, a magnetic sea scene, sandpit and pebbles (not for under 36 months), even a mirror in the old photographs section where children are asked to hold an expression for 30 seconds, as if having their photo taken in 'olden days'. A great grassy expanse is ideal for picnics and ball games, and the café serves a good range of family-friendly items – plus Troy Town farm ice cream (p. 230). A real must.

Open *10am–5pm Easter–end Oct daily.* **Admission** *free (donations).* **Amenities** *café, highchairs, picnic area, shop.*

Gardens

Tresco Abbey Garden ★ ★ ★

Tresco TR24 0QQi; ☎ *01720 424108; www.tresco.co.uk. Southern end of Tresco.*

No visit to Scilly is complete without a trip to Tresco Abbey Garden, created in the 19th century by Augustus Smith, who took over the lease of the islands from the Duchy of Cornwall in 1834. Smith collected plants from all over the world and brought them home: today there are over 4,000 species from the Mediterranean, South Africa, California, New Zealand and the Canaries. Wandering past stands of banana

Tresco Abbey Garden

FUN FACT >> Gig Racing

Pilot gigs are 9.7 m six-oared traditional wooden working boats dating from the 19th century, when competing pilots would race out to assist sail ships as they entered port or negotiated tricky waters. On Wednesday (ladies) and Friday evenings (men) you can hop on a boat and set out to sea to watch **gig racing.** Gigs are rowed out from each island to compete – there are 13 gigs on Scilly – and it's great fun to watch. Boats depart from the quay at 7.45pm, and the races start at 8pm. It's a popular sport: there are gig-racing clubs all around the coast of Cornwall and the Isles of Scilly.

palm and bamboo it's hard to believe you're only 45 km off mainland Britain. It's a wonderfully exciting garden to explore – sheltered, still, warm – a series of exotically planted terraces and avenues linked by steps and twisting paths, many of which lead to intriguing ponds, grottoes, artefacts and sculptures. Don't miss the lovely Shell House mural, craggy Father Neptune and the graceful Tresco Children. The Valhalla Museum at the bottom of the garden houses ships' figureheads and memorabilia collected from the numerous ships that have foundered on Scilly's rocks.

Open 10am–4pm daily all year. **Admission** £9 adult, children under 16 free, £20 weekly ticket. **Credit** MC, V. **Amenities** café, disabled access, picnic area, shop.

FAMILY-FRIENDLY ACCOMMODATION

INEXPENSIVE

The cheapest way of staying on Scilly is to camp; rates range from around £6–8.50 per person per night. It means you have to travel to Scilly on the *Scillonian*, and transport everything you need for

your stay, but it's perfectly possible to manage (and quite adventurous!) – as you land on your chosen island you will be met by the campsite owner who will transport your luggage to the site. Be warned, however, the campsites get fully booked for the summer many months in advance.

St Mary's

℡ 01720 422670; *www.garrison holidays.co.uk*

A sheltered site inside the historic Garrison, with brilliant sea views and a well-equipped shop, near the island tennis court and new playpark.

St Martin's Campsite

℡ 01720 422888; *www.stmartins campsite.co.uk*

In Middle Town, just behind the long, sandy Middle Town beach: a lovely sheltered site, divided into small fields, behind the sand dunes. Local seasonal produce for sale including milk fresh from the cow; boat hire on the beach.

Bryher

℡ 01720 422886; *www.bryher campsite.co.uk*

Periglis Beach, St Agnes

The campsite is situated in a sheltered valley near the northern end of the island, with good views towards Tresco.

Troytown Campsite

St Agnes, 📞 *01720 422360; www.troytown.co.uk*

A magical campsite on a rocky and sandy beach, with fantastic sunsets over the Western Rocks and Bishop lighthouse. Sheltered granite walls, nooks and crannies – and homemade ice cream (p. 227) from the farm!

MODERATE

Mincarlo Guest House ★★★
GREEN

Carn Thomas, St Mary's TR21 0PT; 📞 *01720 422513; www.mincarlo-ios.co.uk. Near the lifeboat station overlooking Town Beach, Hugh Town.*

A solid family house in a glorious position overlooking the harbour at Hugh Town, with a big sunny terrace and steps down to the Town Beach – ideal for children. The house has been beautifully renovated – the breakfast room is spacious, light and airy, and simply furnished, flooded with light from the huge bay window, with local artists' work on the walls. The owners (Scillonian born and bred) have young children and fully understand the needs of a young family: buckets and spades, fishing nets, beach towels and so on are all supplied. The breakfast menu is great: children can have eggy bread, boiled egg and toast soldiers, beans on toast. Every effort has been made to be as environmentally aware as possible (the use of showers rather than baths to save water, and a nappy-washing service for example). Details of how to carbon offset your holiday are given on the website under Green Tourism.

Rooms 7 double/twin, 4 single; 3–4 suitable for families. Rates £30–35 (low) £31.50–37.50 (high) pppn. Credit MC, V. Amenities cot (charge), extra bed (child £10 pppn), Cornwall

Real Nappy Project. **In room** Internet access, showers (1 bath), TV.

Trevean ★★

Throrfare, St Mary's TR21 0LN; 📞 *01929 471210; www.treveanisle sofscilly.co.uk*

It's rare on Scilly to find a good-sized house that can accommodate an extended family, and Trevean fits the bill perfectly. This is a real gem of a house, metres from the harbour and with a slipway onto the Town Beach – within easy walking distance of everything you might need (just round the corner from the Co-op for those late-night purchases!). This solid three-storey homely retreat accommodates eight people in four bedrooms extremely comfortably. The top floor is an open-plan kitchen-cum-living room, with great views over the rooftops and harbour and loads of sunshine. The house is very well appointed and decorated in bright, cheerful colours – there are basins in all the bedrooms, plus two shower rooms and a bathroom – and a utility room and sunny little courtyard. Because it is often used by the owners and their family there are children's videos, DVDs, books, beach equipment and games, and a really good-size kitchen table for family meals.

Rooms 4 doubles (8 max). **Rates** £1200 (low)–1700 (high) whole property. **Amenities** cot (free), cooker/microwave, dishwasher, fridge/freezer, TV/DVD/video, beach a few metres away, small courtyard area.

INSIDER TIP
Seaways Flower Farm (p. 233) offers three self-catering cottages, each suitable for five people (plus cot). Hugh Town is only a 15-minute walk away, passing three beaches en route – a perfect location for a family holiday. 📞 *01720 422845; www.seawaysfarm holidayhomes.co.uk*

Polreath Guest House ★★
GREEN

Higher Town, St Martin's TR25 0QL; 📞 *01720 422046; www.polreath. com. Inter-island boat from St Mary's.*

Polreath is ideal for couples with one or two young children. It's a lovely, solid, granite-built family house in the southern part of St Martin's, about a 10-minute walk uphill from Higher Town Quay. Some of the comfortable bedrooms are in the roof of the house, with sloping ceilings and lovely views, and can accommodate a cot or extra bed. Guests have their own sitting room, with TV and children's books, games and toys (the owners have young children) and the large flat garden opposite the house is kept for guests. Polreath Tearoom, renowned for good local food (homegrown where possible), has a lovely conservatory and loads of outside seating in its flower-filled garden. Check out the old glasshouse, with cane furniture and flourishing vine – see if you can find the tortoise! Evening meals are available on four nights of the week (Monday curry nights are very popular). Polreath is open from March to the end of October.

St Martins, Polreath

Rooms *3 (1 double en suite, 1 twin en suite, 1 double).* ***Rates*** *£40 (low)–50 (high) pppn B&B; children (0–12) sharing £10–25 pppn.* ***Credit*** *MC, V.* ***Amenities*** *baby monitor, cot, extra bed, shower/bath, laptop in guest lounge if required, TV, large private garden, tea room.*

St Agnes Lighthouse Farm ★ ★ ★

Middle Town, St Agnes TR22 0PL; 📞 *01720 422514; www.rowan.pwp. blueyonder.co.uk.*

St Agnes' lighthouse – dating from 1680, and maintained by Trinity House as a daymark – is the focal point of the island. The owners of The Gatehouse, Lowertown Farm and The Threshing Mill live at the lighthouse. St Agnes is an idyllic spot for any family, and these three properties are all real finds. Much of Scilly's self-catering accommodation is pretty cramped: these properties provide spacious living. The Gatehouse stands near the lighthouse, and has use of a huge garden area, with all-round views. Lowertown Farm (the owners are flower farmers; the family has been on St Agnes for 400 years) is just down the lane in its own extensive grounds, sleeps 10 and has a separate sitting room for children. The Mill (a former threshing mill) is a newly converted single-storey building that sleeps four. The beautiful white sandy beach at Periglis is a few minutes' walk away, as is the Big Pool, the most westerly freshwater pool in the British Isles.

3 s/c cottages, 2–10 people. ***Rates*** *£200 (low)–1200 (high).* ***Amenities*** *cot (free), disabled access (Mill), in*

Troy Town Farm

On St Agnes make sure you go to Troy Town Farm (☎ *01720 422360*; *www.troytownscilly.co.uk*), and try their delicious homemade ice cream. A dairy farm for 20 years, the family started producing ice cream in 2006 and you can now find it all over Scilly. Try hazelnut, coffee, forest fruits – topped off with a fudge stick, chocolate flake or dollop of clotted cream. The farm also does the island milk round.

cottage shower/bath, TV/DVD/video, garden.

Harbour View ★ ★ GREEN

Bryher TR23 0PR; ☎ *01720 422222;* *www.bryher-ios.co.uk/hv*

Bryher is an island of two halves: the wild and windswept west coast, where the Atlantic waves crash onto the granite rocks, and the very different calm, tranquil, sheltered east side facing Tresco. Harbour View has three properties on the eastern shores, near the Bar Quay (low water landing) and the licensed Fraggle Rock restaurant (open for lunch, tea and dinner). Two spacious wooden chalets, Thrift and Bracken, in their own gardens, sit right on the water's edge overlooking Cromwell's Castle, built in 1651 on the northern end of Tresco. Castle View, one of the oldest cottages on Bryher, has a similar outlook and provides comfortable accommodation for four to five people. The cottage has a glass porch, ideal for catching the morning sun, and has an enclosed garden.

2 s/c wooden chalets and 1 cottage, 4 and 4–5 people. **Rates** *£470 (low)–960 (high).* **Credit** *MC, V.* **Amenities** *babysitting, cot (free), disabled access possible to chalets.* **In chalet** *cooker/microwave,*

fridge/freezer, bath/shower, TV/video. **In cottage** *cooker/microwave, fridge/freezer, washing machine/drier, dishwasher, TV/DVD.*

EXPENSIVE

Star Castle Hotel ★ ★ ★

St Mary's TR21 0TA; ☎ *01720 422317; www.star-castle.co.uk*

A wonderfully atmospheric place to stay – an eight-pointed star-shaped castle, surrounded by dry ramparts and a moat (plus two ghosts – a maid and a soldier!) with a bar in the old dungeons. The property and grounds are beautifully maintained; the castle compact, historic, cosy. Built by French prisoners of war in the 16th century (part of a chain of similar castles along the English south coast – including Pendennis p. 179), the Star Castle sits on the slopes of the Garrison fortress, the highest ground on St Mary's with wonderful views to the out islands. The 'family-friendly' part comes in the form of a variety of garden suites around a large, level garden area above the castle, where there is also an indoor swimming pool and the lovely Conservatory restaurant, where children's high tea is served. There's lots of room to roam here, as well as all sorts of

Star Castle, St Marys

secret corners to explore, a knock-about tennis court and toys, buckets and spades to borrow.

Rooms *8 double/twin, 3 single in castle/ramparts; 12 garden suites suitable for families.* **Rates** *£60 (low)–138 (high) pppn dinner/B&B. Children in family rooms, £30 high tea, £50 dinner pppn.* **Credit** *AmEx, MC, V.* **Amenities** *babysitting/listening service, bar, cot (free), extra bed (charge), disabled access possible (garden suites/conservatory), laundry service (charge), indoor pool, restaurant, Internet access in reception.* **In room** *shower/bath, TV.*

> **INSIDER TIP** ⟩⟩
>
> What could be better on a sunny evening than sitting on Porthcressa beach eating fish and chips and watching the sun go down? The fish and chip van is there Mon–Sat from about 5.30pm–7.30pm – how long he stays depends on the weather and the length of the queue! Watch out for the seagulls – they quite like fish and chips too...

FAMILY-FRIENDLY DINING

INEXPENSIVE

Dibble & Grub ★★

The Old Fire Station, Porthcressa, St Mary's TR21 0JQ; ☎ *01720 423719. On Porthcressa beach in Hugh Town.*

A brightly painted, cheerful, simply furnished café (with a hard-wearing floor) on Porthcressa beach in the middle of Hugh Town, named after two firemen characters from the 1970s animated show *Trumpton* – a place you could come to straight off the beach. Simple wooden chairs and tables and a comfortable sofa, and outside seating. There are no special meals for children but they are welcome all day and evening. Local fish features strongly on the menu, with reasonably priced tapas on Friday evenings, and an original evening menu that changes weekly. Brunch is available from 10am–12pm – scrambled eggs (£3.50), pancakes with fresh fruit (£4.50) – then there's a tempting selection of wraps, sandwiches, pannini and salads, and great platters for two: vegetable antipasti (£11.95), cured meat antipasti (£11.95), whole baked camembert (£9.50).

Open *10am–6pm Mon–Sat, 7–9pm Wed–Sat.* **Main course** *(lunch) £4.95–6.95.* **Amenities** *on beach, disabled access, reservations accepted (essential for evenings).*

Little Arthur's, St Martins

INSIDER TIP ❯❯

One of the best suppers on St Martin's is takeaway pizza from **St Martin's bakery** (☎ 01720 423444). Order it in the morning – Moo Green Melter, Red Hot Sunset, Seafarer's Smokey – pick it up before 5.30pm and take it down to the beach at Highertown Bay for a blissful meal. The small traditionally run (and brilliant) bakery is open from 9am–5.30pm and makes and sells all manner of tempting and delicious fare: pasties, filled rolls, flapjacks, pecan pie, caramel slice, pain au chocolat, real Cornish lemonade...worth a visit at any time of day! Also don't miss **Glenmoor Cottage gift shop** near Moo Green – a treasure trove of trinkets.

Little Arthur's Wholefood Café ★

Little Arthur Farm, Highertown, St Martin's TR25 0QL; ☎ 01720 422457. Above Highertown Bay, past Pool Green.

A rough uphill track – tough for buggies on a hot day! – leads to a little group of red-roofed buildings which make up Little Arthur organic farm. The owners run a quirky little café during the summer months. Seating in a vine-filled conservatory is limited, and space at a premium, but the food and drink are simple and delicious and the views fantastic. It's a fun place to go for coffee and cake or a lunchtime snack: filled rolls (£3.95–5.25), tomato and basil soup (£4.95), ploughman's (£6.50) or ice cream with toffee sauce. Ingredients come straight from the sea or from the organic farm. A three-course meal may be had on Mondays – bistro night – and the owners' fisherman son produces fish and chips on Tuesday and Thursday evenings (eat in or takeaway).

Open *10.30am–4pm Mon–Fri Apr–end Sept; bistro from 6.30pm Mon (bring own wine).* **Main course** *£3.95–6.50 (café).* **Amenities** *reservations, fish and chips 6pm–8pm Tue/Thurs.*

If you're interested in sustainable living why not stay at Little Arthur's eco-cabin. The cabin – just two minutes from the beach – sleeps 4–5 people, and (like the farm) has a low impact on the local environment: a windmill generates electricity, a wormery and recycling system dispose of cabin wastes. For more details ☎ 01720 422457.

MODERATE

Juliet's Garden Restaurant ★ ★ ★

Seaways Flower Farm, St Mary's TR21 0NF; ☎ 01720 422228; www.julietsgardenrestaurant. co.uk. Overlooking Porthloo beach, below the golf course and above boat park and craft studios.

A fabulous place for morning coffee, lunch, tea or supper – or all four! – with excellent views over the harbour towards Hugh Town and to the out islands. Seaways is a working flower farm, growing scented narcissi, and many ingredients used in the restaurant are homegrown – lettuce, rocket, potatoes – and also on sale in the small farm shop. A lovely terraced garden sits beside the big, light wooden building, with roof lights and panoramic windows, part of which was an old flower packing shed. It's a big place but somehow still manages to feel intimate. Children are welcome throughout the day and early evening. All food is freshly prepared and delicious: the children's evening menu is all homemade and includes beef burger and chips, plaice goujons, vegetable bake and omelette (£3.95–5.95). There's a great range of tempting dishes – ciabatta platters (£7.75–8.20), landowner's lunches, mackerel pâté and a hunk of granary bread, even a 'slimmer's substantial snack'. The cakes and puddings are to die for: sticky date

Juliet's Garden, St Mary's

and walnut, chocolate fudge slice, and Roskilly's ice cream.

Open 10am–5pm daily, 6pm–last orders 8.45pm every day except Tues. Main course £10.50–17.95 (dinner), £4–12.50 (lunch). Credit MC, V. Amenities children's menu, half portions available, highchair, large terraced garden, disabled access, reservations accepted, sandwiches/cakes to take away.

The Turk's Head ★ ★ ★

St Agnes TR22 0PL; ☎ 01720 422434. Porth Conger, St Agnes (near the quay).

The Turk's Head has the best position of any pub on Scilly. The converted lifeboat house stands at the top of the slipway near the quay at Porth Conger, with views towards the island of Gugh, accessible along a sandbar at low tide. The pub is full of atmosphere and nautical memorabilia, and food is more reasonably priced than at many of the islands' eating places. St Agnes can easily be circumnavigated in a morning, giving ample time for lunch at the pub. Try an island pasty (£4.95) or cullen skink (smoked haddock and potato chowder, £4.55), or a good range of sandwiches. Children can choose from pasta, deep fried fish and chips, grilled chicken fillet or ham salad (£3.25–4.25). There's a tempting range of homemade puddings on offer too, all served with St Agnes clotted cream – and delicious chocolate and St Agnes brandy ice cream, made at Troy Town farm (p. 230).

Open 10.30am–11.30pm Apr–end Sept (phone for winter opening). Main course £4.25–8.95 (lunch); £7.95–11.75 (dinner). Credit MC, V. Amenities children's menu (under 13), highchair, disabled access possible, garden, live music some summer evenings.

Try These Too

- **The Atlantic Hotel:** Old-fashioned, friendly and comfortable hotel, a couple of minutes' walk from the quay with great views. Hugh Street, St Mary's TR21 0PL; ☎ *01720 422417; www.smallandfriendly.co.uk.*
- **St Mary's Hall Hotel:** Elegant town house on a peaceful street with three family suites and enclosed garden. Church Street, St Mary's TR21 0JR; ☎ *01720 422316; www.stmaryshallhotel.co.uk.*
- **Round Island Bar & Bistro:** Expansive views across the edge of Tean to Round Island lighthouse and good food and reasonable prices to match. St Martin's on the Isle, Lowertown, St Martin's TR25 0QL; ☎ *01720 422090; www.stmartinshotel.co.uk.*

The Lost Land of Lyonnesse

As if the Isles of Scilly weren't sufficiently romantic already, legend has it that the ancient kingdom of Lyonnesse lies beneath the waters of the Atlantic Ocean between Land's End and the islands.

It is said that after the death of King Arthur his followers fled from his slayer, Mordred, across the kingdom of Lyonnesse. When King Arthur's men had reached Scilly Merlin caused Lyonnesse to be flooded, and Mordred and his followers were drowned. Some say that on a calm day you can still hear the bells of Lyonnesse's 140 submerged churches chiming gently, moved to and fro by the tide.

Less romantically it is known that the islands are part of the same huge granite sheet that erupts on Dartmoor, Bodmin Moor and Penwith. Bronze Age peoples colonised the islands 4,000 years ago when they were linked to the mainland; soon after rising sea levels marooned Scilly – then a single island. The remains of walls are still visible in some places beneath the shallow waters.

EXPENSIVE

The New Inn ★★

Tresco TR24 0QE; ☎ 01720 422844; www.tresco.co.uk. At New Grimsby, north end of Tresco.

The main part of the New Inn – which has a well-deserved reputation for excellent food – is a traditional dark, beamy pub. About nine years ago the pub was enlarged with the addition of the Pavilion, a glass-sided single-storey wooden building with extensive outside decking and views over the quay (and Internet access). Coffee and cakes are available from 10am, and more substantial meals from midday to 9pm. Food is mainly locally sourced – the Atlantic cod and chips is renowned – and ranges from mushroom and brie burger (£8.50) and chicken Caesar salad (£12.50) to rib-eye steak (£16) and fruit de mer 'to share' at £55!

The sandwich menu (£6.50–8) is interesting: Cornish brie and grape, smoked salmon and crème fraiche, smoked chicken, mango and rocket. The children's menu (under 14) is good and varied: Tresco beef burger, fish and chips, papparadelle, chicken goujons (£5.50), and salads, sandwiches and crudités (£4.50) at lunchtime. Turn the children's menu over and borrow some crayons from behind the bar – or make your way to the pub's swimming pool for a refreshing dip, rounded off with a delicious Roskilly's ice cream.

Open 10am–11.30pm Mon–Sat, 10am–10.30pm Sun. Main course £8.50–16 (lunch). Credit AmEx, MC, V. Amenities children's menu/half portions available, BBQs, hog roasts etc. in high season, highchair, disabled access, reservations accepted, swimming pool/showers.

Out and About on Scilly

Boat Trips Go to the TIC or walk along the quay and find out what's on offer. Book a trip on *The Wizard*, a fantastic high-speed jet boat that will whisk you away to see seals, seabirds (including puffins), the Western Rocks and Eastern Isles in comfort (☎ *01720 423999; www.scilly boating.co.uk*).

Cycling **St Mary's Bike Hire** on The Strand in Hugh Town on St Mary's (☎ *01720 422289*) supplies all kinds of bikes (including child carriers and tag-alongs). Bikes can also be hired at the **Bike Shed** on Tresco (☎ *01720 422849; www.tresco.co.uk*).

Horse Riding If you have pony-mad children (minimum age 4) go exploring on horseback from **St Mary's Riding Centre** at Maypole (☎ *01720 423855; www.horsesonscilly.co.uk*) – beginners welcome.

Rockpool Rambles The **Isles of Scilly Wildlife Trust** runs free sessions – perfect for children – exploring the strandline and learning about marine species (☎ *01720 422153; www.ios-wildlifetrust.org.uk*).

Sailing The **Sailing Centre** at Porthmellon on St Mary's offers courses and taster sessions in sailing, windsurfing, kayaking and power-boating for all ages and abilities. During July and August the Centre also operates out of its Ravensport Base by the Island Hotel on Tresco (☎ *01720 422060; www.sailingscilly.com*).

Snorkelling **St Martin's Diving School**, in partnership with the Isles of Scilly Wildlife Trust, run 2-hour guided snorkelling trips from the beach: great for younger or inexperienced snorkellers (☎ *01720 422153; www.ios-wildlifetrust.org.uk* or ☎ *01720 422848; www.scillydiving. com*).

Swimming Swimming is possible on any number of wonderful beaches all over Scilly. On St Mary's check out **Normandy swimming pool**, a lovely public outdoor pool in the grounds of a big house near Pelistry Bay (small charge). If you're feeling more ambitious **Swimtrek** organise week-long swimming trips between the islands (☎ *020 8696 6220; www.swimtrek.com*).

Walking Join a guided walk (2–3 hours) to learn more about the islands' natural history and archaeology with local archaeologist, Katherine Sawyer (*www.scillywalks.co.uk*).

Wildlife Watching Go on a one-hour or two-hour **Island Sea Safari** and find shipwrecks, seals and seabirds. Viewing boxes and a hydrophone bring the sights and sounds of what goes on under the sea to life. Booking essential (☎ *01720 422732; www.scillyonline.co.uk/ seasafaris*).

The Insider

Family Travel

Travelling to Devon and Cornwall as a family doesn't require any specific preparation, but the journey to the southwest can be unbearably long, especially in peak holiday times, and particularly when the majority of self-catering accommodation and campsites operate a Friday or Saturday changeover in peak holiday periods. In 2005 around 79% of visitors travelled to Devon and Cornwall by car (7% by train, 3% by bus and 2% by plane), and the main routes – the M5, A303, A38 and A30 – get horrendously busy. There's little you can do to avoid this; be aware that the journey may take longer than the actual distance to be covered suggests, and plan accordingly. Allow plenty of time for your journey and build in a time allowance for unforeseen delays. Take plenty of food and drink with you – avoid queuing for hours at service station cafés – and make frequent stops to stretch legs and get some fresh air.

When trying to find your holiday destination – be it an out-of-the-way campsite or self-catering cottage – don't rely on your car's sat-nav system to get you there. The system is unreliable in rural and sparsely populated areas, and it's much safer to get good directions from the accommodation provider, and use the local OS map. Remember too that mobile phone coverage is patchy in many parts of Devon and Cornwall, regardless of which network you use.

Many of the family travel websites focus on holidays abroad: the following are all relevant to travelling with children within the UK.

www.rac.co.uk Great ideas on how to entertain children in transit, plus in-car games to download.

www.busybags.biz A fun site offering specially compiled activity bags to occupy 3–5 and 7–10 year olds, plus other in-car entertainment.

www.travellingwithchildren.co.uk Loads of hints and tips on planning the route, in-car toys and activities, travel cots, baby carriers and so on.

www.babygoes2.com Largely about international travel but with a useful section on travel toys and essential equipment to take on holiday, child seats etc.

www.parentlineplus.org.uk 'Because instructions aren't included...'. Good travel tips plus section on 'fun that doesn't cost the earth' – relevant at home or on holiday.

www.netmums.co.uk Unique local network for parents – excellent advice on packing, travelling, staying in hotels – plus holiday recommendations.

Responsible Tourism

The Green Tourism Business Scheme (**www.green-business.co.uk**) has been championing sustainable tourism in the UK since its inception in 1997; and the southwest – and Devon in

You'll know when you're in Kernow (the Cornish name for Cornwall). The minute you cross the Tamar you'll spot typically Cornish place names, starting with Tre, Pol or Pen. An old rhyming couplet states 'By Tre, Pol and Pen shall ye know all Cornishmen', and it's true that these prefixes dominate in place names over most of the county. Tre means settlement or farmstead; pol is a pool or pit; pen a headland.

You're not likely to have to speak Cornish to make yourself understood when on holiday, but it's interesting to know that there are now around 300 fluent speakers, that it's an ancient language closely related to Breton and Welsh, and it's now taught in some schools. See how you get on with the following tongue twisters (***www.cornishlanguage.org; www.bbc.co.uk/cornwall***):

Dydh da	Good day
Fat la genes?	How are you?
Meur ras	Thank you
Marpleg	Please
Dyw genes	Goodbye
Nos dha	Good night
Pasti	Pasty
Howlyek yw hi	It's sunny
Yma glaw puptydh, dell hevel	It rains every day, it seems

particular – now has more GTBS award-winning businesses (more than 200) than anywhere else in the country; the Isles of Scilly has the greatest proportion of GTBS businesses. Businesses are assessed on a large number of criteria, and if you are concerned about the effect of your holiday on the environment pick an accommodation provider who has joined the scheme and who has achieved a gold, silver or bronze rating (depending on the level of 'greenness' demonstrated). The relevant criteria cover such aspects as efficient use of energy and water, good environmental management, recycling facilities, minimisation of waste, the reduction of food miles by buying locally, cutting down on car use by providing information on cycle hire and local transport, and encouraging wildlife in the locality (and information for visitors). Businesses displaying the GREEN icon in this book have all signed up to GTBS and have either been assessed or are waiting assessment – but remember that businesses are continually joining the scheme, so some of those included may now merit the icon too. Equally many of the businesses included in this book follow 'green' principles but are not part of the GTBS scheme.

Eliminate, reduce, reuse, recycle Take bags with you when you go shopping to save accumulating unwanted plastic ones that are almost impossible to dispose of. Stay with an accommodation provider who encourages recycling, and use the recycling banks that sit in car parks all over Devon and Cornwall.

Buy local, eat local Did you know that more than 50 different cheeses are now produced in Cornwall? The last few years have seen a huge increase in interest in local food and in the region's specialities: early potatoes, old-fashioned apples, rare breed sausages and bacon, sea-fresh fish. There's no need to bring your food with you when you holiday in Devon and Cornwall (we do have supermarkets too!). Why not 'go French' and do your shopping at farmers' markets and farm shops, or even from farm gate sales? (listed in each section of this guide). Do your bit by cutting down the food miles and supporting local producers, and enjoy eating food that really has come fresh from the farm or market garden – or straight out of the sea. For further information visit *www.cornwalltasteofthewest.co.uk* and *www.tasteofthewest.co.uk*.

Leave the car behind One of the best ways of seeing the southwest is by bike or on foot. You'll end the day full of fresh air and comfortably tired, and can give yourself a pat on the back for cutting down on your personal carbon imprint – and the whole family will have had fun. And then there's the bus: although public transport services are limited in some parts of Devon and Cornwall, special Rover bus deals do operate in some areas – ask at the local TIC (which will also have information on bike hire). And in much of South Devon and South Cornwall there are loads of opportunities for getting around by boat or ferry (see individual sections) – and in the Isles of Scilly you have no choice but to take to the water.

Watch your water use The population of the southwest swells enormously in the holiday season: Devon alone had an estimated 33 million 'tourist nights' in 2005. If existing accommodation is full, the population of Cornwall and the Isles of Scilly swells from just under 500,000 to over 750,000; Devon's from just over one million to around 1,335,000. This puts an enormous strain of the provision of natural resources such as water – particularly in years when the previous winter has seen low rainfall. Follow the now well-publicised advice concerning sensible water use (and remember to turn off lights and standby buttons when not in use).

Follow the Countryside Code Devon and Cornwall are rural areas; farming still plays a vital role in the local economy. It is important that visitors follow the Countryside Code for the benefit of themselves, the local population and the environment. Be safe, plan ahead, and follow any signs; leave gates and property as you find them; protect plants and animals; take your litter home; keep dogs under close control; consider other people.

Index

See also Accommodations and Restaurant indexes, below.

General

A

Accommodations

Restaurants